PAPYRI AND THE SOCIAL WORLD
OF THE NEW TESTAMENT

In this book Sabine R. Huebner explores the world of the New Testament protagonists and the early Christians using the rich papyrological evidence from Roman Egypt, a resource which gives us unparalleled insights into the everyday lives of a nonelite population. What were the daily concerns and difficulties experienced by a carpenter's family or by a shepherd looking after his flocks? How did the average man or woman experience a Roman census? What obstacles did women living in a patriarchal society face in private, in public, and in the early church? Given the flight of Jesus' family into Egypt, how mobile were the lower classes, what was their understanding of geography, and what costs and dangers were associated with travel? This volume gives us a better understanding of the structural, social, and cultural conditions in which figures from the New Testament lived.

SABINE R. HUEBNER is Professor of Ancient History and Head of the Doctoral Program in Classical Civilizations at the University of Basel. Her research focuses on social and religious history and the everyday life of common people in antiquity. She has published monographs including *The Family in Roman Egypt* (Cambridge, 2013) and is co-editor of *Growing up Fatherless in Antiquity* (Cambridge, 2009), *The Encyclopedia of Ancient History* (2012), *Inheritance, Law and Religion in the Ancient and Medieval Worlds* (2014), *Mediterranean Families in Antiquity* (2016), and *The Single Life in the Roman and Later Roman Worlds* (Cambridge, 2019).

T0381685

PAPYRI AND THE SOCIAL WORLD OF THE NEW TESTAMENT

SABINE R. HUEBNER

Universität Basel, Switzerland

CAMBRIDGE
UNIVERSITY PRESS

Shaftesbury Road, Cambridge CB2 8EA, United Kingdom

One Liberty Plaza, 20th Floor, New York, NY 10006, USA

477 Williamstown Road, Port Melbourne, VIC 3207, Australia

314–321, 3rd Floor, Plot 3, Splendor Forum, Jasola District Centre, New Delhi – 110025, India

103 Penang Road, #05–06/07, Visioncrest Commercial, Singapore 238467

Cambridge University Press is part of Cambridge University Press & Assessment, a department of the University of Cambridge.

We share the University's mission to contribute to society through the pursuit of education, learning and research at the highest international levels of excellence.

www.cambridge.org
Information on this title: www.cambridge.org/9781108455701

DOI: 10.1017/9781108556453

First published 2019

A catalogue record for this publication is available from the British Library

ISBN   978-1-108-47025-4   Hardback
ISBN   978-1-108-45570-1   Paperback

To Stéphane

Contents

Illustrations

Cover image: "Flight into Egypt" by Eugène Alexis Girardet (1850–1907) © The Picture Art Collection/Alamy stock Photo

The system of abbreviations used for editions of papyrological texts is the *Checklist of Greek, Latin, Demotic and Coptic Papyri, Ostraca and Tablets* edited by J. D. Sosin, R. S. Bagnall, J. Cowey, M. Depauw, T. G. Wilfong, and K. A. Worp.

Acknowledgments

My heartfelt thanks go out to all of the colleagues and friends who have supported me over the course of this endeavor. I offer sincere and heartfelt thanks to AnneMarie Luijendijk, whose scholarship has been a great inspiration for my work. I wish to extend my gratitude to John Kloppenborg, Peter Arzt-Grabner, Cillier Breytenbach, Roger Bagnall, Ernst Baltrusch, Elaine Pagels, and Paul Schubert for invaluable and insightful comments on chapters of this book, and to Malcolm Choat for letting me read beforehand his forthcoming work. I presented aspects of this book at various lectures in the US and Europe and thank my audiences in Berlin, Basel, Princeton, Vienna, Leiden, Bonn, Marburg, Kassel, Rostock, Tübingen, Fribourg, Neuchatel, Oxford, Zürich, Rome, and Paris for helpful comments and references.

This project has been made possible by a generous grant from the German Research Foundation (DFG), who awarded me a five-year Heisenberg fellowship. During these years I enjoyed the hospitality of the Institut d'histoire et Civilisation de Byzance at the Collège de France's site on rue du Cardinal Lemoine (2011/12). My special thanks here go to Jean-Claude Cheynet and Beatrice Caseau for their kindness and generosity. While working on this book I also spent two years in Rome (2012–14) and got to know the scholarly bounty and intellectually stimulating environment of the British School at Rome as well as the Institutum Romanum Finlandiae at Villa Lante. I would like to thank Christopher Smith as well as Katariina Mustakallio for welcoming me with open arms into their scholarly communities and research libraries. I wrote the final chapters at the University of Basel, where I made use of the wonderful resources at the university's library. I am particularly grateful to my colleagues and students at the University of Basel, especially Matthias Stern, Graham Claytor, Irene Soto, Matthias Mueller, Audric Wannaz, and Dario Giacometti, who, combined, create an intellectually and personally supportive environment that encourages me to pursue my many

xi

research endeavors and helped me in particular to finish this book. Thanks are due as well to Florian Setz and Victoria Landau for help with finding fitting illustrations. My special thanks go to Sarah J. Johnson, participant in my graduate seminar at Princeton University, for reading the entire manuscript and offering valuable editing ideas. I also want to thank the Princeton University Humanities Council for granting me a Stewart Fellowship in Religion in 2018 that allowed me the free time to finish the manuscript in the inspiring scholarly community of Princeton.

This book has benefitted considerably from the comments I received from the anonymous readers of Cambridge University Press – I thank them deeply for their constructive criticisms and suggestions for improvements. A special thank-you goes to my language editor Sarah Swift, who always knows what I want to say in English even if I am not saying it. Last but not least, I would like to express thanks to Michael Sharp, who shows a continuous interest in my work, to Mary Bongiovi for seeing this book through production as well as to Hilary Hammond for her valuable skills in diligently copy-editing the final manuscript. I dedicate this book to my family, Stéphane, and my children Nina, Marla, and Tristan for their love, patience, and surprising curiosity even about the most intricate details of my subjects of study.

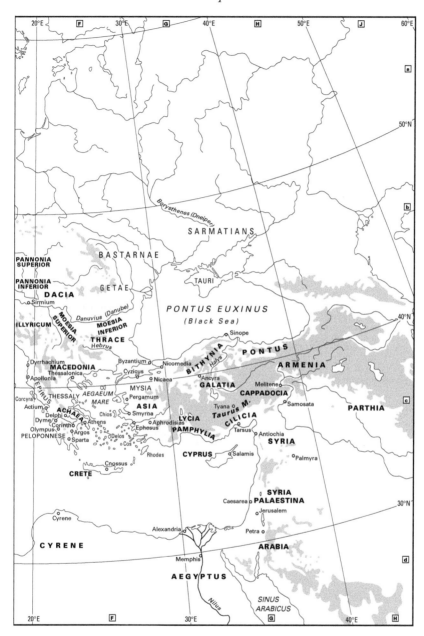

Eastern Roman Mediterranean.

Maps

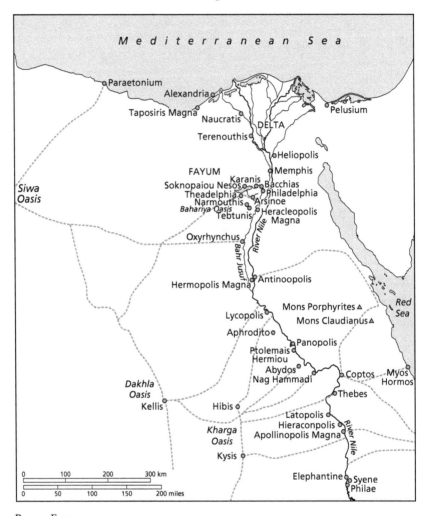

Roman Egypt.

Satellite image of Egypt, 2015.

CHAPTER I

Egypt and the Social World of the New Testament

An Everyday History of the New Testament

Research into New Testament literature has increasingly, albeit slowly, opened up to include in its exegesis historical studies of the society and economy of the Hellenistic and Roman worlds.[1] New insights into Roman social structure, the role of the family, ancient associations, and Roman law, as well as economic aspects, have all enhanced research into the sociohistorical dimensions of events depicted in the Gospels and the history of early Christian communities, and have helped to illuminate the origins of early Christianity in its ancient social context. However, the sociohistorical studies that have been employed are based primarily on historical accounts, biographies of emperors, honorary inscriptions, and Roman jurisdiction which inform us first and foremost about the elites of the Roman world. As such, they tell us very little about the common people who predominate the Gospels and early Christian writings. Individuals of the lower social classes are occasionally mentioned in passing by Roman historians and lawgivers – representatives of the Roman elite – but their thoughts and words are not transmitted.

Common people held no high offices and composed no histories, epics, or poems – in fact, most were not able to write at all. Their everyday lives and deeds were generally of no importance to the writing of history. Roman law had little personal relevance to those who did not own or bequeath anything and could not afford to start legal proceedings. A commoner did not have the means to dedicate a portico to the civic forum; nor did the city have any reason to honor them publicly with a monument. Their offspring could rarely afford to mark their tombs with a stone inscription. It was only in later centuries that accounts of the acts of martyrs and hagiographies started to focus on members of the lower classes, whom classical historians had never hitherto considered the main historical actors.

Consequently, New Testament scholars, church historians, and modern readers of the Gospels often fail to properly set into context the events described in the Gospels due to the fact that so little is known about the everyday lives and concerns of the lower social classes in the provinces of the Roman Empire. Moreover, medieval and modern misinterpretations of and anachronistic analogies to the New Testament texts have led to the formation of persistent and erroneous beliefs about ancient daily life. This state of affairs, I believe, must be addressed.

Papyri and the Social World of the New Testament aims to focus on the lower classes of Roman provincial society. It privileges micro-approaches in order to contribute to a better understanding of the structural, social, and cultural conditions that the protagonists of the New Testament, as well as its early readers, experienced in their everyday lives.

The upper class is defined in this study as the imperial and provincial elite, including great landowners, Roman senators, city councilors of the major cities of the empire, and high-ranking officials in the imperial administration and the military. It represented 1 to 2 percent of the free population. To the middle classes belonged individuals of modest, comfortable wealth – that is, middle-sized landowners, city councilors of provincial towns, well-to-do merchants, and contractors – who comprised another 6 to 12 percent of the free population. Finally, the lower social strata, who were living at subsistence level – the peasants, small peddlers and craftsmen, shepherds, and day laborers – constituted between 86 and 93 percent of the entire free population.[2] Despite their numbers, their reality has been vastly obscured by ancient sources and consequently muted in modern historical accounts. As a result, learning more about the living conditions and everyday existence of these common people represents one of the most urgently felt *desiderata* within the field of ancient studies.

From the 1960s onwards the humanities and social sciences have witnessed a "quotidian turn" or shift toward a scholarly concern with nonelites and common, everyday life.[3] However, daily life in the Gospels and early Christian communities from the first to third centuries CE has, until now, been vastly neglected. There is a surprising lack of interdisciplinary working between New Testament scholars based in departments of religion and Roman social and economic historians, as well as between epigraphers and papyrologists, who belong to departments of classics or history. Not only are New Testament scholars generally unaware of the latest research on the periods and social strata with which they are concerned in their texts; ancient historians also commonly refrain from using early Christian literature as sources for studying the everyday lives of the common people in the Roman provinces.

Admittedly, conducting in-depth studies of the common people in Roman Galilee or Judaea, where most of the New Testament accounts are anchored, is nearly impossible due to a lack of sources. It is in the nearby Roman province of Egypt – and there alone – that we find sources in large quantities that provide information on the everyday lives of the Roman provincial middle and lower classes. Hundreds of thousands of papyri, preserved by favorable environmental conditions, report on details of life in Roman times, including individuals' daily fears and worries, which are unavailable with this degree of quality and in this quantity in any other sources.

Papyrus – the ancient form of paper – was the everyday writing medium in the ancient world, available to almost every social class and put to a variety of uses. Among the papyri we find dated official and private letters, tax receipts, census returns, petitions, wills, marriage contracts, and land leases alongside a wealth of other documents. Whether they have been found in their best-known scroll form or were lost, discarded, or used as packaging in the mummification process, the information they record has been preserved over the centuries by Egypt's dry desert sands (see Figure 1.1).

In those circumstances where no papyrus was at hand or was considered too costly, *ostraca* were used for a wide variety of purposes. Ostraca are broken-off pieces of pottery that cost nothing and were always available (see Figure 1.2). The immediate and personal character of papyri and ostraca grants us insights into the lives and ordinary existences of the majority of the population, thereby constituting a particularly fascinating type of ancient source. The documents permit the ordinary people of the ancient world to speak to us just as they spoke to one another. The voices of those who never appear in ancient literature – artisans, peasants, shepherds, and fishermen, their wives and children – are suddenly heard.

The difference between the transmission of papyrological and literary sources is remarkable. Recorded and copied through late antiquity and the Middle Ages, the great literary works reflect the priorities and interests of previous mediating agencies. They were judged by ancient scribes and medieval monks as worthy of repeated transcription so as to preserve them from oblivion and for posterity. Their contents continued to fascinate people down the centuries. In contrast, the preservation and discovery of papyri were mainly accidental. They lay for two thousand years in ancient rubbish heaps. No medieval monk would have spent time copying the everyday documents of common people; often these texts had been discarded by their own

1.1 Apollinarius, a young Egyptian recruit in the Roman Army writes home to his mother, Taesion: papyrus letter sent from Rome to the Egyptian village of Karanis (Fayum) (*P.Mich.* 8.490 from the second century CE).

authors. But for us, they reveal much about the everyday routines of ordinary people, about their economic situation, family and married life, dietary habits, health issues, illness and death, and generational as well as gender relations and roles. And so, anyone seeking insight into the lives of ordinary families from the middle and lower classes of the ancient world must turn to the unique sources offered by Egypt.[4]

1.2 Receipt for 4 drachmas written on a potsherd, dated to the Egyptian month of Thoth (*P.Duk.inv.* 233).

The evaluation of the papyri from Hellenistic and Roman Egypt for New Testament scholarship has in recent years principally been carried out by Peter Arzt-Grabner, John Kloppenborg, and Mauro Pesce. Their scholarship has extended our understanding of key New Testament linguistic terms and supplemented existing biblical commentaries.[5] Yet the potential of the papyri for a better understanding of everyday life and the circumstances described in the New Testament has only been realized and exploited in a rudimentary way. This book thus draws on documentary papyri shedding light on everyday life in order to provide the social context for key issues covered by the New Testament accounts.

The Special Status of Egypt

Aegyptum imperio populi Romani adieci – "Egypt I added to the Empire of the Roman people." Thus runs Emperor Augustus' concise record of the incorporation of Egypt into the Roman Empire in 30 BCE.[6] Roman provinces were traditionally ruled by a governor drawn from the senatorial aristocracy, but in view of the political and economic significance of Egypt as a province, Augustus instead selected an equestrian, most likely so as to avoid placing such a potential key to power in the hands of a man of excessive ambition. Tacitus tells us:

> Ever since the time of the Divine Augustus, Roman knights have ruled Egypt as kings, and the forces by which it has to be kept in subjection. It has been thought expedient thus to keep under home control a province so difficult of access, so productive of corn, ever distracted, excitable, and restless through the superstition and licentiousness of its inhabitants, knowing nothing of laws, and unused to civil rule.[7]

Although based in Alexandria, the *Praefectus Aegypti* traveled extensively through the region, dispensing justice and supervising the local administration. With the exception of his social status, the legal position of the Praefectus Aegypti was no different from that of the other magistrates of senatorial rank, whether the *legati Augusti* in the imperial provinces or the promagistrates in the public provinces.[8]

Egypt has always been considered exceptional by both ancient and modern authors. In fact, its exceptionalism within the empire was an idea proposed by Tacitus in the *Annals*:

> That prince, among other secrets of imperial policy, had forbidden senators and Roman knights of the higher rank to enter Egypt except by permission, and he had specially reserved the country, from a fear that anyone who held a province containing the key of the land and of the sea, with ever so small a force against the mightiest army, might distress Italy by famine.[9]

The idea of Egypt's special status among Roman provinces was taken up by Theodor Mommsen. Mommsen's now dated notion of Egypt as the emperor's private possession – something approaching a crown colony to which he appointed the Praefectus Aegypti as a viceroy – was developed further by Wilcken, who warned of generalizations for other Roman provinces made on the basis of the rich source material from Roman Egypt.[10] In summary, Tacitus and his modern followers explained the special status of Egypt basically by reference to the nature of its establishment as the private property of Augustus Caesar. This political dimension later became enmeshed with economic considerations: Egypt provided the lion's share of Rome's grain and constituted one of the richest provinces of the empire. For this reason its special status became an economic one.[11]

The most striking difference between Egypt and the rest of the empire lies, however, in the source base it left us. In fact, the contemporary prevailing idea of Egypt's unique status within the empire stems above all from the papyrus finds starting in the late nineteenth century. The tremendous papyrus discoveries in Middle and Upper Egypt and the relatively new field of papyrology revolutionized research in ancient history, which until then had largely relied on literary sources, and enabled scholars to challenge the existing *communis opinio*.[12]

One consequence of Egypt's rich papyrological documentation is that historians ask different questions, investigate different social classes, and explore different aspects of life when studying Egypt than when studying other parts of the Greco-Roman Mediterranean world. Some scholars remain sceptical as to the representative nature of this source base for the empire as a whole, even if papyrologists and historians specializing in Roman Egypt have come to broadly reject the idea of Egyptian exceptionalism, at least for the Roman and late Roman periods. They instead attempt to demonstrate the existence of economic, administrative, and social commonalities between Egypt and other areas of the empire – particularly Asia Minor, Syria, and Palestine. Furthermore, they argue that the results drawn from an analysis of the papyri for understanding Roman Egypt's demography, economy, society, and administration are transferable to other provinces of the Roman Empire.[13]

Today, the majority of historians focusing on the economy, administration, and society of Roman Egypt generally reject the idea that Egypt had any form of special status within the Roman Empire and assume that the elements previously considered peculiar to it could actually have been found in many other Roman provinces if we had comparable evidence. Martin Goodman has written:

> It is important to be aware of the probability that many of the apparently unique elements of life in Roman Egypt in fact may have been shared by other provincials in the Empire, and that Egyptian society differed primarily in that it left behind a detailed record in the sand.[14]

Papyri and ostraca found outside Egypt, as well as wooden writing tablets such as the Vindolanda tablets from northern Britain, the tablets from Vindonissa in Switzerland, or the Bloomberg tablets from London, show many similarities in terminology with the Egyptian papyri, testifying to a common mindset and shared understanding across the Roman provinces. Roman Egypt thus distinguishes itself from other provinces above all by its incomparable level of documentation of everyday life. Simply put: Egypt was not exceptional within the Roman Empire; it is only exceptionally well documented thanks to its climate, which allowed the everyday writing medium of the ancient Mediterranean, papyrus, to survive in the desert sands.

The Christianization of Egypt

Soon after its establishment by Alexander in 331 BCE, Alexandria was harboring the largest Jewish community outside Palestine. A thriving center of trade and commerce, this Mediterranean city was near the Jewish mother-land and was a popular destination for Jewish migration. Accorded con-siderable legal autonomy by the ruling Ptolemaic dynasty, the Jews constituted the majority in two of the five city districts of Alexandria at the beginning of the Christian era, and maintained close economic and cultural ties with Jerusalem. While Jerusalem had about 100,000 inhabitants by the beginning of the common era, Diodorus Siculus estimated the Jewish population of Alexandria at around 300,000.[15]

There can be little doubt that a Christian community developed early in Alexandria, although we know relatively little about it. A tradition first recorded in the early fourth century CE by Eusebius of Caesarea holds that Mark the Evangelist launched a missionary journey to Alexandria. According to Eusebius, Mark was said to have come to Egypt during the reign of the Emperor Claudius (41–54 CE): "And they report that this Mark was the first to be sent to Egypt, in order to announce the gospel which he had written. He was the first to found churches in Alexandria."[16] The recently published *Historia Episcopatus Alexandriae*, a medieval Ethiopian version of a Greek composition from the fourth century, on which more will be said later, builds upon this tradition but gives a different date for Mark's entry into Alexandria: the seventh year of Nero (60 CE).[17] Since neither Acts nor Clement of Alexandria nor Origen know anything about Mark visiting Egypt, we might have to do here with an entirely fabricated story of the early fourth century when the Alexandrian church was competing with Rome, Jerusalem, Constantinople, and Antioch for supremacy of status and authority and therefore claimed an apostolic foundation for itself as well.[18]

A Judeo-Christian from Alexandria named Apollos appears as early as around 50 CE in the Book of Acts:

> Meanwhile a Jew named Apollos, a native of Alexandria, came to Ephesus. He was a learned man, with a thorough knowledge of the Scriptures. He had been instructed in the way of the Lord, and he spoke with great fervor and taught about Jesus accurately, though he knew only the baptism of John. He began to speak boldly in the synagogue. When Priscilla and Aquila heard him, they invited him to their home and explained to him the way of God more adequately.[19]

Apollos was indubitably an educated man – probably an Alexandrian Jew – but it is not clear whether he picked up Christianity in his hometown or elsewhere on his travels to Asia Minor. Acts also reports that Egyptians were present at Pentecost in Jerusalem in 33 CE. Jewish pilgrims from all over the empire had come to Jerusalem to celebrate Pentecost, fifty days after Passover: "Parthians, Medes and Elamites; residents of Mesopotamia, Judaea and Cappadocia, Pontus and Asia, Phrygia and Pamphylia, Egypt and the parts of Libya near Cyrene; visitors from Rome; Cretans and Arabs."[20] About 3,000 of those present were reportedly baptized on that day of Pentecost and might have proselytized after their return to their homelands.[21]

Apart from these legends, however, we have no reliable sources for Christianity in Egypt or for the Alexandrian church or its leadership. Writing in 1902, Adolf von Harnack summarized the situation thus: "The greatest gaps in our knowledge of the history of the early church are constituted by our almost complete ignorance of the history of Alexandrian Christianity and Egypt . . . to 180".[22] The first discoveries of early Christian papyri preserved in the sands of the Egyptian desert thus caused a sensation among late nineteenth-century classicists and the public alike. The new findings kindled hopes of learning more about the first centuries of Christianity and the first Christian communities in Egypt. New societies were launched in Europe and North America to search for further caches of papyri and an entirely new discipline – papyrology – was established to collate and interpret them.

At the turn of the twentieth century British researchers Bernard Grenfell and Arthur Hunt discovered and shipped to Oxford some 400,000 papyrus fragments from the ancient refuse site at Oxyrhynchus, a Greco-Roman settlement in Middle Egypt.[23] They found among the fragments works by ancient authors, some long thought lost and others completely unknown, as well as thousands of records of everyday transactions such as purchase agreements, marriage contracts, private letters, and wills. These novel insights into the ancient world are largely inaccessible anywhere else and unprecedented in scope and quantity. Intensive study of the finds carried out over the course of the ensuing twentieth century means that we now know more about the economic, religious, and social life of Egypt than we do about any other place in the Greco-Roman world.

Scholars interested in the study of the earliest Christian period in Egypt, however, were quickly disappointed by their first examination of the Christian papyri. Copies of the New Testament were found – among the Christian writings was even an entire series of hitherto unknown texts entitled, for example, the Gospel of Thomas, the Gospel of Peter, the Gospel of Judas, and even the Gospel of Mary, written in the style of the known Gospels and reporting the teachings and works of Jesus Christ.[24] However, none of these literary Christian papyri date from a time before the second quarter of the second century at the earliest, but probably rather even fifty to a hundred years later.[25] Furthermore, apart from two exceptions we lack any reference to Christians in the documentary papyri until the second half of the third century.[26] While the earliest epigraphic references to Christians in other regions of the empire such as Asia Minor, Greece, and Italy originate from the middle of the second century,[27] there are no more than a few dozen papyri from the second half of the third century which may have been written by Christians – and the identification of some of these as Christians remains dubious.[28]

Recent research suggests that Alexandrian Christianity developed in the first century in the shadow of the older synagogue. Embedded, however, as it was in the city's Hellenized Jewish diaspora, Alexandrian Christianity most likely suffered severely from its suppression under Trajan during the Jewish revolt of 115–117 CE.[29] Several hundred thousand Alexandrian Jews fled or were killed or enslaved during the Roman countermeasures.[30] It was only at the end of the second century that Jews and Jewish settlements were once again recorded in Egypt.[31] The composition of the Greek Gospel of the Egyptians, which is dated to 120–150 CE, shows, however, that Christianity must have expanded earlier outside the established Jewish quarters. The Gospel of the Egyptians seems to have been popular in the second and third centuries among the indigenous Egyptian population.[32] Clement of Alexandria (ca. 150–215 CE) was familiar with the text and quotes from it in his *Stromata*.[33] A sign that Christianity also appealed to the classical intellectual milieu of Alexandria are two Christian intellectuals of Alexandrian origin, the philosophers Basilides and Valentinus, who taught their respective interpretations of Christian doctrine in the second quarter of the second century. Basilides, a member of the Peripatetic school of Alexandria according to Hippolytus,[34] is said to have composed the first commentary on the Gospels and to have publicly taught his Christian beliefs in Alexandria during the reign of Hadrian (117–138 CE).[35] Origen claimed that Basilides had even composed his own gospel.[36] Later condemned as a heretic, most of his work is lost apart from a few fragments. That Valentinus originally came from Egypt is less certain. According only to a late fourth-century tradition, he was born in Phrebonis in the Nile Delta and received his education in Hellenistic philosophy in Alexandria, where he might have heard Basilides.[37] He is said to have started teaching in Alexandria, but left around the middle of the 130s for Rome, where he founded his own school.[38]

The first recorded leader of the early Alexandrian Christian community about whom we know more than his name is Bishop Demetrius. Demetrius of Alexandria rose to office in 189 CE, about a century after Clemens I of Rome, and about seventy years after Polycarp of Ephesus, these being the first historically identifiable Christian bishops. Irenaeus, the early church father and apologist for the Christian faith from Lyon, recorded in his polemic *Against the Heresies* (*ca.* 180 CE) that Alexandrian Christianity at that time accommodated a range of doctrinal positions.[39] When Demetrius rose to office in 189, he was the only bishop in the entire Roman province of Egypt. At a time when most major towns in the Eastern and Western Empire had their own bishops, the only representative of the episcopal order in Egypt was thus the bishop of Alexandria. Demetrius led the church in Alexandria for forty-three years until his death in 232, and is said to have been the first to ordain bishops for the Egyptian hinterland.[40]

Details regarding the church over which he presided are provided by Clement of Alexandria and Origen, both of whom were based in the city. Nonetheless, only sparse evidence points to Christians in the Egyptian hinterland, the *chora*, in these decades: a letter quoted in Eusebius' *Church History* from Alexander, bishop of Jerusalem, written in about 213 CE and addressed to a Christian community in Antinoopolis on the east bank of the Nile in Upper Egypt, is the earliest reference.[41] Persecutions of Christians under the Roman provincial governor Laetus, in office from 200 to 203, also led to the martyrdom of Leonides, the father of Origen, and a number of other Christians in Alexandria.[42] Decades of peace followed for the church, and Heraclas, former leader of the catechetical school of Alexandria and Demetrius' successor to the bishop's seat of Alexandria in 232 CE, ordained another twenty bishops for the Egyptian countryside.[43] Heraclas was himself succeeded by another leader of the catechetical school, Dionysius, who led the Egyptian church from 248 to 264 CE through a number of crises, such as famines, natural disasters, persecutions, and plague. Eusebius includes several of his letters in his *Church History*. Already in the reign of Philip the Arab (244–248 CE), Dionysius reports famines leading to uprisings and spontaneous persecutions of Christians as scapegoats by the Alexandrian mob. Christians living in Alexandria were dragged from their houses and stoned or thrown into fires.[44] In 250 the Emperor Decius issued an edict ordering everyone to perform sacrifices to the gods and the well-being of the Emperor in the presence of a Roman magistrate. A signed and witnessed certificate was issued in return. Thirty-five of forty-seven known certificates of sacrifice (*libelli*) issued in response to the edict have been found in the village of Theadelphia in the Fayum.[45] Claytor suggested that these documents, which were found together, represent the remnants of a public archive of the village.[46] Alternatively, it seems possible that the official certificates, like most other documents found in Theadelphia, were brought there from the district's capital, Arsinoe. They may actually represent only copies of certificates, while the originals were issued to the individuals mentioned in them. Around a thousand documents found in Theadelphia belong to the vast archive of Heroninos, a manager on the estates of the well-known Alexandrian magistrate Aurelius Appianus. Heroninos and his many subordinates, active in Theadelphia around the middle of the third century, regularly reused the blank sides of older documents originating from the city council of Arsinoe for their business notes.[47]

Dionysius states that those unwilling to sacrifice according to the Decian edict fled or were arrested. He himself was taken by the Roman authorities to Taposiris, west of Alexandria on the Mediterranean, but managed to escape.[48] Dionysius identifies some of those who died as martyrs during this persecution as "Egyptians".[49] Christianity, it seems, had also firmly established itself in the Egyptian hinterland by this time. Dionysius affirms that "also many brothers in the towns and villages were torn to pieces."[50]

During the next persecution, launched by Emperor Valerian in 257 CE, Dionysius with a few men from his clergy were led before the prefect of Egypt, Aemilianus, who asked him to renounce, in the hope, as Dionysius writes, that his men would follow him.[51] He refused and was exiled first to Cephro (modern Kufra), an isolated oasis in the middle of the Sahara Desert in Libya.[52] Dionysius reports that upon their arrival there were not yet any Christians in this district, but that, disregarding the prohibition on Christian assemblies, he successfully proselytized and gained many converts among the local population.[53] Later he was deported to Colluthion, which was closer to Alexandria, and here he could meet more easily with the Christians from Alexandria. Upon his arrival, however, there were no Christians yet among the local population.[54] The persecution thus probably had the unintended effect that Christianity gained a firmer foothold in the towns and villages up the Nile. The first few dated papyri from the late 250s referring to Christians confirm the reports of Dionysius about the spread of Christianity to the Egyptian hinterland.[55]

After the death of Valerian in 260 CE, his son Gallienus ended the persecutions. During the last few years of his life Dionysius witnessed civil war, famines, and plague in Alexandria. The prefect of Egypt, L. Mussius Aemilianus, revolted against the emperor, a conflict that, as Dionysius reports, held the city in its clutch and caused many to die.[56] Famines and the civil war might have helped to give rise to the mass mortality event that followed.[57] Egypt was particularly susceptible to plague due both to its status as a crossroads for trade between East and West, and to its high rate of urbanization and large and dense population. The plague wreaked havoc and the situation in Alexandria seemed so dire that Dionysius – like his contemporary Cyprian in Carthage – believed that the end of the world was nigh.[58] Dionysius' reported figures for plague victims in Alexandria imply a death rate of 62 percent,[59] which seems implausibly high but is broadly in line with the estimated population decline due to death and flight caused by the Antonine plague a century earlier.[60] Plague – which was considered a divine punishment – possibly also contributed to the surprising success of this Judaean newcomer on the religious market. In his recent *Early Christian Books in Egypt*, Roger Bagnall estimates the percentage of Christians in Egypt at the start of Demetrius' tenure in the late second century to be a mere one per thousand of the entire population. Despite a steady growth during Demetrius' episcopate, Bagnall argues that Christians comprised only 1 percent of the entire population by Demetrius' death in 232 CE, and merely 2 percent around the middle of the century.[61] Then a rapid expansion of Christianity occurred. Mark Depauw and Willy Clarysse, expanding Bagnall's study from 1982, have recently argued that by 300 CE 15 to 20 percent of the Egyptian population were Christian.[62]

Moreover, while in 200 CE Christianity seems to have been broadly limited to Alexandria, the Egyptian church a hundred years later could boast several dozen bishoprics extending from Libya and the Delta up the Nile to Upper Egypt.[63] Did Christianity have more to offer in times of fear and uncertainty than traditional religion? The plague afflicted Christians and pagans alike, but Christian church fathers claimed that the Christians continued to bury their dead according to custom. Christian communities may even have enjoyed a growing clientele because they were the ones that cared for the sick and maintained orderly burial practices.[64]

From the last decades of the third century and increasingly into the fourth century we find growing evidence of Christian names, Christian forms of greeting, *nomina sacra*, and indications of ranks within the Christian community among the papyri. Papa Sotas, the first recorded bishop of Oxyrhynchus, appears in letters dating to the third quarter of the third century. In his archive we also find mentions of the first

Christian presbyters originating from Heracleopolis.[65] The first house church dates from the end of the third century and was excavated in Kellis in the Dakleh Oasis.[66] The archeological and papyrus finds appear to confirm the relatively late Christianization of Egypt that also becomes apparent in Eusebius' *Ecclesiastical History*.

Interestingly, the major theological controversies dominating literary accounts of Christian Egypt between the fourth and eighth centuries, and which culminated in the formation of the monophysite Coptic Church, receive little to no mention in the papyri. While the reasons for this might lie to a certain extent in the nature of the source material, as purchase agreements or inventories do not generally deal with the finer points of theology, they might be explained by geography as well. Middle and Upper Egypt were areas far removed from the channels of theological and intellectual exchange, which centered on Alexandria – where due to the climate no papyrological sources have survived.[67]

A recent edition of an Ethiopic manuscript from the fourteenth century transmitting the lost Greek *History of the Episcopate of Alexandria* has raised hopes of learning more about the early Christian period in Egypt. While the original Greek version was composed in the early fourth century, the Ethiopic translation dates to the late fourth century in the Aksumite period. It refers to the founding legend by Mark the Evangelist and lists subsequent bishops on the Seat of Mark. More importantly, however, it then gives a list of bishops ordained by the Alexandrian bishops since Demetrius.[68]

The *History of the Episcopate of Alexandria* also confirms Eutychius' report that Demetrius was the first to appoint bishops for the Egyptian hinterland; before then, the bishop of Alexandria had, as far as the other nomes were concerned, just ordained presbyters and deacons, whom he visited in secret.[69] Contrary to Eutychius, who speaks of three bishops, the *History* lists ten bishops appointed by Demetrius (189–232), although only the district of the first is preserved. Demetrius appointed the first Egyptian bishop for the nomos of Ptolemais, which lay just outside the city southeast of Alexandria on the shore of Lake Mareotis.[70] Unfortunately the following folium of the manuscript is missing, so it is impossible to tell how many bishops Heraclas (232–248) and Dionysius (248–264) ordained and for which places. In the following pages the names and dioceses of twenty-nine men appointed by the Alexandrian bishop Maximus (264–282), fifty-two men ordained as bishops by the latter's successor Theonas (282–300), and fifty-five men ordained by Peter (300–311) are listed.[71] The author of the *History of the Episcopate of Alexandria* undoubtedly had access to the

archives of the Alexandrian bishop's seat, and provides us with unparalleled and so far otherwise unknown information about the early history
of the Egyptian church. From the bishops' names and sees preserved from
the period of tenure of Maximus (248–264), it seems that it was Lower
Egypt, the Delta region, and Libya that were the earliest strongholds of
Christianity in Egypt. Oxyrhynchus probably received its first bishop,
Sotas, under Maximus (264–282).[72] The Arsinoite nome seems to have
been ruled solely by presbyters and deacons up to the time of Theonas
(282–300), who appointed a certain Philippus as its bishop.[73]

Placing the Stories about Jesus in their Sociohistorical Context

This chapter has presented a theoretical reflection on the methodological
approach of the study, and has debated the special status of Egypt among
the many provinces of the Roman Empire. The next chapter identifies the
first readers of the New Testament Gospels, and looks at their social and
economic environments. Who were the people who met to read and study
the accounts of the life of Jesus of Nazareth? Who owned or had access to
these manuscripts, and who were able to read these texts? What use did
they make of these texts in their daily lives? And to what extent did these
writings influence their own prose? Knowing more about early readers
sheds light on how contemporaries in the second and third centuries CE
understood and interpreted these New Testament texts. What associations,
memories, or feelings did the stories of the life of Jesus elicit in them?
Which elements of these accounts did they consider ordinary and which
exceptional (and potentially contrary to those a modern reader would
identify)?

Chapter III focuses on the Augustan census mentioned in Luke's
Gospel, which forced Mary and Joseph to travel the 124 miles from their
home in Nazareth in Galilee to Bethlehem in Judaea. After years of civil
war and internal strife, Augustus, self-proclaimed restorer of the Republic,
reestablished the Republican instrument of the census, both as an aid to
military recruitment and as a basis for taxation. The census also impressed
upon its subject peoples the level of organization and efficiency of the
Roman dominion. Several questions arise regarding the Roman census
mentioned in the Gospel of Luke. What population did this census set out
to record? How did it proceed? When was it held? Dating the birth of the
historical Jesus depends on the dating of this census. Information gathered

from the papyri about the function of the Roman provincial census provides clues to this puzzle.

Chapter IV unravels the status and role of women in the Greco-Roman world, examining their property and inheritance rights, their level of education, and their public role. In the Gospels of John and Matthew, Jesus appears to his female followers (above all Mary Magdalene) before his male disciples. Instructed to inform the disciples of Jesus' resurrection, Luke records that the women's testimony was not believed by the male disciples. The apocryphal gospels, wrested from one and a half millennia of oblivion by the papyrus finds of the twentieth century, report on conflicts between the men and women of the earliest Christian communities. In contrast to the canonical New Testament texts, the apocrypha grant a much greater role to Mary Magdalene, who has been incorrectly identified in Catholic tradition since Gregory I as the anonymous sinner who anointed the feet of Jesus. The Gospel according to Mary enjoyed a certain popularity in Roman Egypt, which contrasts with the exclusion of women from positions of leadership within the Egyptian church.

Chapter V focuses on the life of a carpenter's family as a representation of a typical artisan family in the early Roman Empire, exploring its size, composition, income, social position, and daily routine; then Chapter VI examines the peripatetic lifestyle of Jesus and his followers, his family, his disciples, and the apostles. Studies of ancient mobility usually restrict themselves to consideration of the Roman elites and other closely associated issues such as the *cursus publicus*. Despite their low social status, the travel patterns of various biblical protagonists did not represent anything unusual within the context of Greco-Roman society. Epigraphic records and literary sources confirm the story told by papyrus customs receipts and private letters indicating a high level of mobility among the lower classes of the Roman Empire.

Chapter VII turns to a group on the margins of Greco-Roman society: shepherds. In the New Testament period shepherds held a position very different from that of the shepherd kings of the Old Testament. New Testament exegesis made use of the symbolism of this profession derived from the Old Testament. It has been on the one hand the motif of the "shepherd of the people," a symbol of the exemplary ruler, and on the other hand the image of the "good shepherd," as allegory of Jesus Christ, that have so far dominated scholarly interpretation. Limited examination of these different terms has hampered research into the actual lives of shepherds in Roman times. The study of the papyri from Roman Egypt enables us to reconstruct this reality.

In closing, Chapter VIII revisits the primary argument of the book: that papyri are valuable for our understanding of the social history of antiquity as well as of the importance of studying everyday history in the Roman provinces for a full appraisal of the New Testament Gospels in their historical context.

CHAPTER II

The Social Milieu of Early Christians in Egypt
Who were the First Readers of the New Testament Gospels?

To my dearest lady sister in the Lord, greetings.
Lend the Ezra, since I lent you the Little Genesis.
Farewell from us in God.

P.Oxy. 63.4365

The Earliest Christian Papyri

There is hardly any other topic in papyrology and perhaps even ancient history that has sparked greater interest among the general public over the past century than the discovery of fragments of the Christian Gospels in Egypt's desert sands. The possibility of discovering manuscripts with the words of Christ written just decades after his death has not lost any of its fascination over the past 150 years. Ever since the discovery of these papyri containing passages from the Gospels, however, papyrologists and biblical scholars have been arguing over their correct dating, a task which predominantly relies on paleographic analysis. Experts' opinions on the age of the handwriting as well as on the general reliability of this exercise to determine even a manuscript's age range vary widely. There have been some researchers who have dated multiple fragments to the late first or early second century, while more recent research argues that none of these texts come from a period before the end of the second century, or even the early third century.[1]

An equally interesting question has rarely been posed: Who were the people who owned and studied these early copies of the Gospels recounting the life and death of Jesus Christ? In early excavations of papyri, little attention was paid to the archeological context, and because of this, we often know little or nothing about the place of discovery of these fragments of New Testament literature. If we want to learn more about their owners and readers, we have to look for documentary evidence in which these individuals might have left traces of their Christian faith and their knowledge of early Christian literature.

A Christian Family Living in the Fayum

A papyrus letter, *P.Bas.* 2.43 (Figure 2.1), which has been housed for more than a hundred years in the papyrus collection of Basel University, sheds light through the general darkness covering the early history of Christian communities in the Egyptian chora. Recently I have shown that this letter comes from the ancient town of Theadelphia, located in the northwest corner of the Fayum. Based on prosopographical analysis, I have argued that it dates to the 230s, which would confirm Wilcken's paleographic analysis and identification of it as the oldest Christian documentary papyrus, a few decades earlier than any other securely dated evidence.[2] All other indubitably Christian letters date to the third quarter of the third century at the earliest.[3] Considering our uncertainty about the spread of Christianity to the Egyptian hinterland in the first half of the third century, *P.Bas.* 2.43 is therefore of great importance. On the front side of the papyrus sheet the text reads as follows:[4]

> Greetings, my incomparable lord brother Paulus. I, Arrianus, salute you, praying that all is as well as possible in your life. [Since] [. . .]menibos was going to you, I thought it necessary to salute you as well as our lord father. Now, I remind you about the gymnasiarchy (?), so that we not be troubled here. For Heracleides is unable to . . . For he has been named to the city council . . . Therefore . . . but send me the fish sauce too, whichever you think good. Our lady mother is well and salutes you as well as our wives and sweetest children and our brothers and all our people. Salute our brothers [. . .]genes and Xydes. All our people salute you. I pray that you fare well in the Lord.

The letter is from a certain Arrianus to his brother Paulus and concerns mainly family matters. Some things remain vague, as the start of each line is missing. The letter is constructed following a format common for papyrus letters: (1) salutation and wishes for the welfare of the addressee, (2) occasion for writing the letter, (3) content, (4) greetings to and from family members and friends, and finally (5) renewed wishes for the welfare of the addressee and closing. The phrases employed in the letter are typical for correspondence during the entire Roman period. Arrianus uses the opportunity of an acquaintance heading to the city to write a letter to his brother. Since there was no public postal service, using this occasion is a motive we often find in Roman private letters. Arrianus also sends greetings to their father, who resides with Paulus. Arrianus remains at home with their mother, their other

2.1 Letter from the Christian Arrianus to his brother Paulus, dated to the 230s CE. Ed.pr. P.Bas. I.16; new edition: *P.Bas.* 2.43.

brothers, and their other brothers' wives and children. They also send their greetings to Paulus and assure him that they are doing well.

In line 7 we have a reference to the gymnasiarchy, the office of the gymnasiarch. The gymnasiarch was the magistrate who presided over the gymnasium (a Hellenistic public institution found in every city of the Greek East) and provided for the expenses connected to it. The office of gymnasiarch was typically held for anything from a couple of days to a whole year, and whoever held it had to use his own assets for the financial expenditures of the educational institution.[5] Paulus and his brother Arrianus thus seem to have come from the well-to-do social strata of their nome, given that Paulus or their father was being considered for the post. Perhaps Arrianus refers to troubles connected with this office because it was time-consuming and expensive.

Furthermore, a third person by the name of Heracleides is mentioned in the letter. As Arrianus reports, Heracleides had been nominated for the *boulē* – the Greek city council. Heracleides was unable to do something (the text is too fragmentary at this point to determine what he was not able to do) because of his new political duties. From other papyrus documents we know that Heracleides, mentioned in the Basel letter, belonged to the urban elite of Arsinoe, was a member of the local boulē, held several civic offices in his hometown, and was also chief administrator of the Alexandrinian notable Aurelius Appianus (239–267 CE) in Theadelphia.[6] These activities were not compensated with wages but with prestige and patronage.[7] Further papyrus documents belonging to the archive of the family show Arrianus and his presumed father Arius administrating large estates of the imperial elites as well as their own holdings.[8] Arius was also a member of the city council of Arsinoe.[9] In sum, these young men were moving within the upper social strata of their nome (cf. Figure 2.2). Arrianus' chosen parlance in his letter, including borrowings from poetry, means that he and Paulus came from a family that could afford to give their sons at least a grammarian's education and probably belonged to the upper 5 percent of their community.[10]

The *Nomen Sacrum*

The letter stands out from the mass of private letters from the Roman period by virtue of its closing greeting. The standard "I pray for your health," which is a final greeting that occurs most frequently in private letters, is expanded here with a Christian technical phrase. Arrianus wishes his brother well-being "in the Lord."[11] Both the closing greeting and the

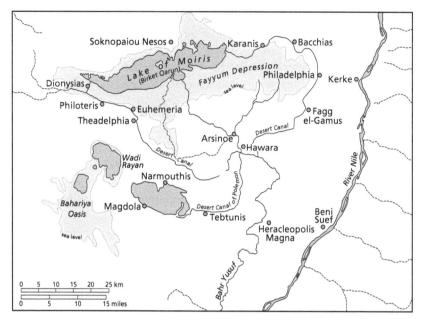

2.2 The Roman Arsinoite nome (Fayum).

distinctive Christian form of abbreviation *en kyriō* (ἐν κυρίῳ) to *en kō* (ἐν κω̄) with a horizontal stroke over it, demonstrate that the author of the letter is unquestionably Christian. This abbreviated form is what modern scholars call a *nomen sacrum*.[12] Recent scholarship has argued that a nomen sacrum should be taken as an explicit sign of Christianity.[13]

Early Christians deliberately used written abbreviations with horizontal stroke indicators for commonly written holy names. The nomen sacrum in *P. Bas.* 2.43 refers to the Lord, which is one of the earliest and most commonly attested nomina sacra in Christian literary texts.[14] In documentary papyri such as private letters, nomina sacra only appear for the first time in the third quarter of the third century.[15] Thus, the Basel letter is not only the earliest known Christian private letter, but also the earliest known evidence for a nomen sacrum in Egyptian documentary source material.

Arrianus' knowledge of the nomen sacrum notation can only be attributed to an independent reading of the Holy Scriptures. The earliest examples with nomina sacra contractions are found in Christian literary papyri such as copies of the Gospel of John, which are dated tentatively to the late second century.[16] Our author must therefore have had these Gospels to hand and read them, as just having heard them would not have imparted knowledge of the abbreviations.[17]

I further suggest that the two brothers did not belong to the first generation of Christians living in the Fayum, but that they had been raised in the Christian faith by their parents. In pagan times, the Latin name Paul was very rarely employed in the eastern provinces of the Roman Empire.[18] It therefore seems likely that Paulus' parents had in fact named their son after the Apostle. Bishop Dionysius of Alexandria (248–264/5), a contemporary of Arrianus and Paulus, observed this trend when he wrote around the middle of the third century that "Believers often choose Paul, but also Peter, as names for their children."[19] As recent research has shown, adults changing their names upon conversion to Christianity was not common,[20] and so we can conclude that Paulus' and Arrianus' parents, both mentioned in the letter, were already Christians when their sons were born in the early third century.

Furthermore, the Basel letter brings further proof of the Christianization of the Egyptian hinterland outside Alexandria during the reign of Septimius Severus (193–211 CE). Eusebius of Caesarea in his *Church History* cites a letter of Alexander, bishop of Jerusalem, written shortly after his ascension to the bishopric in 213 CE,[21] exhorting the Christian community in Antinoopolis, a city on the east bank of the Nile in Upper Egypt, to unity. Alexander had been, together with Origen, a student at the catechetical school in Alexandria under Pantaenus and Clemens.[22] It certainly does not sound too far-fetched to think that many more sons from curial families from the Egyptian metropoleis, sent to Alexandria by their parents to complete their higher education, also attended the school and later brought the Christian faith back with them to their hometowns.

In summary, we are clearly dealing here with a Christian family originating from the curial class which owned considerable estates in Theadelphia and other villages of the Fayum, and which, in addition to their political duties and the administration of their own assets, also acted as administrators for the estates of the imperial elite.

The Social Milieu of the Earliest Christians

It is hardly surprising that we find the first Christians among the landed elite – that is, the local gentry from which the members of the city councils were appointed. City councils had been part of Egyptian urban life since 202 CE, when Septimius Severus granted municipal status to Egyptian nome capitals.[23] Membership of the city council of one's town was a mark of distinction, social prestige, and political influence. Membership was not hereditary, but since a certain amount of wealth was required (100,000 sesterces was the minimum census requirement for council members in many Roman cities), political power remained in the hands of a few rich families. If the council of Arsinoe numbered 100 members, then Arrianus' family belonged to the 100 wealthiest families of the administrative district.[24] Antony, the famous early Christian monk from Middle Egypt, also came from the landowning local elite. Antony was born around 255 CE, by which time our Christian brothers Arrianus and Paulus were already in their fifties or sixties. Antony's parents were Christians who had raised their two children, a son and a daughter, in the faith. From an early age, Antony attended church with his parents, listening to the Gospels being read aloud. Shortly after his parents died around 275 CE, he decided to give away his inherited worldly goods. According to his biographer Athanasius, he owned 300 arouras of fertile land (roughly 83 hectares), which would have easily qualified him for a seat on the local city council.[25] Wealth was important because city councilors were expected to fund public buildings and special events, as well as use their own resources to guarantee the collection of taxes. Over the course of the third century, however, city council membership increasingly became substantially more of a burden than a privilege. Massive personal expenditure was required of local landowners, and many sought ways to escape this duty.[26]

Where did the brothers or their parents pick up the new faith? I suggest that it was the mobility of the local elite that fostered the spread of Christianity to the Egyptian hinterland in the early third century.[27] Quite often, the papyri report that a resident of the Fayum or Oxyrhynchus, in Middle Egypt, had to travel to Alexandria for a court date or to conduct business,[28] and since the sons of wealthy families were typically sent to the regional capitals or to Alexandria for their higher education, parents would visit their children where they studied, and their children regularly returned home.[29] It was perhaps by virtue of one of these occasions that, in the early third century, Arrianus' father came into contact with the new faith. Christianity was flourishing in Alexandria by then, and it was easy to buy copies of the sacred texts which Arrianus had apparently studied in detail.[30]

Arrianus and Paulus had grown up in a period of peace for their faith during the long bishopric of Demetrius of Alexandria, who took office in 189 CE and led the church for forty-three years until his death in 232, presiding over a period of growth and harmony for the church. Nevertheless, Arrianus, the author of the Basel letter, when mentioning two public offices – the gymnasiarchy and membership of the city council – insinuates potential challenges arising from both these duties, and one might wonder whether he is referring here to their Christian faith, which meant officeholders faced new obstacles, rather than to the financial burdens increasingly weighing down members of the curial class.

Nonetheless, the Christian brothers apparently managed to combine their Christian faith with public duties – two ways of life that were seen by many Christian contemporaries as mutually exclusive.

Interestingly, the only other clear early evidence for Christians in the Fayum from the first half of the third century again concerns public liturgies.[31] This papyrus also originates from the metropolis Arsinoe and was later recycled by the Heroninus administration in Theadelphia, and is an official document drawn up by at least three officials of the civic administration of Arsinoe. One official was responsible for drawing up the list of the candidates' names, a second for inserting additional descriptions after each candidate's name, such as their profession and where they lived ("Isidorus is a good man, a manufacturer of oil," "Theodorus is the son of Isidorus who lives in the ------- building" or "Ammonius is a blabbermouth, a construction worker"), and a third for the eventual rankings of candidates. A certain Antonius Dioscorus, son of Origenes, from Alexandria, is considered for the compulsory service (liturgy) of taking care of the water supply for Arsinoe. His Roman *gentilicium* Antonius and his Alexandrian provenance sets him apart from the workers and small traders listed alongside him, while the addition of "Dioscorus is a Christian" (ἔστ(ι) Χρηστιανός) by the second official is apparently in the belief that his superior, whose task it is to rank the candidates, will now know which Dioscorus was meant.[32] The official might have actually considered "Christian" to be a characterization as well as a profession or an office.[33] In a papyrus from Oxyrhynchus from the third quarter of the third century CE, the likely pagan author of the document refers to Sotas, whom we know was the bishop of the Oxyrhynchite, as the "Christian" (δι<ὰ> Σώτου τοῦ χρησια ...). Referring to Dioscorus as the "Christian" might thus have signaled for the pagan scribe that Dioscorus held a position in the local Christian clergy and was even the bishop of Arsinoe.[34] Nevertheless, the fact that he was a "Christian" did not stop the third official from placing him second in the list of men considered suitable to take over responsibility for the city's water supply. While we do not know in the case of Arrianus and Paulus whether their gentile peers knew about their Christian faith, there remains no doubt that in the case of Dioscorus the public officials were well informed and yet did not see any reason not to consider him for this position in the city's administration.

Evidence for Later Readers of the Gospels

If *P.Bas.* 2.43 documents the earliest Christians known from the Egyptian hinterland and represents the first evidence for independent readership of the New Testament texts, who were the readers decades later for which we have more papyrological evidence? The next Christian known by name and in whose life the reading of the Gospels even takes a central place is a certain Coracion. He figures as the protagonist in the story Dionysius, bishop of Alexandria, tells about a visit he made to the Fayum which took place most probably in the mid 250s: Dionysius' reason for traveling to the Fayum was to defeat a heresy that had been very popular there for quite some time, as he says. A certain Nepos, called "bishop of the Egyptians" and at that time already dead, had written a treatise interpreting the Book of Revelation in a literal, physical sense and defending the expectation of a reign of Christ on earth that would last for 1,000 years (a millennium) prior to God's final judgment (followers of this teaching are called "milleniarists"). We do not know where Nepos had been a bishop: a bishopric "of the Egyptians" is not known, but the expression is reminiscent of the "Gospel of the Egyptians" that is believed to have been read in the third century by gentile Christians in the Egyptian countryside. Another bishop who was styled "bishop of the Egyptians" was a certain Hierax, a contemporary of bishop Dionysius of Alexandria.[35] It might be that the bishop of the Arsinoite nome was called "bishop of the Egyptians," but an even wider area of authority originating from the early decades of Christianity in Egypt seems possible.[36] Nepos, who had already passed away when Dionysius visited the Fayum, might have been the first bishop of Arsinoe; Hierax, with whom Dionysius corresponded by letter in the early 260s, may have been his successor.[37]

Coracion had made Nepos' book popular in the Fayum, and Bishop Dionysius saw the need to travel to the Arsinoite nome to defend the orthodoxy in person. In a three-day conference, Dionysius gathered the presbyters, teachers, and lay Christians from the surrounding villages and set out the errors of Nepos' teachings to the gathered brethren. In the end, he managed to convince even Coracion himself.[38] Nonetheless, Dionysius found it necessary to put down his arguments against the milleniarists in the Fayum in writing – the result was his two books *On the Promises*.[39]

What do we know about Nepos and Coracion apart from their names? Next to nothing, it seems. Nepos, the "bishop of the Egyptians," was dead when this episode took place. Coracion is called by Dionysius not by an ecclesiastical title, such as priest or bishop, but simply "leader and introducer of this doctrine" in the Fayum villages.[40] Both men had Greek names, but this does not mean they could not have been Egyptians.

A search in the papyrological databases shows that Coracion (Κορακίων) had a very rare personal name. We have only seven attestations of this name in total across a span of 1,000 years, with six of these from the Arsinoite nome, one from the Oxyrhynchite, and all seven belonging to the first or second half of the third century CE.[41] In one of these papyri dated to 239 CE, a certain Coracion appears as the colleague of the city councilor Heracleides discussed above.[42] It is a request for seeds by village men. Heracleides and Coracion are being appointed by the city council as officers responsible for the watering of agricultural land in parts of the territory of the village of Theadelphia in the Fayum. Is it possible to identify the leader of the Christians in the villages of the Fayum mentioned by Dionysius of Alexandria with this city councilor Coracion? Considering the fact that our earliest documented Christians, the brothers Arrianus and Paulus, originated from the same social stratum, and that they both knew Heracleides, an identification of Coracion the city councilor of Arsinoe with Coracion the Christian leader in the Arsinoite seems at least plausible. We have another attestation of a Coracion from third-century Egypt: in a private letter found in Oxyrhynchus. In this letter, a certain Nepos writes to his lord brother Sarapion asking him to turn to Coracion for help.[43] The letter belongs to the archive of Aurelius Sarapion, alias Apollonarius, who is attested from the late second to the middle of the third century CE. Aurelius Sarapion was a city councilor and gymnasiarch of Oxyrhynchus who later became *strategos* (chief administrator) of the Arsinoite and Hermopolite nomes.[44] Again, we have references to the curial class, the local landowning elite. Nepos is likewise a rather rare name. It therefore seems possible, even if unprovable, that this Nepos and this Coracion are in fact the bishop of the Egyptians and his disciple mentioned by Dionysius of Alexandria.[45]

Be this as it may, we have one Christian family in the Fayum from the 230s who most likely also possessed Christian literature, and although there is no reference yet to a Christian community or ecclesiastical offices, the episode of Dionysius meeting Coracion and the Christian presbyters and catechists in the Fayum implies the existence of blossoming Christian communities in the Arsinoite villages in the 250s.

While the Christian brothers Arrianus and Paulus, as well as the leader of the Christian community Coracion, lived in the Fayum, the ancient territory of the metropolis Arsinoe, the evidence from another Egyptian metropolis, Oxyrhynchus, has been studied much more extensively.[46] Oxyrhynchus, which lies to the south of the Fayum, has been a treasure-trove of papyri finds.[47] Our earliest secure evidence for Christians in Oxyrhynchus, however, dates from several decades later than for the Arsinoite nome.

Luijendijk, according the documentary attestations the attention they deserve, has dealt in detail with the earliest records of individuals from

Oxyrhynchus using nomina sacra in their everyday writing (she rightly argues that nomina sacra used in everyday writings betray the writer's Christian education and familiarity with Christian literature).[48] Evidence for the use of nomina sacra in documentary papyri from Oxyrhynchus is later than the Basel letter. Luijendijk finds eleven examples of the pre-Constantinian use of nomina sacra, the earliest dating perhaps from the later 260s. A certain Sotas, who was most likely the first bishop of Oxyrhynchus ordained by the Alexandrian Patriarch Maximus (in office from 264 to 282), uses nomina sacra in his letters to what seem to be other clerics (see Figure 2.3).[49] Nomina sacra figure here in the same place as in the Basel letter, in the greeting formula. Sotas greets his correspondent "I wish you good health in the Lord" (ἐρρῶσθαί σε εὔχομαι ἐν κῳ),[50] as Arrianus also wrote to his brother Paulus in the 230s. The use of nomina sacra in texts dating to the very end of the third century or the beginning of the fourth century is more complex. While in the Sotas letters only the nomen sacrum "in the Lord" appears, later letters from the end of the third century bear as well the nomina sacra "God," "Emmanuel," and "Father."[51]

Conclusions

P.Bas. 2.43, originating from the village of Theadelphia in the Fayum and dating to the 230s CE, is the earliest documentary evidence for the spread of Christianity to the Egyptian countryside. Author and addressee Arrianus and Paulus were brothers and most likely the sons of Christian parents in what was at that time a generally classical environment. Arrianus' use of the nomen sacrum in the final greeting shows his familiarity with Christian manuscripts. He must have had access to the sacred texts and perhaps even owned them.

The earliest evidence for Christians in the Egyptian chora thus points to a well-traveled, well-read local elite (see Figure 2.4). The Basel letter tells us that Christians at that time were not hindered from taking public offices in their hometowns. In fact, they were called upon along with their pagan fellow citizens of some means; their financial situation was the decisive factor, not their faith.

Later evidence for Christian leaders in the Fayum points to the same social milieu: members of the curial class – thanks to their education and social authority – play a leading role in the early Christian communities. Even though individuals from the lower social strata undoubtedly joined these early Christian communities, due to the fact that they did not leave written traces, we are not able to catch them in our evidence.

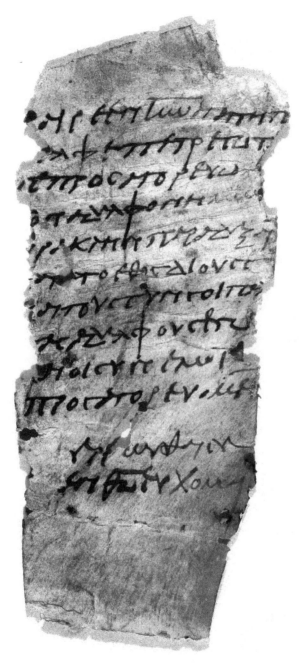

2.3 Letter from Bishop Sotas to Petrus (*PSI* 3.208).

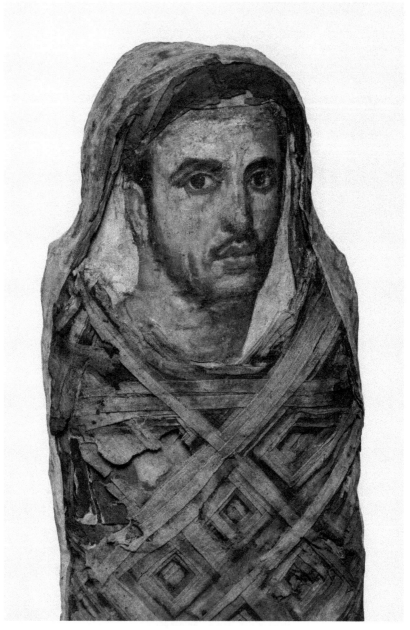

2.4 Mummy portrait of a man belonging to the local elite of the Roman Arsinoite nome, Hawara, 25–75 CE.

CHAPTER III

"In those days a decree went out ..."
The Herodian Kingdom and the Augustan Provincial Census System

> In those days Caesar Augustus issued a decree that a census should be taken of the entire Roman world. This was the first census that took place while Quirinius was governor of Syria. And everyone went to their own town to register.
>
> Luke 2:1–3

The resistance by Jewish protesters encountered by the Syrian governor Publius Sulpicius Quirinius and the troops accompanying him is unlikely to have unduly surprised him. Only by force of arms were he and his men able to subdue the uprising and restore calm and order. Caesar Augustus, for whom he had already fought many a battle in the east, had recently appointed him *legatus Augusti*, legate governor of the province of Syria, then the second-richest province in the empire after Egypt. Augustus had also charged him with administering an additional region, Judaea, which had been ruled over by a Roman client king until very recently. To begin with, Augustus had tasked Quirinius with carrying out a census in order to gain an overview of the economic strength of the inhabitants. There was nothing unusual in this: the emperor placed a high value on collecting numerical data on his empire. Right at the beginning of his sole rule, he had ordered a first census in Gaul.[1] While all had gone well on that occasion in 27 BCE – the Gallic tribes had allowed themselves to be registered with only minimal resistance – a rebellion had broken out fifteen years later during the second census,[2] and it had taken some time for the province to calm down again. The newly created Roman province of Egypt had seen similar developments. There too Octavian, later styled Augustus, had ordered a census to be carried out relatively soon after the establishment of the province in 30 BCE, and rebellion had erupted there as well.[3] The trigger for the turmoil in the provinces in each case was not so much the census itself, the simple recording of the population, but the purpose behind it: the information obtained made it possible to assess the annual tax liability of each individual to the Roman state with precision. Quirinius had to admit to himself, however, that the uproar in Judaea this time seemed qualitatively different. The malcontents were not merely disgruntled at the prospect of paying tribute to their new overlords; the count in and of itself seemed to be agitating them. Their leader, who called himself Judas of Galilee, had been fomenting popular unrest with speeches opposing Roman occupation, castigating the planned tallying as a sign of the subjugation of the Jewish people, and even denouncing the census as sacrilegious. It would be a disgrace, he had been preaching, for the Jews to recognize any ruler above them other than their Lord, the one true God. In light of his insistence that their God would only help those who helped themselves, quite a few people had heeded his call to arms.

Judaea had until recently been ruled by the client king Herodes Archelaus. After complaints about misrule, however, Augustus had decided to remove him and place Judaea and Samaria under the rule of the governor of Syria. Galilee remained under the client king Herodes Antipas, brother of Archelaus (see Figure 3.1). Quirinius, the governor of Syria, was an experienced commander in his prime who had reached the highest political office some time before – he had been a consul in Rome more than fifteen years earlier – and had gone on to accumulate years of experience defending the ever-expanding borders of the empire in the east. He had even been rewarded with triumphal honors in Rome. He probably did not doubt that he would be able to complete his task of taking a census successfully in spite of the uprising led by Judas – and he did complete it, registering the population and collecting the tributes due. We know from Tacitus, Strabo, and Josephus that the following years were also successful ones for the governor. He remained governor of Syria for six years, twice as long as his predecessors had, and when Augustus died, in 14 CE, and his adoptive son Tiberius took up the reins of government, Quirinius also enjoyed the favor of the new emperor, which was by no means a given in those days. When he finally died at a ripe old age in 21 CE, the Emperor Tiberius even honored him with a state funeral.

What Quirinius certainly cannot have suspected at the time, however, was that the census he was about to conduct would mark a dramatic turning point for two world religions, one which would still be remembered after two millennia. For one, it marked the beginning of one of the worst disasters in its history; for the other, the census and the name of Quirinius would forever remain connected with the birth of the founder of their religion, a man whose influence would outlast the Roman Empire.

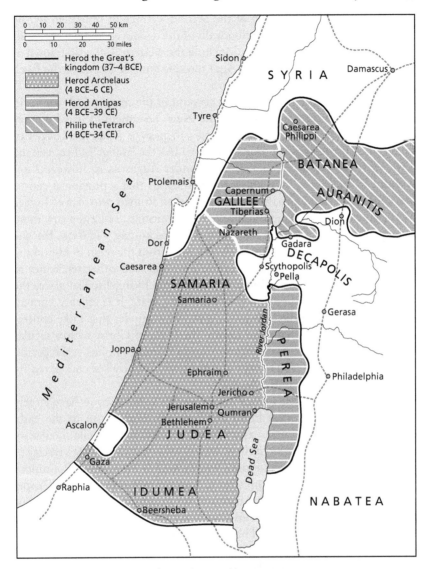

3.1 Judaea and its neighboring regions.

Flavius Josephus, the first-century Romano-Jewish historian, gives a detailed account of the census conducted by Quirinius in 6 CE in his *Antiquities of the Jews*.[4] Josephus views the uprising incited by Judas of Galilee as the beginning of the Jewish rebellion against Roman rule that culminated in the destruction of the Second Temple in Jerusalem by the Romans in 70 CE. The foundation walls of the destroyed and never rebuilt Temple are still extant today and include the western wall, also known as the Wailing Wall. Today, the al-Aqsa mosque and the Dome of the Rock are both located on the Temple Mount.

An even more widely popularized account of the census of Quirinius in Judaea can, however, be found in the New Testament. Virtually every Christian will be familiar with the relevant passage from the Gospel of Luke. The historical connection drawn by Luke the Evangelist between the birth of Jesus and a census in Judaea under Augustus is, however, not without its problems.[5] We know from Josephus that a provincial census was conducted in 6 CE in the newly established Roman province of Judaea by the governor of Syria, Publius Sulpicius Quirinius. Luke appears, then, to be placing the birth of Christ – in modern reckoning – in 6 CE. But the Gospel of Luke also places the birth of Jesus within the reign of Herod the Great, who ruled over Judaea, Galilee, Samaria, and other territories as a vassal king supported by Rome.[6] Matthew the Evangelist also places the birth of Jesus within the reign of Herod the Great.[7] It is reliably known, however, that Herod died early in 4 BCE. This implies that Luke contradicts himself in his attempt to situate the birth of Christ within secular history, since the historical dates he uses as reference points – the period toward the end of Herod's reign and the provincial census conducted by Quirinius – lie almost a decade apart.

The approaches taken toward resolving this contradiction have largely fallen into two categories. From the sixteenth century up to the early nineteenth century countless attempts were made to reconcile the dating of the above-mentioned events in order to avoid questioning the veracity of the biblical record. The question was tackled by a variety of eminent figures, including John Calvin, who in a 1556 commentary on the Gospel of Luke surmised that historical inaccuracies were more likely to have crept into the account given by Flavius Josephus than into the Gospel of Luke. Other scholars, among them Theodor Mommsen, believed that Quirinius must have been governor of Syria twice, once during Herod's lifetime and then again from 6 CE onwards. However, the governors of Syria during the reign of Herod and after his death are known, and the list does not leave room for a second governorship for Quirinius.[8] A further popular theory embraced by many suggested that the translation of the relevant passage should read "This registration was taken before Quirinius was governor of Syria." From the first half of the nineteenth century onwards, doubts were then cast on the historical accuracy of the Gospel of Luke. The account of the birth of Jesus given in this gospel increasingly tended to be seen as a legend of salvation that was irreconcilable with the historical facts; its author had aimed primarily, it was suggested, to move the birth of Jesus to Bethlehem and to establish a connection between Jesus and his descent from the house of David.[9] This version has now become widely accepted by the majority of New Testament scholars pursuing historical-critical approaches.[10] The hypothesis nevertheless jars with the claim to historical authenticity made for his own work by the author of the Gospel.[11] As is spelled out in the Introduction above, Luke places his work within the tradition of Greek history writing. His phrasing is reminiscent of Thucydides, and it is clear from the emphasis he places on his desire to give an exact record of events that he wishes to be taken seriously as a historian.[12]

I turn to the question of the dating of the birth of Jesus in the Gospel of Luke not because I wish to claim that I have found the definitive solution to this puzzle, which has occupied the minds of New Testament theologians for centuries. I am interested in the topic primarily because of the census mentioned by Luke and the insights we can gain into it from considering another Roman census and taxation system originating in the Augustan period, the Roman census in the province of Egypt.

In the third and second centuries before Christ, censuses of the Roman people were held at regular five-year intervals and concluded with a religious festival, the *lustrum* (see Figure 3.2).[13] Rome was expanding territorially in this period, and was establishing provinces which required regular censuses to be held. From this point on, distinctions were made between censuses of Roman citizens, be they in Rome itself or in the provinces, and censuses to register the inhabitants of the provinces who did not possess Roman citizenship. In the first century before Christ civil wars led to breaks in this regular cycle, but once Octavian, the great-nephew and principal heir of Gaius Julius Caesar, had won out in the power struggles that ensued upon the latter's murder in 44 BCE, he reintroduced the institution of the census – albeit no longer at five-year intervals – as part of his program to restore the former order.[14]

Augustus also had provincial censuses held in every part of the empire. Ordered by the emperor, if no special *legati* or *procuratores* were dispatched to oversee them they were conducted by governors by means of an edict. Governors delegated responsibility for taking the census in individual cities, judicial districts, or rural areas to equestrian officials (particularly *procuratores*) or to officers. While the census in Egypt took place regularly at fourteen-year intervals from early in the first century CE onwards, we

3.2 Census registration of Roman citizens from the Altar of Domitius Ahenobarbus
(late second century BCE).

know little about the time intervals between censuses in other provinces. It is known for certain, however, that the provincial censuses were not held at the same time throughout the entire empire.

New papyrus finds in recent decades have expanded our knowledge of the beginnings of the Roman provincial census in Egypt.[15] In Egypt, as in Gaul, the earliest reference we have to a Roman census dates from the early years of the sole reign of Augustus. Registration was initially annual, but from 11 BCE onwards a census covering the population was carried out every seven years, from 11 CE onward every fourteen years. The purpose behind the provincial census was to capture the population size and tax-raising potential of the subjected people of the relevant province; in the first century after Christ, this group still vastly outnumbered that of Roman citizens, who were exempt from poll and land taxes. Tax assessment cannot, however, have been the only objective behind the Roman census, since women, minors, and old men (those over age 62) were registered even though these population segments were all exempt from the poll tax. Taking censuses may well have served symbolic aims as well as more practical purposes: through the taking of a census, the Roman state could demonstrate its might, control, and efficiency in a form which reached into even the most obscure provincial backwater, while regular registration made it clear to each and every inhabitant of the empire that they lived under Roman rule.[16]

Surviving census declarations show that individuals were recorded on a household by household (*kat' oikian* in Greek) basis – a single census declaration related to all the members of a given household.[17] Luke uses the verb *apographô* for the census and, in another place, the noun *apographê*. *Apographô* does not mean "to count," however, but "to write down." The census involved far more than simply counting the population: large quantities of personal data spanning a considerable range of categories were written down. The Roman Egyptian census declarations contain correspondingly detailed data on parameters including age, sex, occupation, place of residence, familial relationships, number of children, and possessions (see Figure 3.3). Census declarations were archived by officials, compiled into lists by the administrators for each nome, and used in the computation of taxes. We currently have information on around 400 households in Roman Egypt and on the approximately 1,500 people who lived in those households, and, as excavations in Egypt proceed, new declarations are still being found, edited, and published every year.

Details in Census Declarations

It is important to stress that the Roman provincial census conducted in Egypt that we are presently discussing is the first census in recorded history, not merely the first from the ancient Greco-Roman world, from which surviving data on a premodern population has come down to us in a quality comparable with Western European censuses from the nineteenth century or censuses held in developing countries today. We possess very little information from other censuses from ancient Babylonia, Egypt and Israel. In the best case, we have the total population numbers arrived at; in the majority of cases, we have no more to go on than a remark by a later historian that a census was conducted. We do not know how people were counted, who exactly was counted, and what attributes were recorded. And we do not have the raw data that was collected, the information provided by individuals. Censuses do not count people purely to determine the number of inhabitants in a given area. This is as true now as it was in ancient times. Citizens are normally required to fill in questionnaires and to disclose personal information in a wide range of categories: name, age,

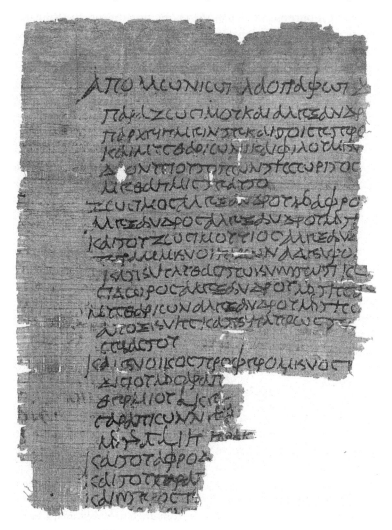

3.3 Census return of five brothers residing together in the city of Arsinoe (SB 10. 10759 dated to 35 CE)

gender, normal place of residence, marital status, household size, occupation, religion, ethnicity, the language used for everyday communication, literacy, family background, birthplace and nationality, the place of residence and the nature of the stay in that place on the day of the census, and perhaps also specific physical features. Statistical information is then compiled from the personal data of individuals.

Census declarations were normally addressed to the Roman officials charged with taking the census, called in Greek *laographoi*, in Latin *censitores*. A provincial census was always initiated through an edict issued by the governor; we know this because declarants often make reference to these edicts in their census declarations. These edicts from the governors proclaiming censuses would certainly have emphasized the will of the emperor in the usual manner. This means that Luke's reference to a decree from Augustus does not contradict the hypothesis that he was referring to a provincial census held by the governor of Syria.[18]

We have here a census declaration from a divorced or widowed single mother called Tatybynchis who was, going by the name, of Egyptian origin. The woman appears together with her guardian, a relative. She registered her household in the summer of 34 CE after the edict proclaiming the provincial census had been issued in 33 CE.

> To Eirenaios and Maron and Herakleides and Ammonios and Petesouchos, *laographoi*, and to Herakleides, village clerk of Philadelphia, from Tatybynchis, daughter of Mareis, of the same village, with my guardian, my relative Patouamtis, son of Ptollis. In the present twentieth year of Tiberius Caesar Augustus I register my son Panetbeueis, son of Kephalon, who lives in my own house; my above-mentioned son Panetbeveis, son of Kephalon, is 5 years old, and myself, Tatybynchis, daughter of Mareis, 35 years old, with a scar on my right thumb, together with my guardian, my relative Patouamtis, son of Ptollis, who is 36 years old and has a scar below his right brow. June 13 in the twentieth year of Tiberius Caesar Augustus. (Second hand:) Registered in the twentieth year of Tiberius Caesar Augustus, June 13. (Third hand:) I, Herakleides, village clerk, have noted it.[19]

After the addressee and the dating by the regnal year of the current Roman emperor, the next piece of information is the name of the person registering his or her household and those who live within it. We typically discover the name of the head of the household here, along with the name of his father and his mother and sometimes also his paternal and maternal grandfathers, and the name of the village or town he is from. Women also appear as household heads, but normally only when the family had no male representative of full age or when they were registering property in another form, such as land or unoccupied buildings. They are normally accompanied by a male guardian, often a kinsman but sometimes also a son or husband. At times they are represented by an administrator, typically one from the slave class. We possess census declarations for land, for houses that were unoccupied or occupied only by tenants, and for households in which the person making the declaration resided along with his family.

After the information on the addressee and the declarant, the date, and the list of property had been given, the next section contains the core element in the census declaration, the list with the members of the household being registered. The first name on the list is the name of the person submitting the declaration. In the largest households, this is then followed by a list of family members. Then the tenants who did not belong to the family are listed, and finally the slaves. Here we discover the name of each resident and normally also the name of his father and his mother, his age and occupation, and how he was connected to the head of the household.

At the end we find the signature of the head of the household submitting the declaration, and sometimes also an oath to confirm that the information given is true, along with the date of submission and acknowledgement of the receipt of the declaration by the official responsible for processing it.

Giving false information or attempting to avoid registration attracted heavy penalties. In the *Gnomon of the Idios Logos*, an administrative manual from Roman Egypt, we read:

> §58: Those persons who register neither themselves nor their family members in the census by household will have a quarter of their property confiscated. If it is discovered that they did not register in two consecutive censuses, a further quarter of their property will be confiscated.
> §59: . . .
> §60: Those who have not registered their slaves shall lose only their slaves.

Most of the surviving documents are from Middle and Upper Egypt, where the climatic conditions exist for the conservation of papyrus: the Nile Delta and the capital Alexandria were simply too damp for their preservation. The poll tax chiefly affected the inhabitants (and mainly the indigenous Egyptian population) of the towns and villages of the chora, the Egyptian hinterland. Residents in rural areas paid tax at the highest rate, while those of the *metropoleis*, a privileged group of town dwellers, paid at a lower rate.[20]

Return to One's Own Town

Coming back to the census described by Luke, we can briefly leave aside the thorny question of its dating as we consider whether the description of the circumstances of the census appears to be realistic.

All went to their own towns to be registered. Joseph also went from the town of Nazareth in Galilee to Judaea, to the city of David called Bethlehem, because he was descended from the house and family of David. He went to be registered with Mary, to whom he was engaged and who was expecting a child.[21]

Census declarations from Roman Egypt can help us here. We know from the dates on the Roman Egyptian census declarations that the population in the cities had to report to the office of the bureaucrat in charge of the census to make their declarations within a certain period of time after the governor's edict had been published – it seems that this could run for up to one and a half years. In the villages, the census recorders seem to have been traveling officials who remained in the village for only a few days or weeks, depending on its size, to collect the required data from residents (the declarations we have from particular villages have all been made within the space of a few days).

If this was the usual procedure for a Roman provincial census, then why does Luke report that Joseph had to go back to the place he was from? Many New Testament scholars pursuing historical-critical approaches do not find Luke's description of a census which required provincial inhabitants to journey to ancestral towns historically plausible. But even if we assume that Luke sends Joseph on a journey from Nazareth to Bethlehem for reasons purely to do with salvation history, we still have a mystery on our hands: would Luke not have had to make some effort to make his report about the census credible to contemporaries? Even at the time of Luke, writing around eighty or ninety years after the birth of Jesus, the Romans were still holding regular provincial censuses on the Augustan model throughout the entire empire, so inhabitants of every province would have been intimately familiar with the procedure.

We know from the tax lists that have survived on papyrus that everybody had to register in the place where they lived. People's places of residence and the places where they owned property were normally identical. But when somebody also owned property elsewhere, such as land or houses, perhaps an inheritance which was now let out to tenants or unoccupied, he also had to travel to that location to declare what he owned there himself. Moreover, several decades ago a papyrus came to light in Egypt which showed that some people were indeed required to return home and register in the place where their families lived. The document in question is an edict issued in Alexandria by the Prefect of Egypt in 104 CE.

Gaius Vibius Maximus, Prefect of Egypt, declares: The census by household has begun and it is accordingly necessary that all persons who are not resident at home for one reason or another at this time return to their homeplaces in order to undergo the usual registration formalities and to attend to the cultivation of land which is their concern. In the knowledge, however, that workers from the countryside are required in our city (i.e. Alexandria), I desire that all who believe they have good cause to remain here have themselves registered with the divisionary commander here in the city, Volsius Festus, to whom I have entrusted this matter. Those who demonstrate that their presence (here in the city) is required will be issued with signed permits. Everybody else must return to the place of residence of their family within thirty days. All apprehended without a permit after this period will be punished without limits.[22]

The difference, however, is that the edict from 104 CE only commanded the rural population of Alexandria to return from their temporary places of work in the city to the places where their families were resident, while Mary and Joseph were expected to return to the birthplace of their ancestors. Or do modern scholars misinterpret this passage in the Gospel of Luke?

It was noted even by ancient commentators that this return to one's ancestors' home in the Gospel of Luke described something which was not self-evident and called for an explanation. John Chrysostom, the Patriarch of Constantinople, explained in a sermon from the late fourth century that the journey had been necessary because Joseph was only temporarily resident in Nazareth but a citizen of Bethlehem, where he likely also owned some land.[23] This explanation is supported by what we have discovered in our Egyptian papyri: various groups – workers from the countryside in Alexandria as well as individuals who owned property in several different locations – needed to leave their places of residence and register elsewhere. In this light, Luke's description seems thoroughly realistic if one accepts that his intent was to leave his readers with the impression that Joseph's family was originally from Bethlehem and owned some property there.

Dating of the Census

Now let us return to the problem of the dating of the census to which Luke makes reference. In the Christmas story, Luke speaks of an order issued by Augustus to record the entire world population:

In those days a decree went out from Emperor Augustus that all the world should be registered. This was the first registration and was taken while Quirinius was governor of Syria.[24]

For this reason, it has generally been assumed that Luke was referring to an imperial census; but a census of the Roman people would not have affected Joseph, since he was not a Roman citizen. Moreover, no imperial census took place during the period in which Quirinius was governor of Syria, from 6 to 12 CE. The account of Augustus' deeds that was widely disseminated throughout the empire after his death makes reference to three imperial censuses during his reign: in 28 BCE, 8 BCE, and 14 CE.[25]

It is beyond historical doubt that Quirinius was governor of Syria from 6 to 12 CE and that he conducted a provincial census in Judaea which caused Judas and his adherents to rise up. To avoid questioning the historical accuracy of the Gospels, historical research on Jesus long posed the question as to whether Quirinius could have been governor of the province of Syria on two separate occasions, once around 7 BCE and then a second time, twelve years later, from 6 CE onwards. Adherents of this theory have advanced in its support an inscription that was found in Tibur/Tivoli near Rome in 1764 and is now on display in the Vatican Museums.[26] The name of the person being honored has not survived, but the text mentions that he had been a consul, a proconsul in Asia Minor, and twice governor in Syria and Phoenicia ("proconsul Asiam provinciam opti[nuit] [legatus pro praetore] divi Augusti iterum Syriam et Pho[enicen] [optinuit]"). Scholars going all the way back to Theodor Mommsen have identified this man who twice served as governor of Syria as Publius Sulpicius Quirinius.[27] But other candidates to whom this acephalous inscription from Tibur may have been dedicated have also been proposed; they include Marcus Plautius Silvanus and Lucius Calpurnius Piso.[28]

A Roman Provincial Census in the Kingdom of Herod the Great?

Another point is that a provincial census which was demonstrably taken by Quirinius in Judaea in 6 CE would not have affected Joseph. Joseph lived in Nazareth in Galilee, which was still ruled by Herod's son Antipas at that time. A provincial census in Judaea after it had been annexed by Rome would not have prompted him to travel there from the formally independent Galilee. For a journey from Nazareth in Galilee to Bethlehem in Judaea for a census to make sense, both areas, Galilee and Judaea, would have to have been under the dominion of a single ruler (cf. figure 3.1).

It is tempting to assume that the author of the Gospel of Luke, writing around eighty years after the event, was not precisely informed about the complicated territorial structures that had been in place at the time. By the time of writing, these regions had all been fully incorporated into the Roman Empire. But to make such assumptions would be to underestimate the author. It is plain from his historical contextualization of the life and work of John the Baptist that he was very precisely aware of which territories had been under the dominion of particular rulers at particular times, and he also matches this information correctly with dates expressed in terms of the regnal years of the Roman emperors.[29]

So could the census in Luke's account have taken place before the end of the reign of Herod the Great? Researchers who have concerned themselves with Herod have typically roundly rejected this theory, since it is normally assumed that Herod reigned autonomously within his territory, although he depended on Augustus for his legitimacy.[30] A passage in the *Annals* of Tacitus suggests, however, that a census in the territory of a Roman client king was not an impossibility.

> At this same time the Clitæ, a tribe subject to the Cappadocian Archelaus, retreated to the heights of Mount Taurus, because they were compelled in Roman fashion to render an account of their revenue and submit to tribute. There they defended themselves by means of the nature of the country against the king's unwarlike troops, till Marcus Trebellius, whom Vitellius, the governor of Syria, sent as his lieutenant with four thousand legionaries and some picked auxiliaries, surrounded with his lines two hills occupied by the barbarians, the lesser of which was named Cadra, the other Davara. Those who dared to sally out, he reduced to surrender by the sword, the rest by drought.[31]

Tacitus makes reference to a Roman census in 36 CE in the kingdom of Archelaus II, the Roman client king of Cilicia Tracheia. The Roman governor of Syria is depicted as having assisted the client king in holding a census on the Roman model in the territory he ruled. This means that we can add an additional category to the two varieties of Roman census normally distinguished: we have (1) the *imperial census*; (2) the *provincial census*; and (3) now also the *client state census*, presumably conducted by client rulers surveying their subjects according to the model of the Roman provincial census, most probably on Roman orders and with the support of Roman units.[32]

This suggests that a similar census on the Roman model could well have taken place in the kingdom of Herod the Great, officially directed by Herod but with military and administrative support from the Roman governor in neighboring Syria. As a vassal king, Herod was dependent on the favor of Augustus and legitimized by his support. Let us call the events of 8 BCE to mind. This was the year in which Augustus ordered an imperial census, and, according to my hypothesis, also ordered a census to be taken in the area ruled over by his vassal king, Herod. A rift had opened up between Augustus and Herod only a year earlier, in 9 BCE, after Herod had mounted a military campaign against the Nabataeans. This had been discussed beforehand with the governor Saturninus, but Herod had neglected to secure the approval of Augustus as well.[33] Augustus then broke their *amicitia*, their political friendship, after more than twenty years, and threatened to treat Herod as a subject rather than as a friend and ally from that point onwards. Could this have motivated Augustus to order a Roman census in Herod's kingdom to assess the tax-raising potential of the region, recalculate the tribute due, and put Herod firmly in his place? A census in Herod's kingdom, carried out by officials dispatched by the governor of neighboring Syria, would have made his dependence on Rome unmistakably clear.[34] A Roman census in Herod's kingdom would not, moreover, have represented the only direct interaction between Augustus and the subjects of his client king. The oath of loyalty to Augustus which Herod's subjects were required to swear in 6 or 5 BCE also indicates an understanding of the nature of Roman rule that was increasingly unfettered by borders and which interfered with the normal autonomy of a client king in interior affairs.[35]

Quirinius or Saturninus?

What do the earliest Christian authors, those still writing in times when Roman provincial censuses regularly took place, have to say about this passage in the Gospel of Luke? Did they, like modern theologians, perceive historical inconsistency in Luke's dating of the birth of Jesus? To my knowledge, only two of these early authors expressly mention a census around the time of the birth of Jesus. These are Justin Martyr, who was from Judaea but lived and worked in Rome at the time of writing, and Tertullian, a Christian apologist from North Africa.

Justin, in his apology for the Christian faith, writes around the middle of the second century: "Now there is a village in the land of the Jews, thirty-five stadia from Jerusalem, in which Jesus Christ was born, as you can ascertain also from the registers of the taxing made under Cyrenius, your first procurator in Judaea."[36] Justin is directly highlighting the possibility of consulting the Roman archives to access the census data given by the family of Jesus here. We know from Roman Egypt that it was quite straightforward for the local population to obtain a copy of census declarations from earlier censuses from the archive in their nome. Historic census declarations could be retrieved from the local archives even after many decades, in order to resolve disputes over inheritance and similar issues.[37] Justin's apology was addressed to Emperor Antoninus Pius and the Senate, and if the census data had *not* actually existed, it would have been quite easy for them to demonstrate that Justin was lying.

It is interesting to note that Justin does not refer to Cyrenius/Quirinius as governor, but as *procurator*, an entirely different office. The governor of an imperial province such as the province of Syria, the *legatus Augusti*, was normally tasked with managing military and administrative affairs and with the administration of justice at the highest level. Financial affairs were, however, normally the responsibility of an independent procurator of finance, who was directly responsible to the emperor and was tasked with collecting taxes and levies, and, above all, with the organization of the provincial census.[38] We have, for example, inscriptions referring to a *"procurator ad census accipiendos Cappadociae et Armeniae minoris,"* a census administrator in Cappadocia and Armenia, and to a *"procurator ad census Pannoniae,"* a census administrator in Pannonia. When Herod died in 4 BCE, Varus was governor of Syria and a certain Sabinus, the man who confiscated the temple treasure of Herod in Judaea, was his procurator. The Greek translation of *procurator* used by Josephus is *hegemon* or *epitropos*; the term *procurator* never refers to a governor. Luke also uses the present participle *hegemoneuon*, "to be a hegemon" (ἡγεμονεύοντος τῆς Συρίας), to refer to the role of Quirinius, indicating that he might in fact have held the position of procurator. Luke certainly does not call Quirinius a governor, a term normally rendered in Greek as *strategos*. Quirinius could, then, have taken a census in the function of a procurator of finance, a treasurer, subordinate to the governor of Syria. But in that case, who was the governor at the time?

Perhaps consulting Tertullian can offer a solution. In or around 208 CE, he writes: "Also it is well known that a census had just been taken in Judaea by Sentius Saturninus, and they might have inquired of his ancestry in those records."[39] Tertullian also makes reference to the Roman archives in which the relevant census records could be consulted. In the source accessed by Tertullian, however, it appears that Gaius Sentius Saturninus is named as the governor of Syria in the period during which the family of Jesus went to be registered. Other sources also make reference to Gaius Sentius Saturninus. Josephus reports, for example, that Saturninus was governor of Syria from 9 to 6 BCE.[40] It was Saturninus who was governor of Syria at the point when Herod fell into disgrace with Augustus in 8 BCE and Augustus formally rescinded their friendship. And it was Saturninus who presided over the proceedings against Herod's sons Alexander and Aristobulus that took place in 7 BCE at the instigation of Herod himself (they had conspired against him and were punished with death): by involving the Roman governor Saturninus, Herod sought to have his course of action officially sanctioned by Rome again. So was it under the governorship of Saturninus that a census in the territory of Herod the Great took place, and was Quirinius in the role of procurator tasked with its actual implementation on the ground? Tertullian specifically says that it was generally known that censuses had taken place in Judaea under Saturninus. This clearly points to a time when Herod the Great was still alive. If this were accurate, then all our problems would be solved.

The purpose of Luke's reference in the Christmas story to the first census would then be to clarify that several censuses took place and that this one, the first one conducted by Quirinius, had taken place during the reign of Herod the Great. He explicitly mentions that this census was the first one because the second census – the one that took place twelve years later, when Quirinius was governor of the province, and a certain Coponius was procurator – would have occupied a much more prominent place in the memory of contemporaries as the census marking the beginning of events culminating in the Jewish War and in the destruction of the Temple.[41] In Gaul, too, it had not been the first provincial census under Augustus in 27 BCE that had led to rebellion, but the second one in 12 BCE [42] – presumably because the local population were aware the second time around that the primary purpose of the census was the collection of tax revenue.

Justin and Tertullian both highlight, independently of one another, that the documents from the census relating to the family of Jesus were available for consultation in the Roman archives. If this had been untrue, it would have been an incredible claim to make in light of the ease with which documents in the archives could be retrieved and consulted.

The simplest solution to the puzzles thrown up by this much discussed passage appears to be that the Gospel of Luke made reference to Quirinius not as governor but as procurator; it is clear from other sources that Gaius Sentius Saturninus was governor in Syria from 9 to 6 BCE. The correct translation of Luke 2:1 should then read:

> In those days a decree went out from Emperor Augustus that all the world should be registered. This was the first registration taken under the procurator Quirinius from Syria.[43]

If the census mentioned in the Gospel of Luke took place during the governorship of Saturninus rather than that of Quirinius, the historical Jesus would have been born between 9 and 6 BCE. We have already seen that the Egyptian census records show that the population had around one and a half years to report to the authorities for the purpose of registration after a census had been decreed. This would mean that a contemporary reader of the Gospel of Luke would have assumed that if Augustus had issued the edict in 8 BCE, Jesus' family had registered in 7 or 6 BCE. This also matches the account of Jesus' childhood given by Matthew (2:1–23), which situates his birth and early childhood in the last few years of Herod's reign.

Conclusions

Octavian (the later Augustus) strove to order and classify his empire comprehensively from the very beginning of his reign. As well as reorganizing structures in the capital, he also had the population of Rome, Italy, and subsequently also all the provinces thoroughly and repeatedly registered and counted. After the turmoil of the civil war years, Augustus revived the census of the Roman people, a measure which was seemingly part of his policy of restoring the Republic. And he had censuses carried out in the provinces from the very beginning of his sole reign. The results of these counts were also used for propaganda purposes: the numbers spelled out how the empire had grown and prospered under Augustus after the turmoil of the civil wars.

In this context, a census of the population in the dominion of a client king dependent on the favor of Augustus does not seem particularly far-fetched; it fits in well with what we know about other aspects of the provincial policy pursued by Augustus. We also have sources which demonstrate that a Roman census took place within the territorial dominion of another client king in Cilicia Tracheia, albeit under Tiberius, although as classifying the entire empire was mainly a preoccupation of Augustus, this Tiberian census may be seen as a continuation of Augustan practice. We can speculate that the level of tribute to be rendered by client rulers depended on the results of these surveys of the population.

The New Testament Gospels, and here principally the Gospel of Luke, are the most important sources for dating the birth of the historical Jesus. It must always be borne in mind, however, that these accounts are only of limited use as historical evidence in light of the programmatic interests pursued by their authors. They are, nevertheless, broadly consistent with the most important historical facts in spite of their literary embellishment and theological molding. Both Matthew and Luke state that Jesus was born during the reign of King Herod, who is definitely known to have died in 4 BCE. Matthew places the birth of Jesus a few years before the death of Herod. According to Luke and Mark, Jesus began his work after being baptized in the Jordan by John, who had begun to preach and baptize people in 28 CE and had been arrested shortly afterwards. Luke reports that Jesus was about 30 years old at this point. This makes it extremely doubtful that Luke was referring to the census of 6 CE in his retelling of the events surrounding the birth of Jesus. If Jesus had been born in or close to 6 CE, he would only have been 21 or 22 years old in 28 BCE and not about 30, and he would have been born more than nine years after Herod's death. Luke's statement about the census would then contradict both the other two dates given by Luke and Matthew. If Luke had been aiming to connect the birth of Jesus with a census under Augustus in order to give credibility to a journey to Bethlehem that was necessary for reasons of salvation history, he would have needed to stick to historical facts and to ensure that his description of how the census was conducted was in itself credible. And I believe he did do this.

It seems considerably more plausible that a general Roman census in the entire territory of Herod would have prompted Joseph to travel from Galilee to the possessions of his family in Judaea than that a later census taking place after the division of Herod's kingdom would have prompted him to travel out of the territory governed by Antipas and into the territory previously governed by Archelaus, which had now been annexed by the Romans. I believe that this census in the kingdom of Herod was part of a general census in the province of Syria under the governor Sentius Saturninus, whose censuses are also mentioned by Tertullian. There would have been nothing new or unusual about a Roman provincial census in the province of Syria; by this point in time, several censuses would undoubtedly already have been taken since the establishment of the province by Pompey in 63 BCE. This time, however, the population was also counted in the neighboring kingdom of Herod, and Quirinius as procurator was tasked with holding the census.

It is also evident that none of the earliest commentators on the Bible, such as Justin Martyr, Tertullian, or John Chrysostom, had any great difficulty with the historical context of the events around the birth of Christ narrated in the Gospel of Luke. Problems only arose in modern times and through the imprecise translation of Luke's original Greek text by translators no longer familiar with the official titles used by the Romans and with the structures of Roman provincial administration. None of the ancient commentators names Quirinius as a governor at the time of the birth of Jesus, not even Luke himself. Both Josephus and Tertullian report that the governor at the time was Gaius Sentius Saturninus. And it appears that none of the early commentators on the Gospel of Luke had any difficulty with the idea of a Roman census being carried out in the territory ruled by Herod the Great during the king's lifetime. We also have a parallel case in the Roman census which took place in the client kingdom of Cilicia Tracheia. Both Justin Martyr and Tertullian even go so far as to highlight the existence of the original census declarations made by the family of Jesus that could, they tell us, be consulted by anyone at any time in the archives – just as in the provincial administration of Roman Egypt.

I am not arguing here that Luke's report of the journey made by Mary and Joseph to Bethlehem *corresponds to historical facts*, only that it is, if it is fictional, at least a story that *could* be true, since the author of the Gospel of Luke knows and respects the historical circumstances of the time in which he places the birth of Jesus. His depiction of the census can be seen as thoroughly realistic.

CHAPTER IV

"But these words seemed to them an idle tale"
Discrimination and the Struggle for Women's Equality in Early Christianity

And returning from the tomb, they told all this to the eleven and to all
the rest. Now it was Mary Magdalene, Joanna, Mary the mother of
James, and the other women with them who told this to the apostles.
But these words seemed to them an idle tale, and they did not believe
them.

Luke 24:9–11

The Gospel of Mary

Among the Christian texts discovered at the end of the nineteenth century
in Oxyrhynchus was a Greek fragment of an unknown Christian tale,
inspired by a vision of a certain Mary, in which Jesus initiates Mary into
some of his secret doctrines, and Mary explains these teachings to the
assembled disciples (Figure 4.1).[1] This small and severely damaged fragment, which has been dated on paleographical grounds to the early third
century CE, originally belonged to a papyrus book, a codex, written in
Greek. It was published in 1983 and is now kept in the Sackler Library at
Oxford.[2]

In 1917 the Rylands Library in Manchester, England, acquired a Greek
fragment of a papyrus scroll which also preserves some text of the same
story about Mary and the disciples (Figure 4.2).[3] This fragment has also
been dated to the early third century.[4]

We also have a later Coptic version of this story (Figure 4.3).[5] It formed
part of a papyrus book of gnostic writings dating back to the fifth century,
today kept in Berlin.[6] The leather-bound codex contains four different
"books" in the Sahidic dialect of the Coptic language,[7] the first of which
is signed "Gospel of Mary," marking it as the only extant early Christian
gospel written in the name of a woman.[8] This Coptic text – undoubtedly
a loose translation of an older Greek original text represented by the two
above-mentioned Greek fragments from Oxyrhynchus – is incompletely
preserved since the first six pages of the codex are missing, leaving us with

51

4.1 Greek fragment of the Gospel of Mary (*P.Oxy.* 50.3525).

a little less than eight pages, or about half of the original text.[9] Most scholars agree that this so-called "Gospel of Mary," later considered noncanonical by the compilers of the New Testament canon, might have been a composition from the early second century; there are a few who suggest that it might have been written shortly after the lifetime of Christ.[10]

In this gospel, lost for almost fifteen hundred years, a certain Mary appears as the central figure. Most scholars agree that these texts refer to Mary Magdalene, who is also mentioned in the New Testament.[11] Because the first six pages are missing, the text begins abruptly in a post-Easter appearance of Jesus in front of his assembled disciples, leaving the disciples distraught and scared. It is Mary who rises and presents words of

4.2 Greek fragment of the Gospel of Mary (*P.Ryl.* 3.463).

comfort and encouragement to the disciples, for she appears to be the only one who has understood Jesus' message. Peter then asks her to tell the disciples of the Lord's words, which are not yet known to them, since the Lord loved Mary more than any other woman. It is interesting here that Peter does not generally compare Jesus' love for Mary with that for the other disciples, but only with that for the other women among his followers. For Peter, Mary is not one of the disciples but above all a member of the female followers, not to be equated with men per se, and not at all equal. Mary, however, bravely answers Peter's request: "I will teach you about what is hidden from you." She then tells of a vision of the ascent of the soul and a conversation with the Lord that guided her understanding of her vision.

Mary appears in the Gospel of Mary as a teacher of the disciples and as someone who is more spiritually advanced than them; she asks the right questions and interprets Jesus' answers for the disciples. At first, she surprises the present-day reader with her resolute appearance in this group of men. She acts without hesitation when a post-Easter appearance of the Lord has left the disciples frightened. It is she who gives the disciples courage, and she is also not afraid to tell the disciples about her vision in detail and to interpret the words of the Lord. It is important to note that Mary here violates gender-specific behavioral norms in Jewish society, as well as those of the Gospels' later readers in the other provinces of the Roman Empire. It was not appropriate for a woman to give a speech in public: men should not listen to women, let alone believe them. However, when Peter then attacks Mary and doubts and rejects her speech, Levi takes her side and puts Peter and Andrew in their place.[12]

If the assumption is correct that the Gospel of Mary was composed in the early second century CE, Christianity was still in its very beginnings, there was no elaborated clerical hierarchy, Christians met in private homes, there were no normative doctrines, and no established leadership groups existed on which one side or another could rely. Each community interpreted the message of Jesus of Nazareth independently, debating the details of Christian belief and practice, the authority of prophetic visions, the authenticity of various Gospels in circulation, as well as the role of women and slaves within the growing Christian communities.[13] The Gospel of Mary seems to reflect these intra-Christian group conflicts. Finally, the three independently developed copies that have been found so far in Egypt show that this gospel must undoubtedly have enjoyed a certain popularity in Egyptian Christian communities from the third to fifth centuries.

All four canonical Gospels tell of the close relationship that Mary Magdalene had with Jesus. According to Luke, Mary Magdalene was one of the women who followed him (Luke 8:3) and, according to Matthew and Mark, also stayed by him during his crucifixion and provided for his burial (Matt. 27:61; Mark 15:47) when most of the disciples fled (Matt. 27:55–56). According to John, Mary Magdalene was the first witness of the resurrection of Jesus, and, as in the Gospel of Mary, Jesus tells her to tell the disciples about this (John 20:11–18). In the Gospel of Luke, Mary Magdalene and the other women receive the order from an angel to tell the men about the

137

© SMB Ägyptisches Museum und Papyrussammlung, Foto: Sandra Steiß

4.3 Folium of the fifth-century Coptic Gospel of Mary.

resurrection of the Lord. The male disciples, however, do not believe them and consider their account an idle tale (Luke 24:9–11).

The same contrast between Mary Magdalene and Peter is also found in other apocryphal gospels, such as the Gospel of Thomas, the Gospel of Philip, the Pistis Sophia, and the Coptic Gospel of the Egyptians.[14] As in the Gospel of Mary, Peter is consumed by jealousy in these gospels as well, and once again cannot come to terms with the fact that Jesus loved Mary, a woman, most, preferring her as the interpreter of his words. Mary Magdalene, however, is one of the closest disciples to Jesus and is open-minded to philosophical themes that require a higher understanding. According to these writings, she definitely counts among the most insightful, rational, and wise of his followers, interpreting Jesus' words for the other disciples. It is repeatedly said that the Lord loved Mary most.

The Position of Women in Roman Egypt

Scornful remarks toward women, like those of Peter and other disciples reported in the Gospel of Mary, were common in antiquity, when explicit discrimination against women manifested itself in many forms and, as one would expect, especially affected women who moved outside of traditional social norms, breaking expectations of gender-conforming conduct. However, women in Roman Egypt traditionally had substantially more rights in comparison to their contemporaries in other parts of the ancient world.[15] Egyptian women could, for example, own property and practice commerce without male legal guardians. As in Roman law, women inherited equally with their brothers and their consent was necessary for a marriage. A husband had no access to his wife's assets, and during marriage it was a rule to separate property. Unlike under classical Athenian or Roman law, however, Egyptian women could also take custody and guardianship of their children, and were allowed to adopt in the case of childlessness.[16] We have hundreds of papyrus documents from Roman Egypt that were composed by women, whether written by women themselves or dictated to a scribe.[17] These documents include private letters to family members, purchase or leasing contracts, and requests to government agencies, and they clearly portray the freedom of action and decision-making responsibilities that Roman Egyptian women enjoyed in family matters and economic affairs. They also represent a unique resource for the position and function of women in one of the Roman provinces. Here, we find women able to manage their extensive businesses independently, hold land and property, organize their household, raise their children on their own, and undertake long travels alone for court hearings or visiting relatives. In addition, women in pre-Christian Egypt held priestly functions in Greco-Egyptian temples.[18]

While the majority of women could not read or write, many were able to recruit someone to perform these tasks for them.[19] They were not afraid to resolutely stand up for their rights and purposefully assert their point of view in opposition to Roman officials and their male family members, be they brothers, fathers, or husbands. These were women who did not keep silent, but gave instructions and spoke boldly;[20] Roman Egyptian women who acted self-confidently and competently in a patriarchal world the strategies of which they exercised to accomplish their goals in a male society. In so doing, it is possible they may have had more influence and freedoms than women in other parts of the Roman Empire.

Meanwhile, women employed stereotypically female tactics to influence their counterparts. When Peter abruptly attacks Mary in the Gospel of Mary, Mary begins to cry and thereby wins Levi's support, and we find similar probably tactical behaviors utilized by other women in Roman

Egypt, when they believed themselves to be in inferior positions. While Roman Egyptian women acted extremely competently and persuasively in private as well as commercial correspondence, they indubitably consciously resorted to female tactics when handling the Roman officials in order to win them to their side, for example, using female helplessness as an argument to produce a verdict in their favor.[21]

Mary's claim to leadership may therefore have appeared less striking to the readers of the apocryphal gospels that had been circulating in Egypt from the third to at least the fifth century, than it did to readers in the early Christian Jewish environment, where women occupied inferior positions in all sectors of daily life.[22] Mary's self-assured appearance may also have seemed significantly more self-evident to Egyptian readers than it does to us, looking back on an almost two thousand-year-old, exclusively male-led church.

The Gospel of Mary, though certainly not written by the historical Mary of Magdala herself, arises from an alternative development in Christianity, which granted women a leading role in the religious community and advocated for a stronger equality of the sexes in society in general. The Gospel of Mary, as passed down to us in its Coptic version, clearly reflects the emerging debate about gender-specific attributes, placing into question the normative subjugation of women under men in Greco-Roman and Jewish societies.[23]

Women in Early Church Leadership Roles

What, then, was the status of women in Egyptian Christianity, and what role did they perform in the Egyptian clergy? For Asia Minor, Syria, Palestine, Greece, Macedonia, Dalmatia, Italy, and Gaul, we possess both literary references and inscriptions relating to female clerics in the first centuries after Christ. Here, female apostles, prophets, theological teachers, deacons, presbyters, and even bishops are attested, who seem to have played a major role in the proselytization and successful spread of Christianity.[24] Considering the comparatively emancipated position Egyptian women enjoyed in daily life as well as the wide circulation of apocryphal gospels advocating a leading role for women in church leadership, we might expect to find a prominent role played by women in their Christian communities in later Roman Egypt. It is therefore all the more surprising that women are not documented for any office in the Christian clergy in Egypt, whether in the papyrological or in the literary sources.

We know that from at least the middle of the second century onwards there were movements in the young church to banish women from any leading position. In his presumably pseudo-epigraphic first letter to Timothy, Paul says: "A woman learns in silence in all subordination. But I do not allow a woman to teach or to rule over the man, and I also want that she stays in silence." The creeping processes of assigning female community leaders to "heretic movements" and excluding women from leadership roles in the self-proclaimed Orthodox Church were well underway in the middle of the second century. The Syrian *Didascalia Apostolorum*, a pseudo-apostolic collection of ecclesiastical-liturgical content that originated at the end of the third century, says: "It is neither proper nor necessary that women teach, especially concerning the name and suffering of Christ." Slightly further down in the same text is the following passage, which can be understood as a direct answer to the Gospel of Mary:

> For the Lord himself, Jesus Christ, our teacher, has sent us, the twelve, to declare his teachings to the public and heathens; and together with us were female disciples, Mary Magdalene, Mary, the daughter of Jacob, and the other Mary, but he did not send them out to teach the doctrine together with us. For if it was necessary for women to teach, our Lord Himself had assigned them to teach with us.

This development culminated in the second half of the fourth century with the Synod of Laodicea (363–364), which stipulated that women could not be ordained as presbyters or leaders of church services (*can.* 11), and that they should generally keep away from the altar (*can.* 44). The view was then repeated in countless later ecclesiastical canons.[25] Nonetheless, women were permitted to give other women religious education as long as it was in the private rather than the public sphere.[26]

The female presbyters and bishops of the third and fourth centuries who are attested in Asia Minor and other regions are generally assigned to heretical communities such as the Montanists. However, the office of deaconess existed in the Orthodox Church in all parts of the empire until at least the seventh century. The diaconate was the only office that was open to women as well as men. We know from Asia Minor, for example, that women dedicated themselves to the community as deaconesses from the time of the travels of the Apostle Paul, in the middle of the first century, until the Byzantine period.[27] In addition, deaconesses are attested in inscriptions from Syria, Armenia, Palestine, Arabia, Greece, the Greek Islands, Macedonia, and also Italy and Gaul.

Female deaconesses were excluded from the offering of the sacraments, they did not preach or teach, but they nonetheless fulfilled an important function in dealing directly with female parishioners, assisting the presbyter or bishop for reasons of decency with the baptism of women and, unlike male clerics, they were able to visit female parishioners safely in their homes.

It is interesting to note that the feminine form *diaconissa*, instead of the gender-neutral term *diaconus*, appears for the first time at the Council of Nicaea in 325 CE, suggesting that at this time the woman's office was formally institutionalized and officially distinguished from the position of the male deacon.[28] However, according to the Apostolic Constitutions[29] and the Council of Chalcedon in 451 (*can.* 15), the bishop ordained the deaconesses in the same way as he did the male clerics. The procedures for the consecration of a deaconess, which are passed down in the Apostolic Constitutions, do not differ in their essential components from those for a male deacon.[30] In the sixth century the Hagia Sophia in Constantinople had forty deaconesses, who ranked below the one hundred male deacons in the hierarchy of offices but above the lower clergy consisting of subdeacons, readers, and doorkeepers.[31]

The Lack of Female Members in the Egyptian Clergy

By the end of the third century, we have evidence for Middle and Upper Egyptian women who openly display their Christian beliefs in writings and letters. We also find several letters of recommendation from clerics in support of traveling Christian women.[32] There is a vast body of papyrological evidence regarding Christian women from late antique and Byzantine Egypt, who come from the middle and lower classes in both cities and villages. In the light of this, it is therefore surprising that there is a total lack of evidence for female clergy from Egypt.[33] That this lack of women in ecclesiastical offices has not yet been noticed or examined may be a result of a general specialization of both epigraphy and papyrology, whereby regional differences in the structure of the clergy are less noticeable because several disciplines are examining them.[34]

Among the papyri of the fourth to seventh centuries we find a great number of clerics, albeit exclusively male officeholders. We have roughly six thousand texts with Christian content, of which 2,400 texts mention members of the clergy. These texts give insights into the everyday lives of the clergy and the world of the bishops, presbyters, deacons, and lower clerics in Egypt.[35] They show how these people entered into and exercised their offices, their activities regarding ecclesiastical administration and ecclesiastical economic life, their secular professions, and offer insights into their everyday problems and conflicts. These texts reveal that the everyday lives of Egyptian clerics actually differed little from the everyday lives of the clerics in, for example, late antique Asia Minor.[36] We do not, however, discover any deaconesses in the papyri, and not even a single example of what is elsewhere called a 'consecrated widow.'[37] This was a woman who took on similar tasks to the deaconesses in some regions, even if she was never counted among the clergy.

That the lack of sources for women in the clergy is the result of the situation regarding our written records seems unlikely, given that we possess some 2,400 papyrological texts in Greek and Coptic that mention male clerics. The proportion of female members of the clergy at the beginning of the sixth century in Constantinople's Hagia Sophia was about 10 percent,[38] so statistically alone, about 240 of the 2,400 papyri should have mentioned female clerics. The situation is even more astonishing given the fact that women in Roman Egypt were relatively more emancipated in comparison to their contemporaries in other parts of the empire. Moreover, Clement of Alexandria, the Egyptian church teacher who lived towards the end of the second century in Alexandria, was one of the few church fathers who explicitly argued for an equal role of women in the church,[39] while Origen, his successor at the Catechism School in Alexandria, also pleaded, like his predecessor, for equality of the sexes.[40] This was entirely in contrast to his North African contemporary Tertullian (ca. 155–240), for example, who stood as the leader of a misogynistic ecclesiastical movement geared towards the complete subordination of women.

Women in Monastic Circles in Egypt

While there seem to have been no women in the Egyptian secular clergy, women played a significant role in monastic circles.[41] The *Historia Monachorum in Aegypto* speaks of 20,000 holy virgins living in Oxyrhynchus toward the end of the fourth century. Even though their number is almost certainly exaggerated, there are papyri from the middle of the fourth century onwards that record Christian virgins – we find mentions of *monachai* ("nuns"),[42] *aeiparthenoi* ("eternal virgins"),[43] and even *monachai apotaktikai* ("nuns secluded from the world").[44]

However, this does not mean that a consecrated "virgin" was just another term for a deaconess, or that it marked essentially the same ecclesiastical office. Consecrated virgins are, in fact, elsewhere documented alongside deaconesses, suggesting they are two different positions. And the difference is clear: while a married or widowed woman with children could be appointed as deaconess, the requirement for admission into the rank of consecrated virgins was virginity. The majority of Christian virgins in Egypt, whether referred to as "nuns," "eternal virgins," or "nuns secluded from the world," seem to have lived unmarried within their family circles or in a household shared with other virgins.[45] The composition of many literary *opuscula*, which were written as educational literature for virgins living in family circles, falls within this period. One example is the anonymous work *On virginity* (*De virginitate*), which is preserved in Syriac and falsely attributed to Athanasius of Alexandria.[46]

At least some women lived as hermits in the Egyptian desert. In addition to the 120 so-called desert fathers (*abbas*), the fifth-century *Apophthegmata Patrum* recounts the lives of three desert mothers (*ammas*). In the representation of these ascetics, we find the same stereotypes that Peter entertained in his speech against Mary Magdalene: the men wonder how they can be taught by a woman, since she generally has less intelligence and does not possess the right to speak publicly. The desert mothers who have to face these accusations find their own answer: they are, in fact, by nature women, but have reached the intellectual qualities and status of men, or rather a status which transcends the gender boundary, through their asceticism. In his *Historia Lausiaca*, written in the early fifth century, Palladius, a bishop of Helenopolis in Bithynia, Asia Minor, and a student of John Chrysostom, also aims to monumentalize the "male women, to whom God gave the power to endure struggles as a man."[47] He reports on several women from Egypt who have pursued a lifestyle of asceticism in various forms in the process of overcoming the boundaries imposed by their sex: as a hermit in the desert, as a monastery founder, within a family.

The right of women to assume positions of authority in the Christian community has been and still is a subject of constant debate, and we can follow its various manifestations over the centuries. Mary of Magdala and the desert mothers are just some of the protagonists in the continued struggle for female recognition and autonomy.

Explanations for Women's Absence in Ecclesiastical Offices

It seems to me that there are two lines of inference to explain the absence of female members in the Egyptian clergy. These two peculiarities of the history of Egyptian Christianity are closely related. On the one hand, there was the relatively late Christianization, not of the capital Alexandria but of the Egyptian chora. The split and destruction of the Jewish community in Alexandria apparently deeply affected and slowed the spread of Christianity, which therefore reached the Egyptian hinterland very late in comparison to other regions.[48] The other reason is the long and decidedly "antiheretic" rule of Demetrius of Alexandria – as mentioned in the introduction to this book, the city's first extensively attested bishop, who took office in 189 CE. According to the reports of church fathers Tertullian (*ca.* 155–240) and Irenaeus of Lyons (*ca.* 140–200), Egypt was one of a group of provinces affected by "heresy" before 189 CE – that is, before Demetrius was credited as the reorganizer of the Egyptian church. In the demarcation of heretic or gnostic groups, Demetrius made an internal change to the Egyptian church and developed a hierarchical form of organization that had already existed in other provinces. He led the Alexandrian church community toward the orthodox way and united the diverse Christian groups in an institutional church. Demetrius also ordained the first ten bishops for the Egyptian chora. Some scholars have stressed the influence of the Christian world beyond Egypt on Demetrius' actions and his ambition as well as will for absolute control.[49]

Demetrius' term in office also coincides with a period of general reorganization of the church in other regions of the Roman Empire: the development of an ecclesiastical hierarchy, the demarcation of heretical groups such as the Marcionites and the Montanists, and the canonization of the New Testament. The writings of Irenaeus against the heresies, which were written around this time, in 180 CE, were especially directed against various gnostic sects, including that of the Valentinians. Irenaeus' writings were read shortly after their composition in Egypt; we have a papyrus fragment of his work dating to roughly 200 CE.[50] In particular, Irenaeus denounced the gnostic practice of allowing women to join the altar services. It is quite possible that Bishop Demetrius was guided by the dogma of Irenaeus during his reorganization of the Alexandrian church. This all happened before Christianity had spread widely in the Egyptian chora. When Demetrius made efforts to Christianize the Egyptian hinterland, women had already been successfully excluded from all teaching and altar services in other parts of the empire, and he was following this trend. Bishop of Alexandria for forty-three years, he had a substantial influence on the development and direction of the young Egyptian church, and was known for his energetic intervention against gnostic groups. While the early Christian tradition of a female diaconate had established itself from early on and lasted in changed form until Byzantine times in other regions of the Mediterranean world, it never had the chance to establish itself in Egypt. The Gospel of Mary, which was originally a text about disputes among early Christians regarding the reliability of visions, might also have been interpreted as an alternative pro-women voice: it likely enjoyed its highest popularity in circles outside the Orthodox Church, where it stood as a voice of disapproval toward the official ecclesiastical stance of excluding women from the clergy.

Conclusion

While secular deaconesses in other parts of the Roman Empire and then the Byzantine Empire even served in metropolitan churches, we find no proof of their existence in Egypt – neither in the extensive papyrological record of the third to eighth centuries, nor in the literary sources. This exceptional exclusion of women from all ecclesiastical positions may be connected to the gnostic-philosophical beginnings of Alexandrian Christianity, which benevolently viewed women as leading members of their Christian communities, something the radically antiheretic bishop Demetrius later strongly opposed in his reorganization of the Alexandrian church. Furthermore, the population of the Egyptian hinterland seems to have come only comparatively late to Christianity compared to other eastern Roman provinces – it was only under Demetrius that the Egyptian hinterland was Christianized. The practice documented elsewhere of consecrating female deaconesses among the secular clergy, a tradition which can be traced back to the early Christian origins of the first two centuries, thus probably never had the chance to establish itself in the Egyptian chora.

However, that this general exclusion of women from all Egyptian ecclesiastical offices did not remain undisputed may be evident in the popularity of some apocryphal gospels circulating in Egypt at the time. These gospels postulate a strong role for women among the apostles and early Christian communities. The writings, which seem to have been popular in the Egyptian chora from the third until at least the fifth century,

repeatedly show the contrast between Mary Magdalene's claims to leadership and the misogynistic position of Peter and the other disciples, who
could be interpreted as representing the Orthodox Church authorities.
The obvious and lasting popularity of these writings, which emphasize
Jesus' belief in women as competent and worthy to teach his doctrine, may
reflect a persistent tension regarding the position of women within
Christian communities that extends far beyond the second and third
centuries.

CHAPTER V

"The Carpenter's Son"
The Family and Household of a Craftsman

Is not this the carpenter's son? Is not his mother called Mary? And are not his brothers James and Joseph and Simon and Judas?

Matthew 13:55

The Trade of Carpenter in the Roman World

The protagonists of the New Testament came from the "working classes," which probably represented around 95 percent of all premodern society, though they barely play a role in Greek and Roman literature. Jesus was raised in a carpenter's household and probably also learned the craft of his (step)father himself. Four of Jesus' disciples had previously earned their living as fishermen, and the birth of the Savior was first announced to shepherds. Furthermore, Jesus constantly uses agricultural motifs in his parables, the lives of crop farmers, gardeners, and winemakers being a central focus. If we call the daily routines of the craftsmen, farmers, fishermen, and shepherds who appear in the New Testament as protagonists ordinary, then the family lives of ordinary people, their daily routines, their livelihoods, and their forms of housing have so far been little researched; ancient historians and biographers had little interest in members of these classes. The ideal of the Greco-Roman elite was leisure, not work; for the lower classes, work was essential for their livelihoods.

The ancient writers had little appreciation for any kinds of craft or wage labor.[1] Similarly, research on the ancient building industry has until now focused above all on the nature of construction, temple architecture, and state building programs. In general, little is known about the social, organizational, economic, and legal background of the building trade itself.

The documentary papyri of Greco-Roman Egypt, the private letters, purchase and leasing contracts, tax receipts, and census entries offer us a different view. Here the working classes are the focus. We learn about

their everyday lives; the structures of their days; their economic situation, health, disease and death; details about their education and the extent of their illiteracy; and about the differences between genders, social classes, and ethnic groups. Here we have an alternative way of approaching Roman society that also elucidates the historical reality of everyday life in the New Testament stories.

The term *tektōn* (τέκτων), which the Evangelists largely called the profession of Joseph and Jesus himself, is often documented as a type of job in the Greek inscriptions of the eastern Mediterranean world. Here the term *architektōn* (ἀρχιτέκτων), meaning the top-ranking construction supervisor, occurs much more frequently than the simple *tektōn* or *domotektōn* (δομοτέκτων) – supposedly for reasons of status, since the architektōn could probably often afford the costly construction of a grave or votive inscription. In the papyri, however, the occupation of tektōn is much more often documented in different contexts, precisely because there were probably more tektōnes than architektōnes.[2]

In these texts tektōnes are working with wood and ordinarily appear in combination with other builders.[3] One can therefore translate *tektōn* as "carpenter." Tektōnes built not only roof structures for houses, but also other wooden structures such as oil mills, furniture, wagons, chariots, wheels, and also barges and boats. Mechanized wooden water wheels that were constructed by carpenters are also frequently documented in papyri.[4] Perhaps the carpenter also handled the production of wooden doors and windows, since, apart from roof structures, doors and windows were the only parts made of wood in mud-brick buildings in Roman Egypt.[5] Together with other builders, the carpenters also built towers, storage facilities, military defense walls, bridges, and siege machines. We also possess several Roman Egyptian mummy labels for tektōnes, which are preserved in the Louvre in Paris. However, they provide us with little more information than the carpenter's name, mother's and father's names, and, in individual cases, the carpenter's place of origin.[6]

Hand tools were among the carpenter's most valuable possessions and were presumably passed on from father to son over many generations. We find accounts of hand tools on carpenters' funerary reliefs, but also in archeological excavations (see Figures 5.1 and 5.2).[7] Two finds are particularly prominent here: the Casa del Fabro, or the House of the Carpenter, which in 79 CE was buried by Vesuvius in Pompeii, and the August 1964 excavations in the Swiss canton of Basel-Land, in which numerous carpentry tools were discovered. However, most of the examples come from England, where metal hand tools were

5.1 Funerary stele of a carpenter found on l'Isle Saint Jacques, France.

submerged in water and so not corroded by oxygen. These included hand-held measuring tools, which were often made of bronze, such as solders and angle irons, and cutting tools such as axes, hatchets, chisels, smoothing planes, hammers, and saws.[8]

In the papyrus texts from Roman Egypt, carpenters are most frequently mentioned in payment lists, and here they appear together with lower craftsmen and day laborers, freedmen, and slaves.[9] A carpenter's wages are mentioned in a lease agreement for an oil mill.[10] According to Diocletian's Edict on Maximum Prices, a carpenter earned 50 denarii a month – as much as a mason, or twice as much as a shepherd, water carrier, or unskilled day laborer. Potential wages were dependent not only on skill

5.2 Fresco of a carpenter at work, House of the Vettii, Pompei.

but also on the construction industry. Since the carpenter mainly worked outside, his salary was probably also subject to seasonal fluctuations.

As with many other crafts, it is well documented that at least in larger cities carpenters organized themselves into guilds (*collegia*), to provide members with a dignified funeral and full care for the surviving family. The question therefore arises as to whether the carpenter Joseph was a member of a carpenters' guild, because Nazareth was a small village and different from the large cities of the empire from which most of our

5.3 Ivory relief of a carpenter from fourth-century Alexandria.

information about craft guilds derives. Since this village probably had no more than one or two carpenters, membership in a guild seems to have held no great importance.

While work tools and the activities associated with the profession of carpenter scarcely differed from one Roman province to another – as suggested by pictorial representations and archeological findings from the most diverse parts of the empire – there is a significant difference between Middle Egypt, from where the great bulk of our material comes, and Galilee, the region in which Jesus lived with his family. Wood was very rare in Egypt and used only sparingly in house construction and furnishing for reasons of cost: intensive grain cultivation was organized along the Nile, while by far the largest part of Egypt was desert, in which no trees grew. The hilly Galilean landscape, on the other hand, was less suitable for agriculture, and here deciduous forests dominated, as well as olive plantations and extensive meadows.[11] Wood was available in abundance, which meant there were many more opportunities to work as a carpenter. Moreover, King Herod's ambitious construction program had boosted the local construction industry,[12] an economic boom which might also have benefited Jesus' (step)father.[13]

A Craftsman's Household

The main source of information for the housing and composition of craftsmen's families in Roman times is once again the census lists preserved on papyrus. With the lists made by the Roman provincial census, we can investigate a source material that is essential for all studies of family and generational relationships in research on the early modern period and yet is also unique for the ancient world: as we have seen in Chapter III, we are much better informed about Egypt as a Roman province thanks to this unique resource. Each resident was recorded by household in the Greek *kat'oikian*. In other words, a census was taken of all residents per household.[14] We possess the original census returns for around four hundred households, and information on about fifteen hundred people who lived in these households.

Households of artisan families often only consisted of two parents and their young children. Unlike in farming families, there were no economic incentives for adults and married sons to remain in their parents' house. The management of a farm or a large herd of cattle could not be done by a couple with children; several adult men were needed. On the other hand, for an artisan's family to be maintained, a couple sufficed. Furthermore, Roman Egypt was characterized by large differences when it came to household size and size of residence. Rural households were often larger and frequently composed of multiple married couples,[15] while in the cities, where living space was limited, around half the population lived in nuclear households (only one quarter of the population in the countryside did the same).[16] Since artisan families were located more in the cities than in the villages, most lived in relatively small households. Both the husband and the wife managed the workshop, with the wife looking after the book-keeping, the maintenance of the household, the parenting, and perhaps also selling the finished goods at the nearest market. Sometimes the family housed one or more apprentices as well. These young men, of around 12 to 17 years old, were given by their parents to a master in the trade and also lived in their master's household, receiving food and lodging there (see Figure. 5.4).[17]

5.4 Apprenticeship contract of a carpenter from Theadelphia in the Arsinoite dated to 128 CE (*P.Mich.inv.* 4238).

The material remains of housing structures inform us about the common organization of family households and workshops. Workshops were typically located at street level, and the craftsman's family lived either in a back room or on the floor above the workshop. The question is whether we should imagine a carpenter's workshop to be similar to that of other craftsmen such as a goldsmith or cabinetmaker. Individual carpenters who mostly built simple residences have so far received no scholarly attention at all.

From the papyri and ostraca, one gains the impression that the individual carpenter was quite mobile; most of the time he did not work in his home village, but probably moved from construction site to construction site together with other specialized craftsmen in the building industry, or worked in stone quarries, presumably building wooden scaffolding.[18] Larger building projects could only be undertaken by traveling groups of craftsmen, who occasionally had to live close to the construction site for several months. For Pharaonic Egypt, several such temporary construction site villages are documented (for example, Deir el-Medina).

According to the four canonical Gospels, Jesus was raised in the Galilean village of Nazareth.[19] However, he may already, through his profession, have been accustomed to moving around the province of Galilee from childhood, long before his appearance as a wandering preacher. He would have been familiar with traveling to the various construction sites of his (step)father, whose profession had taken him to other small Galilean towns far from their home village of Nazareth. Jesus and his (step)father Joseph may even have profited as builders from the private and public building projects ordered by the Roman governor to improve the infrastructure and stimulate the construction industry. The Gospels thus depict Jesus growing up in a comfortably off craftsman's household, certainly not belonging to the landowning elite, but better off than the unskilled landless majority of the population.

The situation of craftsmen seems to have deteriorated between Jesus' time in the early Roman Empire and the fourth century CE. Late antique authors paint a picture of misery and abjection; of men who earned their living as craftsmen seemingly having to live just above subsistence level. They relate this demise directly to the fact that Constantine introduced a gold and silver tax in 326 CE called the *auri lustralis collatio* (also *chrysargyrion*), which every person who had a workshop or craft had to pay.[20] It was initially estimated every five years, and then became every four years in the fifth century.[21] At the end of the fourth century, Libanius complained about the injustice of this trade-related income tax, which, he said, led to great suffering and fright every five years.[22] According to his likely biased account, tax collectors followed the fleeing merchants and craftsmen like dogs, allegedly even giving parents no choice but to sell their children into slavery in order to raise the money for their taxes.[23] Zosimus also draws the same horrific picture, according to which, whenever the time for the collection of taxes approached, misery and lamentation arose in every city, while those who were too poor to pay were tortured with whips and other instruments. Thus it came about, he says, that mothers sold their children and fathers offered their daughters to foreign men in order to pay the tax collectors.[24]

In addition, craftsmen and merchants had the obligation to perform *munera sordida* such as dike work and agricultural labor, whose implementation was organized by the town.[25] According to Libanius, these obligations imposed an additional heavy burden.[26] John Chrysostom accuses the tax collectors and elites of abusing free citizens like slaves, stealing from them and beating them. He reprimands the powerful and urges them not to scorn the small craftsmen and merchants, and reminds them to bear in mind that the apostles and Jesus himself had come from these social layers.[27]

A Family with Five Sons

We know of the following names in Jesus' family: Joseph, his (step)father, Mary or Miriam, his biological mother, and his brothers James, Joseph (or Joses), Simon, and Judas.[28] Typically, brothers were named in order of age, at least in the Roman census surveys.[29] Jesus is also described as the "first-born son" of Mary in Matthew 1:25 and Luke 2:7. From this wording alone we can conclude that there were also "later-born sons." James, who was also identified by Paul as the "Brother of the Lord," later assumed leadership of the early Christian community in Jerusalem (Gal. 1:19; Gal. 2:9). He may have been the oldest brother after Jesus. The Gospel of Matthew mentions several sisters, but does not give us their names,[30] while siblings are also included among the relatives in Mark 3:20, 31–35. The family thus had at least five sons and an unknown number of daughters.

However, in the Gospel of John, the scene in which the dying Jesus places his already widowed mother Mary under the care of John actually excludes the possibility that Mary had other sons.[31] This is because, after the death of the first-born, the other sons would have been in charge of caring for the mother and widow, especially since James, who was likely the second-oldest son, was already one of Jesus' followers. However, only John reports this scene – the Synoptic Gospels do not mention that Mary was present at the crucifixion of her son – and so its place in his gospel thus probably mainly serves the purpose of legitimizing John's authority and trustworthiness as the author .

Considering the high infant mortality rate in the ancient world, the large number of children in Jesus' family is striking. Quite in contrast to today's Western world, in which the majority of people die at the end of a natural lifespan from chronically degenerative diseases, most people in antiquity did not die of old age but much earlier as a result of epidemics and infectious diseases. Child mortality rates were particularly high: one-third of children died in infancy, and almost half of all children did not live to see their fifth birthday.[32]

Historical demographics has assumed an important role in the study of history in recent decades, and demographic issues are also increasingly entering into ancient historical research. Roman Egypt, with its many preserved census entries, offers us a unique window into the population structures of an ancient society.[33] Before the Florentine census lists of the fourteenth century, we have nothing comparable for a premodern society.[34] Thus by analyzing the Roman-Egyptian census data, we can learn something about the average life expectancy of ancient Mediterranean peoples for the first time. We can learn about the average number of children they had, their ages at marriage, the age differences between spouses, the percentage of men to women, child mortality, and mortality rates during the course of an adult life – data which are of great interest for historical demographics, as well as for ancient social and economic history.

There have been many other studies of these subjects, such as, for example, the study of epigraphy to determine the average life expectancy in antiquity (most notably, of course, using tomb inscriptions). But it has now been repeatedly shown that these studies are hardly ever reliable for any calculation of ancient life expectancy; rather, they mainly follow social patterns and cultural practices.[35] So, for example, children and especially women only very rarely received a tomb inscription on stone. Men are significantly more represented than women, and indications of age are often rounded and greatly exaggerated, especially among older people. This is quite different from the census entries from Roman Egypt, where great emphasis is placed on correct information. Information on age, for instance, was checked by Roman officials against earlier data from the census fourteen years earlier, or compared to birth reports, which were all kept in local archives. Correctly recording data on age and the number of inhabitants was crucial for maintaining the most efficient tax policy, which squeezed the greatest amount possible out of the province.

The demographic profile of the Roman Empire's population was undoubtedly characterized by high mortality rates, high fertility rates, and low population growth. This demographic profile was typical for many premodern societies before the demographic transition, which began around the mid nineteenth century and continues into today's Western society, which is characterized by few children and a high life expectancy.

Given the high mortality rate compared to modern societies, the overlap of generations in antiquity was low. Most fathers did not live long enough to see either their sons marry or their sons' children. Since daughters married at a considerably younger age, for them, more fathers were still present. As women were significantly younger than their husbands at the birth of their first child, many more children were able to enjoy maternal grandparents and a grandmother rather than a grandfather.[36] The age difference between spouses was on average eight years in Roman Egypt. Roman Egyptian men married in their mid twenties, while there is evidence to show that Jewish men married somewhat earlier, in their late teens or early twenties. Most girls in Roman, Greek, and Jewish societies were married right after the onset of puberty. Not a few women thus found themselves already widowed in their twenties and thirties, often with still very young children. Likewise, it was not uncommon for a man to lose his wife in childbirth, marry a second time, and then form another family.[37]

At the age of 30, an imaginary cohort of 100,000 live births would leave only a quarter of the people alive.[38] Only a little more than a quarter of all men still had a father by the age of 30, but at least one in two still had a mother.[39] At the age of 30, a young man had on average only 0.8 living brothers.[40] Yet the Gospel of Mark says that Jesus had four brothers as an adult man. Five adult sons and an unknown number of daughters constitutes a very rare phenomenon, therefore, in societies with a demographic profile similar to that which must have prevailed in Egypt and the Galilee of Jesus' time.[41] A contemporary of Jesus or a later reader of the Gospels would undoubtedly have considered this family quite blessed with good fortune.[42]

The Gospels indicate nothing about Mary's or Joseph's parents – perhaps they played no role in the story, they were already dead, or they did not live locally. The only close portrayal of Mary's childhood is found in the so-called Protoevangelium of James, where Jesus' maternal grandparents, Joachim and Anna, are also introduced. According to this childhood story, they were still alive when Jesus was born. We hear nothing about his paternal grandparents. This combination would have been quite common, as one can see from the demographic profiles of ancient societies. A 15-year-old girl – about the same age as Mary is described as being at the time of Jesus' birth – had according to models estimating mortality rates a 62 percent chance that her father was still alive and a 71 percent chance that her mother still lived at this time.[43] According to model life tables, Mary's father Joachim might have been around 50 years old at this time, and her mother Anna around 42 years old. If Joseph had previously been married and had already been an old man by the time of his engagement to

Mary, as the apocryphal Protoevangelium of James reports, then it is not surprising that we no longer hear of Jesus' grandparents on his (step) father's side.

When Jesus begins preaching as a 30-year-old, Joseph no longer appears in the Gospels – either because he performed no role or because he was already dead at this time. Statistically, as a 30-year-old, Jesus had only a 28 percent chance that his father was still alive, but a 46 percent chance that his mother was still alive.[44] In fact, his mother Mary, probably in her mid forties at the time when Jesus started preaching, sometimes followed him on his wanderings. She is present at the marriage at Cana (John 2:1–12) and is also mentioned by John as a witness present at the crucifixion of her son in Jerusalem (John 19:25).

Jesus' education

> When he came to Nazareth, where he had been brought up, he went to the synagogue on the Sabbath day, as was his custom. He stood up to read, and the scroll of the prophet Isaiah was given to him. He unrolled the scroll and found the place where it was written . . .[45]

Thus, the Evangelist Luke reports on the beginning of Jesus' work. According to his testimony, Jesus was able to read and write and knew the Scriptures well. Was it common that a craftsman's son could read? Since the publication of William Harris's *Ancient Literacy* in 1989, the scholarly *opinio communis* maintains that the percentage of literate people in the population of the ancient world was less than 10 percent. At first glance, it therefore seems unusual that Jesus so casually and naturally takes a book in his hands and reads it aloud. How can this information be understood within his specific social and cultural context? Had Jesus and his siblings possibly enjoyed access to education, and, if so, what did this look like in the village of Nazareth in Galilee?

It is precisely through the surviving Egyptian papyri that the role of writing in everyday Roman life becomes clear. From the entire Roman administration to the functioning of the household, the smallest unit of society, everything depended on the written record.[46] Alan Bowman has emphasized that even the illiterates of ancient society took part in the written record in an important way.[47] The required registration in the provincial census, the obligation to register births and deaths within the family, the need to issue written contracts for purchases and leases, the possibility to draft a marriage contract in the case of marriage or a divorce settlement in the case of separation, the option to draft a will, the importance of knowing Roman laws in order to assert one's claims against an adversary or counterparty, and the custom to issue receipts for purchases all made contact with writing an almost everyday experience for people, except perhaps for the poorest of society. On the other hand, the high rate of social mobility, the migration of workers to larger cities, and the recruitment of young men from the local population into the Roman auxiliary forces made it desirable to be able to keep in contact with far-away family members through regular written correspondence. However, it was not necessary to be able to write in order to participate in the omnipresent experience of writing and the written record. And the great majority of the population was not able.

Three different levels of writing can be noted for the population of Roman Egypt.

(1) Being incapable of writing one's own name, thus being illiterate (*agrammatos* or *grammata mē eidōn*). This included, as we shall see, most of the male and almost the entire female population.

(2) Being a slow writer (*bradeōs graphōn*).[48] Herbert Youtie describes slow writers as "persons of very limited education. They may as children have spent a year or two with a teacher. Some of them may have learned to read, but most would have lost this acquisition through the many subsequent years in which they read nothing. None stayed at school long enough to develop firm habits of writing, and what little progress they may have made was dimmed through lack of use."[49] A slow writer was at least able to write his own name under a document with effort, struggle, and stiff lettering. However, despite being able to do so, he was probably not able to read the contract he had signed, and as we will soon see, a slow writer often did not even understand what he was copying with his own hand. According to today's definition, this would classify him as illiterate.

Raffaella Cribiore emphasizes that it was precisely the common use of ostraca (potsherds), which were available for free at any time, which opened up an informal way of writing to even the least educated social layers. This contrasts with the Egypt of earlier centuries and millennia, where writing was limited to the priestly caste, professional scribes, and high-ranking administrative officials. According to her, "the extemporaneous and casual quality of Greek and Roman writing technology successfully counterbalanced the limiting and intimidating factor that strongly characterized it in ancient Egyptian and medieval times and that created definite problems of access to writing."[50]

(3)   Being able to write fluently. This third group was actually capable of writing. Only a small percentage of the population belonged to this group, although naturally they are greatly overrepresented in the documentary papyri. However, one must also distinguish here between someone composing an awkward but original letter in colloquial language to his brother, and someone who could compose elegant prose with literary allusions.[51] For the elite and rising layers of society, the ability to read, write, and even express oneself skillfully and precisely in writing was a prerequisite for a career in the upper echelons of the civil service. For craftsmen, merchants, administrators, and other service providers, writing was probably mainly functional.

In general, reading and writing were considered skills that were useful but not absolutely necessary. Thus one could participate in public life and even hold public offices without being able to read and write. The village scribe Petaus, who lived in the Fayum at the end of the second century CE, is known to have been illiterate, even though he tried to disguise this fact from his colleagues.[52] Indeed, a village scribe who is not skilled in writing seems a curious phenomenon, but only at first sight: Youtie argues that the Roman administration in a largely illiterate society would have had difficulty finding a new candidate for the position of village scribe every three years, had they only accepted skilled writers.[53] But it does not seem to be as simple as that. Petaus pretended to be able to read and write in order to avoid threats of dismissal, as had happened to his illiterate colleague Ischyrion; however, he could only keep up this appearance because of his brother Theon, who completed his scribal work for him. Many illiterates were probably therefore able to hide behind the mask of the slow scribe if their literate family members or friends stood in for them.

It is harder to explain why even in the urban middle class we find men who could not write. Why could one brother write and not the other? Why were some elite daughters provided with a higher education by their parents, while others could not even write their names? Ewa Wipszycka explains these discrepancies as due to the inclinations and skills of the individual.[54]

In contrast to the comprehensive interest of scholars in the *artes liberales* (which were higher studies such as rhetoric, law, and philosophy, meant for the sons of the elite), the structures of education for the bulk of the ancient population are still comparatively little researched. There was no free public school system and no compulsory schooling. Parents had the option – but not the obligation – of giving their children to a teacher for instruction.[55] The most favorable option was certainly to send one's child to a teacher in a public place, such as the front hall of a temple or synagogue. Here, the teacher instructed several children lecture-style on the main components of reading, writing, and arithmetic. This was definitely the preference when resources were limited. Families of the local upper class could also likely provide a private teacher to teach their children, both boys and girls, at home.[56]

Saller assumes that urban craftsmen enjoyed at least a few years of rudimentary education in reading, writing, and arithmetic.[57] Harris also agrees with him that urban craftsmen could at least read and write in a rudimentary fashion.[58] Yet the poor rural population, especially small-scale farmers and day laborers, could not raise the small amount of money necessary to give their children a basic education. Sons of these families had to start contributing to the livelihood of the family at a young age. Diocletian's Edict on Maximum Prices lists the cost of an elementary teacher who was paid by the child's parents: the lessons should not cost more than 50 denarii per month. If several parents shared the cost of a teacher, as was common, the cost would be less per person. That still means, however, that a simple worker who earned around 30 denarii per month and who lived with his family at subsistence level could probably send no more than one of his children to school. According to the Price edict, even a skilled craftsman only received a monthly wage of 50 denarii.

If Harris assumes a literacy rate of a maximum of 10 percent of the Roman population, the proportion of so-called slow scribes was probably considerably larger. Relevant here is a recent study by Yiftach-Firanko based on the signatures (*hypographai*) in land leasing contracts for the province of Arsinoe in the first three centuries of Roman rule. The parties involved in such contracts had to sign in their own hand, and so one had at least to be a slow writer in order to be able to put a name and a few other words of information on the document. A representative could only sign if it was explicitly stated that the contracting party was not able to write. According to Yiftach-Firanko, an analysis of these documents produces the following results: 80 percent of the documented women who leased land wrote a few lines of information on their promissory note with their own hand. With male landowners, it was as much as 96 percent. The percentage of land renters was different. The proportion of the population that could write lagged far behind: only one-third of male tenants signed by themselves, while female tenants who signed with their own hand are not documented at all.[59] Differences can once again likely be mapped on to the social strata. The landowners were probably the urban landowning elite, and the tenants were probably the working rural population. The rate of illiteracy was therefore linked to social class, urban or rural residence, and ultimately gender.

It should again be emphasized that this does not mean that a third of the total male population was actually able to write. The documents show that many people were only able to painstakingly copy texts letter by letter in a shaky script. To sign with one's name, one would not have to know how to write. In fact, one did not even have to speak Greek to put this desired information on the documents.

We must also remember that we are mainly dealing with a bilingual society – a fact the importance of which we can hardly overestimate. The indigenous population of Egypt spoke Egyptian, not Greek, the language of the documents. In fact, the Egyptian language remained the colloquial language of the ordinary population throughout the entire Hellenistic and Roman periods. Before the birth of Coptic, every context which demanded the written word required a knowledge of Greek, which was the only regularly available literary language. However, Coptic only became customary for private correspondence and private contracts in the Byzantine era. Thus, many of our Greek letters to family members may have been translated from Egyptian before they could be written down by a scribe. Men and women who could sign a contract in their own hand may only have been able to understand and write their own names and a few formulaic phrases in Greek. The fact that for a very large part of the population learning to read and write first required the acquisition of a foreign language, undoubtedly significantly reduced the proportion of people who truly acquired this ability and were able to apply it as adults in everyday life. Furthermore, it seems that more women than men only spoke Egyptian rather than being functionally competent in both languages, simply because they appeared much less frequently in public Greek-speaking spaces.[60]

Again, there is no evidence to suggest that the situation in Roman Palestine was any different.[61] It shared a multilingual environment with Roman Egypt, where the everyday language differed from the language of administration. Egyptian in Egypt and Aramaic in Galilee held the same status as spoken languages, while Greek was the language of Roman administration. Literacy rates were low; only sons of the better off would have enjoyed a formal education.[62] When the ancient reader learned that Jesus and perhaps even some of his brothers were good at reading and writing, he or she had to conclude that their father Joseph was a financially well-off craftsman.

Jesus as an Apprentice Craftsman

When Jesus began teaching in the synagogue of his home village of Nazareth, the Gospel of Mark reports that the villagers asked in astonishment: "Is not this the carpenter, the son of Mary and brother of James and Joses and Judas and Simon, and are not his sisters here with us?"[63] As already mentioned, according to the Gospel of Matthew, Jesus was the son of a carpenter. According to the Gospel of Mark, he had learned the craft of carpentry himself.[64] As was customary at that time, Jesus probably held the same vocation as his (step)father as a young man. Most sons followed their father's profession, whether he was a farmer, a shepherd, a wageworker, or a craftsman. Learning a profession mostly happened informally via daily observation of one's father, grandfather, or uncle, and via the completion of small auxiliary tasks before moving on to more complex projects.[65] In his *Republic*, Plato says: "Or have you never noticed, for example, the practice in the art of craftsmanship, where potters' sons stand near their fathers as assistants long before they touch the clay themselves?"

While most sons learned the craft of their father or other male relatives, others were sent to a master in the nearest city to learn the trade. The apprenticeship contracts from Roman Egypt, which were commonly created between a master and the apprentice's parents, testify to the apprentice's age at the start of his training, and to the duration of the process. Apprentices were usually aged between 10 and 13 years at the beginning, and their apprenticeship lasted a few years depending on the craft. In most cases, the duration of the contract was two years. One of the few apprenticeship contracts for a carpenter that we have is dated to 16 CE and comes from Karanis, a village in the Fayum of the Arsinoite nome. In it we read:

> . . . his son for six years, the tax on individuals for the builders' trade for the third year of Tiberius Caesar and clothing and the poll tax (being a charge on the master), and (the master agrees) that after the term he will give him a chiton (worth) eight drachmai and a carpenter's adze (worth) four drachmai.[66]

This document speaks of an apprenticeship of six years, which was an unusually long time. Working as a carpenter was therefore probably considered especially challenging and multifaceted, so that a six-year-long apprenticeship was considered reasonable. The master most likely provided his apprentice with house and board, had the obligation to clothe him, and was required to pay the builder's tax and poll tax for him. The master also pledged to provide him with a new *chiton* (in Latin *tunica*) – a unisex garment usually covering from the neck to above the knee, and a new axe, the carpenter's most important tool, at the end of his service.

Craftsmen among the First Christian Clergy

The documentary sources from the Roman and later Roman periods, most notably inscriptions in Asia Minor and papyri in Egypt, show that the clergy was recruited from the same social class from which Jesus also rose: the craftsman class. While the bishops mainly came from the local elite, rich landowners and members of the city councils, presbyters, deacons, and lectors were recruited from the local middle class, if we may call them that. For Asia Minor, we have evidence, e.g., of subdeacons who were professional makers of fishing nets[67] or cider merchants,[68] and presbyters who worked as professional goldsmiths,[69] sewers of ships' sails,[70] potters,[71] gem cutters,[72] blacksmiths,[73] or butchers.[74] Most of these attestations come from Korykos in Cilicia. Nevertheless, we should not conclude that Korykos was an isolated case. In other parts of Asia Minor it was not common to include the profession of the deceased in the epitaph, as was the case in Korykos and its surrounding area. A letter by Gregory of Nazianzus mentions a tradesman-deacon named Euthalius,[75] and elsewhere in the letter Gregory asks for the exemption of another tradesman-cleric from the business tax.[76] Many of the fourth-century clerics at the church of Caesarea in Cappadocia also seem to have followed a craft or trade.[77]

The papyrological sources for Egypt tell a similar story. Schmelz has compiled evidence for craftsmen among the Egyptian clergy and shown that they were employed as bakers, workers in the textile industry, potters, silversmiths, blacksmiths, locksmiths, goldsmiths, and nail-smiths. Clerics were also employed in woodworking as carpenters, chair or saddle makers, bow makers, and sculptors, and in the transport industry as camel drivers.[78] In the biography of John the Merciful, two lectors who worked as shoemakers are mentioned at a church in Alexandria.[79]

Earlier, we read how tax collectors of the fourth and fifth centuries spread anxiety and terror among the small-scale craftsmen and merchants, even if many of the sources probably paint an exaggerated picture. Because of this, craftsmen and merchants, like workers in many other professions, had an interest in obtaining an office in the church, and this was particularly the case after 343 CE, when all clerics undertaking a trade or craft were granted exemption from the business tax by Constantius (they were also assured that they would not have to perform menial service or corvée labor – *munera sordida*).[80] Moreover, the Edict of Constantius insinuates that the exemption of the clergy from the business tax had already been put in place by Constantius' father Constantine, and that it was being confirmed here by his son.[81] An edict from 346 reinforces the fact that members of the clergy did not have to perform menial services and would not have to pay for the maintenance of roads and bridges. All clerics employed in commerce were again assured that they were exempt from the business tax, albeit now with the added restriction that they should support the poor with their profits.[82]

Mother and Son

In all ancient societies children were obliged to care for their parents in their old age. Care for the elderly included not only the provisioning of food, clothing, a roof over their heads, respect, dignified treatment, protection, assistance, and company, but also the organization of a proper burial and the performance of common funerary rites after a person's death. Daughters and sons were involved in the care of elderly parents, though in varying degrees and in different ways. Forms of support depended on the particular child's financial situation, physical capabilities, housing situation, and the quality of the emotional attachment they felt towards their parents. Other diverse motives also encouraged children to provide help, such as sympathy, the feeling of commitment, imminent social ostracism, and the prospect of inheritance. The reality was usually a complex combination of all of these motives. However, the sources also show that in return and just as often, parents were morally obliged to care for their children, to provide their sons with an education, to see their daughters married with a dowry, and to transfer their property to their descendants at their death.

In Roman Galilee, as well as in many other eastern regions of the Roman Empire, an elderly father had control of the household until his death, although not with such extensive authority as a Roman *paterfamilias* had. The elderly father managed his family's assets and was the highest authority in the household regarding the taking of decisions. Due to his paternal control of the family's productive sources of income until his death, he could be relatively sure he would receive support and care in his old age. In contrast to classical Athens, it was not common in the Hellenistic Roman world to transfer wealth to the next generation while the father was still alive. If a patriarch's wife died before him, this did not alter his situation; the old father kept his position of authority. Finally, some widowers remarried at a fairly old age to substantially younger women.[83]

The patriarch's widow was much less secure. When her husband died before her, a widow's eldest son typically took over as head of the household. The paternal inheritance was evenly distributed among the children, but the widow herself did not inherit, receiving at most a lifetime right of abode in the family house.[84] Now, the first woman of the household was no longer the widow, but the wife of her eldest son, her daughter-in-law.[85] The death of the patriarch thus severely weakened the position of his widow. In only a few cases in the Roman-Egyptian census lists do we see a patriarch's widow taking over as head of her household; most of these women still had children who were minors, for whom they took over management of the paternal inheritance until they reached the legal age of adulthood.[86]

If her sons were already adults, a widow was completely dependent on their goodwill.[87] Private letters between family members, which have been preserved among the papyri of Greco-Roman Egypt, show that mothers cultivated an especially close emotional relationship with their sons – a phenomenon also known from many other traditionally patriarchal societies. This is not very surprising considering that in such systems the most important insurance for a woman's old age lay in her sons; most women would have had every interest in assuring their sons' loyalty and lifelong fidelity.

From these private letters between family members, we also see that both sons and daughters who had left their parents' house remained in close contact with their parents, and especially with their mothers. Letters were regularly accompanied by small gifts, and there was a constant exchange of various foodstuffs and textiles between the households. Sons wrote home when they were away on business trips or served in the military far from their hometown. Letters home from adult children are mostly addressed to mothers, but also contain greetings to the rest of the family. All reflect a close emotional relationship between adult children and their mothers, full of respect and childlike love. The children try to reassure their mothers that they are doing well, and say that they are very concerned for their mother's wellbeing. For their part, mothers ask for regular news and for their children to come home for a visit.[88]

Most of the older widows in the cities and villages of Egypt lived with one or more of their children. Many lived with their adult sons, their young wives and children, and occasionally with their unmarried or already divorced daughters. While the great majority of old men were still married, often with a considerably younger partner than themselves, two-thirds of women over 60 years of age no longer had a husband.[89] While women did not usually marry a second time after the death of their husband or after a divorce, men still regularly took a new wife in their old age – a pattern found in many traditionally patriarchal societies. These gender-specific differences are then rereflected in the living situations of old women and men. As a rule, it was a married son and not a daughter with whom the old mother lived in a household. This is quite clearly due to the fact that married sons stayed in their parents' house while daughters left their parents' home at the time of their marriage, and relocated to their parents-in-law's house. For a son-in-law to live in his parents-in-law's household was looked upon as a stop-gap measure, and it only happened if the father had no sons of his own, or if the son-in-law's parents' house had no room for another couple. A son was thus the greatest support for a widowed mother.[90]

According to his contemporaries, Jesus' abandonment of his profession and his family, his controversial attitude toward the authorities, and his voluntarily sought death strongly neglected the traditional role of a widowed mother's son. Whether Jesus' attested brothers were Mary's biological sons, or came from Joseph via an earlier marriage, we will never know. However, as the oldest and possibly the only son of Mary, Jesus would have been responsible for his elderly widowed mother, who anticipated a difficult financial, social, and emotional situation in her old age.

Conclusions

In demographic terms, there is little to differentiate Roman Galilee from Roman Egypt. Both exhibit high levels of mortality and fertility as well as a correspondingly low population growth. These are common features of many premodern societies before the mid nineteenth century. Furthermore, there is no evidence to suggest that Jewish families in Roman Palestine differed from pagan families in Roman Egypt with regards the composition of families and households. Roman Egypt and Roman Galilee also feature similar ages of first marriage for men and women, similar rates of divorce and remarriage, and similar levels of social differentiation regarding access to formal education. With an average difference of eight years between the age at marriage for men and women, men married in their mid 20s while their brides were between 15 and 18 years old. Thus, a considerable number of husbands died before their wives, leaving many widows aged 20 to 30 with young children. This fate probably also befell Mary, the mother of Jesus. By the same token, it was not uncommon for men to lose their wives in childbirth. While it was improbable that a widow over the age of 30 would remarry, widowers would often marry into their fifties, establishing a second family in the process. For these reasons, and in view of the rich evidence that we possess, we can with confidence extrapolate insights into aspects of everyday life to Roman Palestine and other (eastern) Roman provinces.

Jesus belonged to the so-called middle class – free craftsmen, who probably profited from the Roman occupation's building program. The average artisan household in the Roman world was smaller than a peasant family, and, in the case of the latter, it was common for brothers to work together as heads of the household with joint responsibility for the farm. This would prevent the inheritance from being divided. Artisan families tended to be small – restricted to parents and children – and the workshop was often set up in the home. Sons of these families received at least a basic education, and were able to read and write. However, by the age of 12 or 13 they would follow in their father's footsteps and learn a craft.

Birth rates during Jesus' time were high, but so were child mortality rates. Almost half of all children died before their fifth birthday. Jesus' family defied these harsh demographic conditions; five sons and several daughters had survived their dangerous early childhood years. It was very unusual that a couple had five sons who reached adulthood. Even at first glance, the ancient observer would have recognized this family as blessed by God.

Finally, as Mary's eldest son Jesus would have been obliged to take care of his widowed mother. For the widowed Mary, her son was her most important old-age insurance. Instead, Jesus transferred this task to one of his disciples before resigning himself to death.

CHAPTER VI

"In those days Mary set out . . ."
Travel by the Lower Classes in Roman Times

In those days Mary set out and went with haste to a Judaean town in
the hill country.

Luke 1:39

Almost anyone prompted to talk about journeys in the New Testament
would be able to enumerate a few immediately. The Gospel of Luke alone
contains several, for example Mary's journey from Nazareth in Galilee to
visit Elizabeth in Judaea and the accounts of the journey of Jesus and his
disciples throughout Galilee and Judaea. Matthew even reports that the
Holy Family fled all the way from Bethlehem to Egypt, and the Book of
Acts describes journeys made by Paul and the other apostles through the
Roman Empire's eastern provinces and across the Mediterranean to Rome.
But what we know about how people traveled in antiquity is quite limited,
especially for those from the social classes we are looking at here – the
protagonists of the New Testament were the kind of ordinary people who
made up about 90 percent of the total population. And since the picture we
have of travel in antiquity is incomplete, quite a few interesting questions
remain open. What social strata did travelers come from? Were extended
journeys normally only made by members of the elite or those on whom
the state depended, or was it also commonplace for ordinary farmers and
tradesmen to travel beyond the immediate environs of the villages or cities
where they lived? Why did people go on journeys? Did they make journeys
for cultural or religious edification, leave their habitual places of residence
in order to attend court hearings, or travel to keep up family relationships
or to work? Interesting questions about gender-specific aspects also arise.
Did men have a larger radius of movement, for example, or did women also
venture out on journeys? If so, did they travel in the company of others – or
even alone? Other seemingly mundane questions are nevertheless interesting enough to merit investigation, including the specific means of transport used for typical journeys, and the costs of transport. Price differences

must also have existed between travelling by water and travelling overland in ancient times – but how significant were they? How did travelers eat while on their journeys, and how did they find secure places to sleep? What hazards did they fear, and did they opt to avoid certain areas entirely?

As these questions show, the travel options open to the lower classes constitute a highly interesting topic that has been largely neglected up to now in research on Roman roads and travel in Roman times. The Roman *cursus publicus*, the state-run transport system, which could only be used with written permission from the governor or emperor, has been investigated and described in depth in a number of publications.[1] It consisted of a network of relay stations, or *mutationes*, and guest-houses, or *mansiones*, which were situated along the Roman highways. At the mutationes, which were located 6 to 9 miles apart, horses and pack animals could be changed, while at the mansiones, larger post stations spaced 22 to 25 miles apart, travelers with the requisite permission in writing found overnight accommodation free of charge. Officials and notables traveling in this way had a bed waiting for them at the end of each day in the rest stations located along the Roman roads. But how did a peasant farmer organize his trip centuries before travel agencies and online booking? Where did he sleep, and how did he replenish his funds? How did he know what terrain or which villages lay ahead of him on his way?

Early Travel Reports and the Significance of the Papyri

The *Histories* of Herodotus, from the fifth century BCE, can be regarded as travel writing – Herodotus certainly reports on observations, experiences, and stories from his travels – but they contain scant practical information about how he organized his travels. For Roman times, the *Metamorphoses* by Apuleius, from the second century CE, represents the main source of insights into the travel and transport system the lower orders were able to use during the Roman *pax Augusta*. While Lucius, the chief protagonist, initially belongs to the aristocracy, he participates in the daily lives of ordinary people in northern Greece after being transformed into a donkey.[2] A report given by Horace while on a journey from Rome to Brundisium in 37 BCE also contains various interesting details.[3] While he was frequently welcomed into the manors of rich friends as he traveled through Latium, Campania, and Apulia, he occasionally had to bed down in a public hostelry. With the Christianization of society in late antiquity, a new literary genre came into existence in the form of the pilgrim's travel report to the Holy Land or other holy sites.[4] As in so many other areas, however, the papyri from Egypt represent the richest seam of source material relating to travel and transport.

Occasions for Travel

Trade and the state-sponsored or private transport of goods were probably the main reasons behind the movement of people from one place to another. Pieter Sijpesteijn has carried out an important study in this area that draws on more than 900 surviving receipts from customs posts in Roman Egypt, and presents incomparable insights into the network of trade routes and the use of camels, oxen, and donkeys for transport. The receipts also contain information on the wares traded within Egypt and beyond its borders.[5]

Letters from travelers to family members who had stayed at home make reference to a wide range of other reasons for undertaking journeys. Special events within extended families such as the birth of a child often prompted people to travel.[6] Birthdays were also a welcome opportunity to pay a visit to family members not living in the immediate vicinity.[7] When news arrived that a family member had been taken ill, people would often set off to visit them as soon as they could: even illnesses that seem harmless to us today could quickly prove fatal in an era that predated modern medical expertise, the discovery of antibiotics, and all we know today about hygiene. When family members died, people also traveled to pay their respects to the dead and to support grieving relatives.[8]

In both pre-Christian times and during the later Christian period, religious festivals of local or supraregional significance also frequently prompted people to go on journeys.[9] Contracts of apprenticeship stated, for example, that apprentices were to be given a certain number of free days every year to enable them to take part in religious festivities in the areas they came from. A cornucopia of temple festivals attracted people from far and wide in Greco-Roman Egypt: these festivals also represented an opportunity to visit family members living some distance away. Such a religious holiday forms the context in which Petosiris writes to his sister Serenia in Oxyrhynchus:

> Be sure, dear, to come up on the 20th for the birthday festival of the god, and let me know whether you are coming by boat or by donkey, in order that we may send for you accordingly. Take care not to forget.[10]

Jews in Egypt also made pilgrimages – for example, members of the Jewish congregation in Alexandria traveled to the Temple in Jerusalem or up the Nile to the Jewish Temple on Elephantine Island.

Sources contain quite a few reports of people living in the Fayum or in Oxyrhynchus in Middle Egypt having to travel to Alexandria to take part in court hearings.[11] Roman military personnel had to travel to reach their bases, and such journeys could take them to the borders of the province or across the sea by ship to the ports of Misenum in Campania or Ostia, Rome's port – and then onward to their deployments.[12] Labor migration was also common. Migrant workers seeking opportunities to help with sowing or harvests did not confine their search to their own nomes: many also found earning opportunities in Alexandria – at least on a temporary basis – and worked there while their families stayed at home in the countryside.[13]

Youths usually began their apprenticeships when they were 10 to 13, and often traveled to another village or town for this purpose. They then lived in the household of their masters for several years, returning home only on holidays.[14] Sons from well-to-do families were sent to the capitals of their nomes or to Alexandria for schooling beyond elementary level. It seems likely that they often stayed with relatives or with family friends there. They were frequently accompanied by a slave, who was tasked with looking after them. Parents visited children where they were studying, and children in turn returned home for regular visits.[15]

The roads and waterways of the province saw busy traffic as people traveled between villages, from villages to their nome capitals, or even all the way to Alexandria. Many seem to have had a good grasp of the geography of their own province at least: people knew in which direction Alexandria lay and how long the journey would most likely take. Most people living outside of Alexandria had friends or relatives in the city, and even people who remained at home in their villages regularly encountered people who were about to travel to Alexandria or had just returned from there. This meant they could give them letters: indeed, travelers acted as an informal mail service connecting the capital with rural Egypt, and quite a few families kept up very intense correspondence with relatives in Alexandria in this way. Only state officials were permitted to avail themselves of the state postal service and its infrastructure, and only the elite could afford their own messengers. Ordinary members of the population who wanted to send a letter had to find somebody who happened to be traveling in the direction of the addressee.[16] Along the main route up and down the Nile, it does not seem to have been difficult to identify people who were going in the right direction and were willing to take and deliver letters. This is certainly the picture conveyed in one son's complaint to his mother:

I have sent you so many letters, yet you haven't sent me back a single one even though so many people have traveled down the river."[17] Another man complains to his brother in a similar vein: "This is now the third letter I am writing you, and you have sent me no reply, although you know that I am worried if you do not write me frequently about your affairs, and in spite of the fact that many persons come here from your vicinity.[18]

Letter couriers could be family members, acquaintances, or complete strangers who happened to be passing through. People who encountered or heard about somebody who was about to travel to an area where a family member lived often took advantage of the chance to give the traveler a message of greeting to take along. A son, presumably in Alexandria, writes to his father further up the Nile in Hermopolis:

Heliodoros to his father many greetings! I have just received your letter and I am pleased that you are well . . . I am always happy when I can send you my greetings with somebody traveling upriver even when I have no real news to share.[19]

Most of the evidence we have is from the Fayum region, the Roman Arsinoite nome. The cosmopolitan port city of Alexandria, at the western end of the Nile Delta, is the most common destination mentioned by people living in the Fayum, even though it was almost 250 miles away. Coptos, in Upper Egypt, some 342 miles from the Fayum, is also mentioned frequently as a destination.[20] The gateway to the desert, it was an important crossroads on major caravan routes leading to the Red Sea: caravans departing from Coptos reached the Red Sea ports of Myos Hormos or Berenike within five days. Most of the travel routes mentioned in the papyri relate to shorter journeys that could be accomplished within a day – trips from one village to the next, or from villages to their respective nome capitals. The number of destinations mentioned which lay beyond the borders of the province can be counted on the fingers of one hand.

Such journeys extending beyond the province were typically to Rome, the center of the Roman Empire. Those who made the voyage across the sea to Rome were largely either wealthy businessmen or recruits for the Roman Army. A certain Antonius, son of Ptolemaeus and evidently a wealthy landowner, traveled from Alexandria to Italy, presumably on business. After landing in Puteoli near Naples, he writes to his overseer in Oxyrhynchus in Middle Egypt:

As soon as I set foot in Italy, I felt compelled to let you know that my family and I are in good health. The sailing was slow, but it wasn't a difficult trip, and my poor little body suffered none of the discomfort one usually expects, especially on one's first voyage. Written in Puteoli on 29 May.[21]

A young recruit named Apollonarius from Karanis, in the Fayum, writes to his mother at home from Portus, Rome's harbor, to assure her that he is well after the long sea journey:

> From Cyrene, where I found a man who was journeying to you, I deemed it necessary to write to you about my welfare ... And now I am writing you from Portus (i.e. the harbor of Rome), for I have not yet gone up to Rome and been assigned ... I arrived in Portus on Pachon 25 (20 May).

This is followed by a postscript: "Know that I have been assigned to Misenum, for I learned it later." The writing on the verso of the folded papyrus reads: "Deliver to Karanis, to Taesion, from Apollinarius, her son." As the letter was discovered in Karanis, a village in the Fayum, it clearly reached its intended destination from Rome (see fig. 6.1).[22]

Travel Routes and the Transport Network

The Nile has been the main traffic artery in Egypt from time immemorial. Since the most important cities were located on the Nile, travel by water was the obvious option for many journeys. The journey downriver from Coptos, Oxyrhynchus, or the Fayum to Alexandria, the capital, could be accomplished rapidly with the help of the current. Travel upriver was more difficult, since boats had to be laboriously towed upriver by draft animals and could only set their sails when the winds were favorable. As there were no bridges spanning the Nile, the river represented a barrier to as well as a facilitator of travel: it could only be crossed by ferry, and ferry passage was expensive.

During the annual flooding of the Nile, entire swathes of land adjacent to the river were submerged. The famous Nile mosaic of Palestrina (see Figure 6.2) includes a depiction of Egypt during the flood which shows the valley submerged and only the villages standing above the floodwaters after the river has burst its banks. Herodotus gives us a similar description:

> When the Nile overflows the land, only the towns are seen high and dry above the water, very like the islands in the Aegean sea. These alone stand out, the rest of Egypt being a sheet of water. So when this happens, folk are not ferried, as usual, in the course of the stream, but clean over the plain.[23]

The tracks along the banks were then also impassable. Only once the floods had receded and the earth had dried out could the towpath along the river be repaired and made passable again for people on foot or riding on donkeys or in wagons (Figures 6.3–6.5). In the second or third century CE, Arsinoe writes to her sister Sarapias living in the Oxyrhynchite nome:

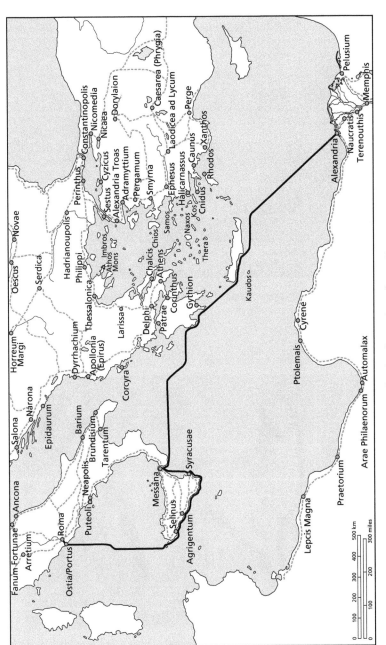

6.1 Route by ship from Alexandria to Rome.

6.2 Nile mosaic detail of a riverboat from Praeneste.

6.3 Roman relief depicting a chariot, first to second century. Church of Maria Saal, Klagenfurt, Austria.

6.4 Reconstruction of a Roman carriage. Römisch-Germanisches Museum, Cologne.

"If the roads are firm (again), I shall go at once."[24] Not only were the tracks along the river destroyed in the annual flood; irrigation systems and field borders were also washed away. After each Nile flood, the fields had to be newly measured out and the irrigation channels repaired. Building a proper road was pointless under these circumstances.

Travel certainly became easier once Egypt had become an integral part of the Roman Empire and the productive capacity of Egyptian agriculture reached new heights. Waterways and a network of roads and tracks were comprehensively developed: Rome was heavily dependent on the enormous quantities of wheat supplied from Egypt, and the wheat had to be transported as quickly as possible from where it was cultivated to Alexandria and then shipped to Rome.[25] Entire armies also had to be moved along the empire's transport network to wherever they were required – and they in turn had to be kept supplied.

Women as Travelers in Roman Egypt

We tend to conceive of women in premodern societies with patriarchal structures as being tied to the home and firmly under the control of their menfolk. We can easily visualize them looking after the hearth, preparing meals, raising children, and making and mending clothes. But the papyri from Egypt reveal that women were able to move around much more freely than is commonly assumed. A treasure trove of evidence shows that women traveled, and while some of these journeys were only between a village and the nearest larger town, others extended considerably further, for example from the Fayum to Alexandria or, in the other direction, upriver from the Fayum to Coptos.[26]

Like men, women embarked on journeys for many different reasons. One of the most common – perhaps somewhat surprisingly – was the arrival of children. Toward the end of pregnancy, women often returned to the houses of their parents. Perhaps they could count on more support and assistance from their own mothers and sisters than was to be reckoned with in the households of their parents-in-law, in the dramatic days and weeks around the birth of a child. The sight of a heavily pregnant woman riding a donkey – as the Evangelist Luke depicts Mary – would not have been unusual at the time.

But women also traveled to assist their pregnant relatives, especially when the health of expectant mothers prevented them from traveling themselves. This is illustrated by the case of the pregnant Didyme from the Thebes area. She had originally intended to travel home to her parents to give birth, but, as the end of her pregnancy drew near, she no longer felt able to do so,[27] and so she sent a brief message on an ostracon to her mother or her sister:

> Didyme to Thesis, greeting! I had prepared myself for coming. Apollos himself told me as he was leaving, "If you are well go to your home to give birth; if you want, write to me and I will come." The bearer of this ostracon told me, "Remain there."[28]

Another document in which a birth and a journey are linked is from a certain Thermouthas from the area around Arsinoe in the Fayum. In the second or third century, she wrote the following lines to her brother:

> Thermouthas to Apolinarios her brother, many greetings. I want you to know, I and Valeria, if Herois gives birth, we are praying to come to you; for it is necessary. We want to bring Demetrous to sail down with her mother.[29]

The document clearly shows that four women wanted to leave for a journey downriver together, but were waiting until they had helped a fifth woman to give birth. Other evidence suggests that pregnant women, in particular, tended not to travel alone. A woman named Serapias, also from the Fayum, writes to her son-in-law to request that he bring her pregnant daughter home to her so she can give birth in her parents' house. She assures him in her letter that she will bear the cost of (renting) a donkey (see Figure 6.5).[30]

But women traveled for other reasons – to follow their menfolk, for example, when the men had found work in their nome capitals or in Alexandria.[31] Wealthy women sometimes also had to travel to attend to

6.5 Man feeding a donkey. Detail of a mosaic floor, sixth century CE.

property matters; for example to check up on tenants, or to ensure that estate managers were doing their jobs. The case of Arsinoe, mentioned above offering to collect the rent from a tenant on behalf of her sister Sarapias, represents one such example of a woman traveling on business.

> If the roads are firm (again), I shall go at once to your tenant and ask him for your rents – if indeed he will give them to me; for you should have sent me a letter for him. All the same, if instead you wrote to him in advance to give them to me, I shall go off and collect them.[32]

The sources we have for Roman Egypt make it clear that women often traveled without male escorts. In practice, however, women would have traveled completely alone only in exceptional circumstances, and would normally have banded together with other women to form groups.

It is difficult to reach a broad judgment on whether the journeying of Egyptian women as a matter of course reflects typical Egyptian attitudes and practices that generally conceded more freedom to Egyptian women than their counterparts in the Greco-Hellenistic world were accorded. Comparable practices are certainly unimaginable for classical Athens; respectable women there did not travel alone, and left their homes only on special occasions or when it was unavoidable.

Interestingly enough, one of the oldest accounts we have of a pilgrimage to the Holy Land was written by a woman in the penultimate decade of the fourth century. Egeria, probably from southern Gaul, traveled from there to Jerusalem and to the holy sites mentioned in the Old Testament in Egypt and Mesopotamia.[33] In contrast to the anonymous pilgrim from Bordeaux whose report from fifty years earlier has survived in fragments, Egeria narrates her travels and experiences in detail for the benefit of her sisters in faith at home. Egeria traveled by water, on donkeys, and on foot. It can be assumed with some confidence that she did not belong to the lower social strata in her hometown: not only was she able to read and write; she had also learned a foreign language, Greek, albeit only to a rudimentary level. She also possessed sufficient means to travel for three years without having to worry about money or to work. The financial aspects of her journey are not once mentioned in her account.

While Egeria describes her experiences mostly in the first person, she did not travel alone but in the company of several co-religionists, who are not described any further; we know neither their number, origin, nor gender. The group relied on the hospitality of monks for food and accommodation in isolated regions, where they were presumably taken in and looked after in exchange for donations toward the upkeep of local holy sites. In other areas, the group seems to have stayed in public inns. The military escort the travelers manifestly needed on the more dangerous routes doubtless also expected remuneration.

Egeria's gender does not seem to have prevented her in any way from traveling, not even in the most far-flung regions. She visited the hermits of the Egyptian desert, eating with them and even spending the night out in the desert. While she seems to have traveled by donkey most of the time, she climbed Mount Sinai (7,497 feet) on foot. Her account makes no mention of any unpleasant incidents that arose during her journey; indeed, she appears to have been contented and to have gotten on well with her guides at all times – she was unfailingly thankful to them and to God.

Travel on Foot, by Donkey, in Wagons, or by Boat

In theory, four travel options were available in Egypt: on foot, in wagons drawn by animals, by boat, or on the backs of donkeys. An oracular decree in hieratic script promising to protect the wearer against all hazards wherever she went mentions three of the usual four options: "I shall keep her safe from anything unpleasant and any abomination on every kind of journey which she will make (by) ship, chariot, or (on) foot, while her breath is alive and well with her."[34] Camels and horses were only used for transportation in exceptional cases: camels were used as beasts of burden only in the Western and Eastern Deserts,[35] while keeping horses was the preserve of the well-to-do elite and state officials, since they were far more expensive to buy and to keep than donkeys.

Short trips from one village to the next were generally made on foot. Irrigation channels created barriers to rapid progress, however; they were presumably spanned by simple footbridges, which could be crossed on foot and perhaps with a donkey, but not with wheeled vehicles. Some of the wider irrigation channels were also navigable at least some of the time, which meant one could choose between traveling by boat or traveling overland with a donkey.[36]

As the Nile itself, the Nile canal, and the river Tomis were all navigable, boats and ships provided a significant means of transportation. Cargo vessels plying the Nile sometimes also took on passengers.[37] Farmers or tradesmen who wanted to travel to the principal city in the nome or all the way to the provincial capital Alexandria had to try to obtain a place on a ship that was making the journey in any case: they did not possess boats of their own or have contacts who owned boats in their immediate family or social circles. But it was not easy to find a boat going to the right place at the right time that had space for passengers and their luggage.

A woman named Eutychis intended to travel with a considerable amount of luggage from Antinoopolis to her mother in Oxyrhynchus, approximately 50 miles downriver on the Nile. First she approached camel drivers, but they refused to make the trip to Oxyrhynchus for unspecified reasons. Perhaps they were deterred by the local unrest frequent in the third century CE. Eutychis then attempted to travel down the Nile by ship, as she recounts to her mother. But she failed to find a suitable ship and ultimately decided to wait in Antinoopolis until a better transport option appeared.[38]

The sources repeatedly report on the difficulty of finding a captain willing to take extra passengers. Travelers like Eutychis with a lot of luggage seem to have encountered particular difficulties. A certain Satornilus ran into a similar problem, albeit with the difference that his "luggage" took the form of an embalmed body, which he needed to transport from Oxyrhynchus to Alexandria. At first, he failed to find a captain willing to admit the corpse and its living escort on board. Eventually the chief priest came to his aid and put a skiff at his disposal.[39] Several further letters testify to the difficulties faced by travelers looking for a passage and to the delays to their travel plans that resulted from not being able to find a boat.[40]

Table 6.1 *Prices in second-century Roman Egypt*

Purchase price	
Donkey	150–300 drachmas
Camel	500–800 drachmas
Boat	8,000 drachmas
Rental price	
Donkey with guide (per day)	2 drachmas
Camel with guide (per day)	6 drachmas
Ferry from Oxyrhynchus to Alexandria	60 drachmas
Wages	
Unlearned worker (per month)	30–40 drachmas

Transport Costs

Donkeys were very useful for transporting goods for trade or luggage. But not everybody owned one; even this humble means of transport did not come cheap. A papyrus dating from 141 CE in the Basel University Library collection cites the sum of 148 drachmas as the purchase price of a donkey (see Table 6.1).[41] In comparison to the sums mentioned in other papyri, it seems that this was very much at the lower limit of what people were liable to pay. An ordinary laborer earned about 8 obols a day. If he worked for about 250 days of the year, his annual wages would have amounted to some 330 drachmas. A donkey, then, cost almost half a year's wages – a considerable sum, especially given that an ordinary laborer would have been living close to the breadline in any case. For most people who wanted to travel any distance with luggage, renting a donkey was more realistic. It is very probable that there were more than enough professional donkey hirers – they are certainly referred to in numerous cases in the papyri.[42]

Travel by ship was even more expensive: even short trips by water seem to have involved substantial costs. Letters often contain agreements on who would pay for the costs of a family member being ferried somewhere. When Mikke and her brother Euthalius wanted to travel home to their mother for Easter, Euthalius assured his mother that she need not worry: he would pay for Mikke's transport.[43] We know from two sources that the price of a boat trip from the Fayum in Middle Egypt downriver to Alexandria in the second century CE stood at 55–60 drachmas, twice the monthly wages of an ordinary worker.[44]

Only members of the most prosperous class in Roman Egyptian society had boats of their own. Prices for boats of several different sizes are given in the papyri, and even small boats cost sixteen or seventeen times as much as an ordinary laborer earned in a year.[45] Even a well-paid legionary in the Roman Army would have had to put six years' salary aside before being able to afford such a boat. Thus it was only really the local aristocracy – imperial officials, members of city councils, bishops, churches and monastic foundations, and large landowners – that owned boats, as Roger Bagnall has shown for fourth-century Egypt.[46] State-owned boats also existed and were used, among other purposes, in the running of the state postal service, the *velox cursus.*[47]

The Pace of Travel

Villages in the Fayum were never more than half a day's walk apart. Even Arsinoe, the capital of its nome, could be reached within a day from anywhere within the district. A journey to Alexandria, the provincial capital, took several days, however, and that was when no unforeseen circumstances arose. A woman called Isis indicates the duration of the journey in a letter from the third century CE addressed to her mother, who had remained at home in Philadelphia in the Fayum: "I want you to know that I have arrived well and safely in Alexandria in four days."[48] That represented relatively rapid progress for a distance of almost 250 miles (see Figure 6.6). Interestingly enough, the journey had not taken much longer 600 years previously, in Ptolemaic times: we know that from letters addressed to a certain Zenon, a large landowner who lived in the Fayum in the third century BCE. His archive, which was discovered under a door sill more than a hundred years ago, contains letters dispatched from the capital Alexandria which reached their destination in the Fayum within four to seven days.[49] Other letters in the Zenon archive from various parts of the Mediterranean world were in transit for much longer. The messenger who brought a letter from Alexandria to Cilicia (southern Turkey) needed around two months to make the journey of some 746 miles, a distance covered largely by ship.[50] The messenger who brought a letter from Sidon in Syria to Philadelphia in the Fayum, presumably also by sea, took fourteen days to cover 404 miles, most probably also by sea.[51]

Eating and Sleeping Arrangements

Surprisingly enough, travelers in the papyri scarcely mention in their letters where and how they found overnight accommodation on their long journeys. Ships pulled into port in the evenings, since travel on a river at

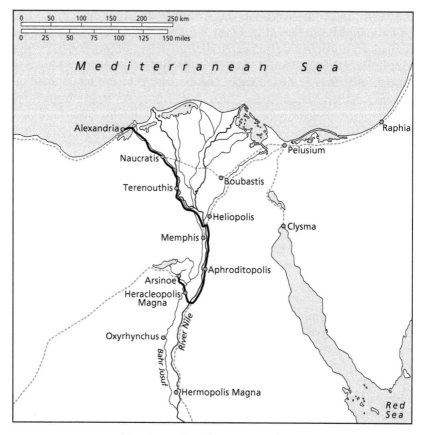

6.6 Travel route from the Fayum to Alexandria.

night was banned to prevent pirates operating under the cover of darkness, but not everybody would have had acquaintances or family members living along the route who could put them up. We know very little about how people passed their nights when traveling, about how secure they felt and about how much they paid for accommodation. We also have very little information about what they ate or whether the food was good, and the letters we have do not contain passages referring to inns or cookshops frequented by travelers. Modern travelers prize accommodation and the taste of foreign cuisines highly; after sightseeing and other attractions, they form a core part of the travel experience. In ancient times, just as today, staples such as bread must have been prepared in different ways in different regions. It also seems safe to assume that variations existed in the range of fruit and vegetables which were available from place to place, but none of the travelers for whom we have records mention such differences. We know from Pompeii that food stalls were a dominant element in the streetscape. Martial reports that grimy cookshops stretching from the ground floors of houses out into the streets were ubiquitous in Rome.[52] In Alexandria and other large cities in Egypt, the picture can scarcely have been different. We do have evidence for the existence of public inns with patrons who met up to dine together in the nome capitals of Arsinoe, Hermopolis, and Oxyrhynchus,[53] and also in smaller villages in the Fayum such as Kerkeosiris and Philadelphia.[54] This kind of public inn is referred to in the papyri as *kapeleion*, a term roughly equivalent to the Latin *caupona*. However, while the letters written by travelers contain complaints about issues like the horrendous price of boat transport, poor weather, the impossibility of obtaining a place on a ship, attacks by brigands, and local disturbances, none of the people writing report on the quality of these local inns or what they served for dinner.[55]

Travel Hazards

Natural phenomena such as heavy rainfall, storms, and the flooding of the Nile, which regularly made tracks and roads impassable for some time, made travel completely impossible at times and far from enjoyable on other occasions. Occasionally travelers found themselves stuck in a harbor for days or even weeks at a time.[56] The apostle Paul relates that he experienced three shipwrecks on his missionary voyages and spent a day and a night drifting on the open sea.

> Three times I was shipwrecked; for a night and a day I was adrift at sea; on frequent journeys, in danger from rivers, danger from bandits, danger from my own people, danger from Gentiles, danger in the city, danger in the wilderness, danger at sea, danger from false brothers and sisters; in toil and hardship, through many a sleepless night, hungry and thirsty, often without food, cold and naked. 2 Cor. 11:26–27

One of the main reasons, however, for the general unwillingness to travel that is often discernible in the papyri was the ever-present danger of being attacked.[57] This is plain in a letter from a husband asking his wife to follow him from the Fayum to Coptos with all she possesses (see Figure 6.7). He instructs her to bring her gold jewelry, but cautions her that she should not wear it during the trip on the boat – evidently to avoid attracting the attention of bandits.[58] A certain Petesouchos from Tebetnou in the third century BCE was less careful – or perhaps just plain

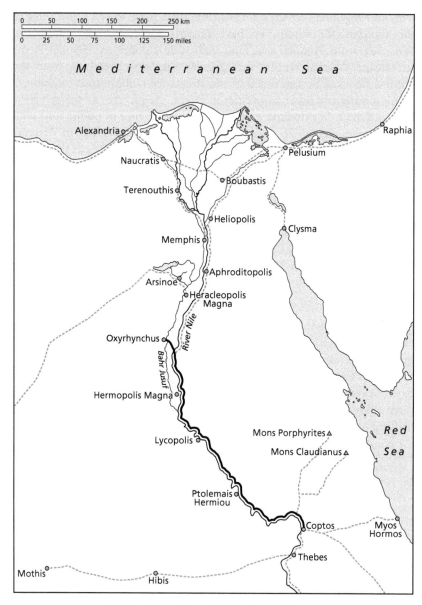

6.7 Travel route from Oxyrhynchus to Coptos.

unlucky. He fell into the hands of robbers on his way to his sister in Corphotoi, and they stole his clothes and his money.[59] Another traveler, Seos, also had his clothes stolen on his way home from the oasis to Hermopolis – as well as his two donkeys.

> To Mnaseas, of the diadochoi and epistatês phylakitôn, from Seos, son of Horos, of those from the Sarapieion in the desert opposite Hermoupolis. On the 24th of Choiach, year 6, I was away from the Oasis with others. A band of robbers set upon us as we were coming back and took off in possession of a male donkey of mine and a female one. With both of these they carried off the merchandise of which they stripped me. . . .[60]

These examples show that encounters with groups of thugs while traveling alone through the countryside rarely ended well: assaults, injuries, and even death were real risks.[61] Whenever it could be arranged, people opted to travel in groups, as the letters which have come down to us on papyrus clearly show. Zois from Oxyrhynchus, for example, wrote to her brother Ischyron in around 30 CE: "If you wish to depart to Alexandria, Apollos son of Theon is going tomorrow."[62] But having company on the road was no guarantee of a safe journey. Despite having joined forces, two swine dealers were attacked and robbed on the open road as they made their way to the village of Theadelphia in the Fayum.[63]

Accidents on the Road

A farmer and veteran by the name of Lucius, living in the hinterland of Oxyrhynchus, set off with his donkey one day for the nome capital, possibly to sell his produce at the market.[64] A group of donkeys driven by a slave and laden with stones came toward him on the road. A collision resulted – it is unclear why – and one of the donkeys the slave had been leading kicked out in the ensuing chaos, probably in panic, and struck Lucius' lower leg. Lucius or rather somebody accompanying him managed to catch the donkey, which had bolted, but Lucius was so badly injured that he was confined to bed after the accident and, as he reports, he was even on the brink of death for a time. When the owner of the donkey demanded the confiscated animal back from Lucius, the latter was, if we believe his story, so incensed that he petitioned the chief administrator of the nome, the strategos.

A woman called Aphrodite suffered a similar accident on her way to Alexandria when a horse trod on her foot. She describes her injury to her sister in a letter outlining the time and expense required for it to heal: "I want you to know that . . . to go to Alexandria, my foot was trodden by a horse and I was in danger, so that I have been healed at great expense, and until today I have been out of action."[65]

By the standards of these injuries, the indignity suffered by another traveler seems almost amusing. A Greek traveler in the Ptolemaic era had traveled to Pysa in the Arsinoe nome on personal business, but as he strolled idly through the city streets, he suddenly had his head wetted by a stream of liquid which also appears to have completely soaked his clothes. On looking up, the unfortunate man discovered that a woman had emptied her chamber pot into the street without bothering to look down first. When he began to complain vociferously, the woman – an Egyptian, the plaintiff mentions – took a dim view of his protests and went on to assault him, tearing his clothes and spitting in his face.[66]

Travel: A Pleasure?

It seems clear when we look at the source material we have from Roman Egypt that hardly anybody actually enjoyed traveling – at least, certainly not in comparison to twenty-first-century travelers. To journey was to put up with discomfort and inconvenience, and those who took the effort upon themselves could expect the kind of gratitude shown in this letter from the second half of the fourth century: "Gratitude toward him should be the greatest because he took upon himself the trouble (to come) to you with us providing him with a compensation."[67] In another document, two young men, Hephaistion and Origenes, thank a certain Theophanes for taking them along with him on his journey to Alexandria: "It is not, sir, that we consider the labors of our journey merit any recompense in (? this) season [since] we elected [voluntarily] to incur them."[68] The two men gladly gave up the pleasures of home life for a while in order to undertake this journey with Theophanes. Elsewhere, a young woman writes to tell her father that he need not make the effort of coming upstream to visit her; she will travel downstream to visit him instead. She mentions that she will bring Persion along, presumably her young son, and she anticipates that the journey will be troublesome.[69]

The idea of travel as a pleasure in itself or as a way of spending free time and discovering and experiencing new things does not seem to have existed – at least as far as we can tell from the papyri.[70] The closest we come to a depiction of travel as actively desirable is a letter from a small boy: Theon in Oxyrhynchus was bitterly disappointed his father had not taken him along on the 310-mile journey to Alexandria. As we can read, Theon was inconsolable:

Theon to Theon his father, greetings. A nice thing to do, not taking me with you to the city. If you refuse to take me with you to Alexandria, I shall not write you a letter or speak to you or wish you good health. So: if you go to Alexandria I shall not take your hand or greet you ever again. If you refuse to take me, this is what happens. And my mother said to Archelaos, "He's upsetting me, take him away!" A nice thing to do, sending me these grand presents, a hill of beans. They put us off the track that day, the 12th, when you sailed. Well then, send for me, I beg you. If you don't send for me, I shan't eat, I shan't drink. There![71]

Travel Descriptions in Early Christian Texts

We can also draw on texts from early Christian sources in the eastern Mediterranean to fill out the picture we have of travel at this time. Both the New Testament and the apocryphal gospels contain many references to journeys undertaken by ordinary members of the population. The protagonists do not travel solely within their own surroundings, but also across provincial boundaries. The flight into Egypt described in the Gospel of Matthew (Matt. 2:13–14) is an event in the childhood of Jesus that is further embellished when retold in later apocryphal texts such as the Gospel of Pseudo-Matthew from the early seventh century and the Syriac Infancy Gospel.[72] While this episode seems unlikely to have taken place as described and can probably be dismissed as fictional, the details relating to food and accommodation on the journey were most likely portrayed in a realistic manner.

In the apocryphal Gospel of Pseudo-Matthew, the baggage train of the Holy Family on their flight into Egypt is described in quite concrete terms: "There were together two oxen drawing a wagon with provision for the journey."[73] Mary and Joseph ate what nature provided while on the journey:

> And it came to pass on the third day of their journey, while they were walking, that the blessed Mary was fatigued by the excessive heat of the sun in the desert; and seeing a palm tree, she said to Joseph: Let me rest a little under the shade of this tree. Joseph therefore made haste, and led her to the palm, and made her come down from her beast. And as the blessed Mary was sitting there, she looked up to the foliage of the palm, and saw it full of fruit, and said to Joseph: I wish it were possible to get some of the fruit of this palm.[74]

These passages also mention various forms of overnight accommodation, for example: "And having come to a certain cave, and wishing to rest in it, the blessed Mary dismounted from her beast, and sat down with the child Jesus in her bosom."[75]

Two well-built Roman roads led from Palestine to Egypt. One crossed the desert, while the other, the Via Maris, hugged the coast and passed through the coastal ports. The Via Maris extended from Damascus, in the province of Syria, through Palestine and on to Pelusium at the easternmost point of the Nile Delta in the province of Egypt. Before reaching it, however, Mary and Joseph had to head for the coast, which was 47 miles from Bethlehem. To traverse the desert successfully, water for people and animals had to be carried in skins. This explains Joseph's remark to Mary in the Gospel of Pseudo-Matthew: "I am thinking more of the want of water, because the skins are now empty, and we have none wherewith to refresh ourselves and our cattle."[76] The route along the coast strikes Joseph as the easier choice: "Joseph said to Jesus: Lord, it is a boiling heat; if it please Thee, let us go by the sea-shore, that we may be able to rest in the cities on the coast."[77] In the version narrated here, Mary and Joseph would have passed through Ashdod, Ashkelon and Gaza before finally reaching Egypt. In Egypt, they did not remain in the border area, but traveled another 310 miles south to Sotina in Middle Egypt. (Travelers from Pelusium to Middle and Upper Egypt normally preferred to travel by ship rather than toiling along the riverside tracks.) When the family arrived in the Egyptian town of Sotina, near Hermopolis (now Al-Ashmounein) they had nobody they could ask to take them in. They seem not even to have tried asking at public inns. Instead, they went straight to the Temple of Sotina, probably in the hope of finding a roof over their heads in a hostel.[78] Pagan temples, Jewish synagogues, and – later – churches often had accommodation for pilgrims in an annex. The hostel at the sanctuary at Epidaurus, for example, with foundations that are still visible today, is from the fourth century BCE and had space for around 160 pilgrims. We have evidence going all the way back to the period of Hittite rule for accommodation in the temple precincts.[79]

An Egyptian named Theophanes took the same route as Mary and Joseph on their flight into Egypt (Matt. 2:13–14), albeit in the other direction, at the beginning of the fourth century. Theophanes set off on his journey in or around 320 CE, when Constantine the Great and Licinius were still struggling for sole control of the Roman Empire.[80] It was to bring him from Hermopolis, on the Nile in Upper Egypt, to Antioch, on the Orontes, the capital of the province of Syria. Theophanes counted among the notables of his home city; he was a member of the city council and a *scholasticus*, a type of lawyer in the service of the Roman prefect. He was also traveling on official business and not for purely personal reasons. On his journey, which lasted for six months, he kept a painstakingly detailed account of the places he passed through, the distances he covered, his expenses, and all overnight stops. His travel journal even includes detailed shopping lists, with the prices of individual foodstuffs purchased as provisions for his retinue. Theophanes covered approximately 30 miles per day and took a mere twenty-five days to reach Antioch, in Syria, from Alexandria (see Figure 6.8). As a member of the

6.8 Land route from Alexandria to Antioch.

social elite traveling on the business of the governor, he was able to make progress much more rapidly, much more comfortably, and, above all, in a much more organized and predictable fashion than Joseph, a carpenter traveling with his small family, could have hoped to do. Theophanes belonged to the limited group of people entitled to use the cursus publicus; he possessed the necessary permission in writing from the governor or the emperor, and was also fortunate enough to possess letters of recommendation from his superior to the governors of both Syria and Palestine, who could be relied on to open all the doors to him.[81] He was able to find accommodation effortlessly each evening in the official guest-houses along the Via Maris – a stark contrast to the experiences of Mary and Joseph portrayed in the apocryphal Gospel of Pseudo-Matthew.

The Gospels also report on numerous other journeys undertaken by Jesus, which took him all around Galilee and Judaea and also to Panias, Samaria, and the Decapolis. He even made it as far as Tyre and Sidon on one occasion, and all the way to Phoenicia. Jesus generally traveled on foot – the cheapest form of travel – and in the company of others. He also made sporadic use of water transport, for example, to cross the Sea of Galilee (Matt. 9:1; 15:39). Jesus only traveled on a donkey once: on the Sunday before his crucifixion, he made his triumphal entry into Jerusalem riding on a donkey, according to the depiction in the Gospels.

The Gospel of Luke contains several other references to travelers and traveling besides the depiction of the journey of the Holy Family to Bethlehem, including the parable of the Good Samaritan (Luke 10: 30–37). The beginning of the parable, "A man was going down from Jerusalem to Jericho," places the traveler on the route linking Jerusalem and Jericho. As a segment of the main trade route between Africa and Asia, this route saw intense traffic in ancient times. It was around 17 miles long and led out of the hills and down into the Jordan valley 3,280 feet below. Jesus goes on to recount that the man

> fell into the hands of robbers, who stripped him, beat him, and went away, leaving him half dead. Now by chance a priest was going down that road; and when he saw him, he passed by on the other side. So likewise a Levite, when he came to the place and saw him, passed by on the other side. But a Samaritan while traveling came near him; and when he saw him, he was moved with pity. He went to him and bandaged his wounds, having poured oil and wine on them. Then he put him on his own animal, brought him to an inn, and took care of him. The next day he took out two denarii, gave them to the innkeeper, and said, "Take care of him; and when I come back, I will repay you whatever more you spend."[82]

Luke uses the term *pandocheion* for this inn or public hostelry. From at least the classical Greek period onward privately run inns existed and were patronized by ordinary travelers who could not draw on their extensive social networks or rely on the hospitality of local elites. These inns, also called *katagōgia* in Greek, were located along the main transport routes and were often to be found on the outskirts of cities or larger villages.[83] They provided travelers from the lower social strata with cheap hot meals and basic accommodation.[84] The word *pandocheion*, literally "all-receptive," indicates that they were public lodging places rather than private residences or the mansiones forming part of the cursus publicus, which were open only to selected travelers.[85]

Pandocheia were widely viewed as disreputable by ancient authors, who were mostly members of the social elite. Strabo gives the following description of the town of Eleusis, near Alexandria, and its inns: "It is a settlement near Alexandria and Nikopolis, situated on the Kanobic Canal itself, having lodging and views for those wishing to engage in revelry – both men and women – a beginning of the 'Kanobic life' and the wantonness there."[86] Drunken guests, adulterated wine, brawls, theft, and prostitution were all rife. Women running or working in pandocheia were invariably regarded as prostitutes.[87] In Apuleius' *Metamorphoses* the landlady takes in a traveler who has been attacked by robbers and treats him hospitably for free, but she ultimately manages to bed him and rob him of his last strength and his last shirt.[88]

It was not uncommon for a landlord's daughter to sell her body as well as wine and a hot meal to travelers.[89] The apocryphal Acts of Thomas, probably written in early third-century Syria, narrates that a young man who had recently been converted by Thomas tried to persuade a girl working as a prostitute in an inn to enter a chaste marriage. When she refused, he slew her with his sword.[90] Another well-known example is found in the Life of the Byzantine ascetic St. Theodore of Sykeon. His birth was the result of a brief dalliance in or around 550 CE between an imperial messenger and a prostitute in Sykeon, a small village in Galatia between Constantinople and Ancyra: "The public highway of the imperial post ran through this village, and on the road stood an inn kept by a very beautiful girl, Mary, and her mother, Elpidia, and a sister Despoinia. And these women lived in the inn (ἐν πανδοχείῳ) and followed the profession of courtesans."[91] The courier spent the night in the hostelry on one of his journeys in the service of the empire, and as a result Mary became pregnant. The author of the Life uses the Greek term *pandocheion* for the inn, the same word Luke uses in the Parable of the Good Samaritan.

Not only considered hotbeds of fornication and vice, pandocheia were also notoriously filthy. The Acts of John, written at an unknown location in the eastern Mediterranean in the mid second century, contains an amusing reference to lice in the beds of an inn. John and his companions had stopped off at a lonely inn on their way to Ephesus. As the bed in their room had no sheets, the brothers all placed their cloaks on it and requested that John repose there while they made themselves comfortable on the floor. In the middle of the night, John's sleep was disturbed by lice, and he commanded them to leave the men of God in peace. The brothers were much amused by this, but in the morning they were surprised by the sight of the massed lice waiting at the door of the room. When John woke, he thanked the lice and allowed them to crawl back into their bed as soon as he had got up.[92]

The apostles also traveled extensively, and their travel experiences are narrated in the Book of Acts. While the depiction of Mary and Joseph on the flight into Egypt shows them thrown back on their own resources, the apostles benefited from their network of friends and co-religionists on their long missionary journeys. It seems that they were received with hospitality and given all they needed wherever they went. The apostles profited from the social networks of their Christian followers. The apostle Paul, for example, was welcomed in private houses on his travels.[93] The Book of Acts also reports that Peter was put up in the house of the tanner Simon for quite some time when he came to Joppa to preach.[94] After that, he was invited into the house of the centurion Cornelius, in Caesarea.[95] When the Jew Apollos came from Alexandria, in Egypt, to Ephesus to learn more about the Christian faith, he was taken in and put up by local Christians Priscilla and Aquila. When he then decided to continue traveling into the Greek province of Achaia, the Christians in Ephesus gave him a letter recommending him to the community in Corinth and requesting its members to welcome him when he reached his destination.[96]

This neatly mirrors the way in which members of the elite approached travel: if stopping off at country residences of one's own was not possible, the residences of friends or acquaintances were acceptable substitutes where one would be well provided with creature comforts at no charge in the name of mutual hospitality. When one knew nobody in the place one was traveling to or through, letters of recommendation from friends with better connections in the region in question came into play, as an example from the mid third century BCE found in the Zenon archive shows.

> Aleximachos to Zenon greeting. Nikanor who is handing you this letter is a friend of ours, and he has gone on a journey to your district on account of his

son being one of the *epigonoi* who have received allotments in the Arsinoite province. Be kind enough then to show him consideration in any matter about which he may speak to you; for you will be doing a favor to me. And write to us yourself about anything that you may desire at any time. Farewell.[97]

Staying in a private household was always considered a much better option than staying at an inn. The same idea is conveyed in the Pseudo-Clementine Writings. The apostle Peter and the brothers accompanying him often stayed in public inns as they made their way through the cities of the province. This is interpreted as a sign of their humility. When one of the most important citizens in Laodicea asked Peter and his men to accept his hospitality, they initially put up some resistance, but their private benefactor insisted: "It is base and wicked that such and so great men should stay in a hostelry, when I have almost my whole house empty, and very many beds spread, and all necessary things provided."[98] This passage highlights what was perhaps the most important difference between how members of the upper and lower social strata made long-distance journeys: social connections seem to have been more relevant than financial resources. The upper class seems to have had much better networks – and not just within their own surroundings. The radius within which ordinary people maintained networks they could rely on seems to have been considerably smaller. Ordinary travelers did not have letters of recommendation to help them when they reached their destinations, or servants who hurried ahead and prepared everything for their comfortable arrival. They did not have business associates who prepared comfortable lodgings for them in their villas, and they could not expect local notables to go to any trouble to aid them.

Conclusions

One thing becomes very clear in this overview of travel in Greco-Roman Egypt, and here we can surely generalize from Egypt to other provinces: travel in ancient times was not the sole preserve of members of the social elite. People belonging to the lower social strata were anything but immobile. People seem to have had a good grasp of the geography of their own province, at the very least. In the Fayum, for example, they knew what lay behind their village and beyond the capital of their nome. They knew how one could travel to Alexandria or Coptos, and how long the journey generally took. Many had family members in other parts of the province or in its capital, and often exchanged letters with them. Travel was not cheap – that much is clear – but everybody, perhaps with the exception of the poorest of the poor, could afford to make necessary journeys.

The significance of travel for religious purposes appears to have been overestimated by scholars over many years, when we compare it to travel motivated by, for example, the desire to visit family members or the need to travel for work.[99] Traders and tradesmen traveled in Egypt to extend the radius within which they could offer their wares and services. Members of the Roman military traveled to their bases, and women and children traveled to follow husbands and fathers to their places of work. Other journeys took place for reasons such as the need to check up on property people owned in other regions. When people lacked the resources to make journeys, other family members often subsidized their travel to enable visits to take place. Women traveled as a matter of course, just as men did, but both women and men avoided traveling alone where possible.

The hazards that lay beyond one's own village were real and never far from people's minds. This also explains why a general dislike of travel is readily identifiable in the sources we have. Travel and surmounting the hazards it entailed was perceived as a necessary evil. People traveled when they needed to, but hardly anybody enjoyed traveling and most presumably breathed a sigh of relief when they reached their destination.

CHAPTER VII

"In that region there were shepherds living in the fields . . ."

An Occupation on the Margins of Society

> In that region there were shepherds living in the fields, keeping watch over their flock by night. Then an angel of the Lord stood before them, and the glory of the Lord shone around them, and they were terrified. But the angel said to them, "Do not be afraid; for see – I am bringing you good news of great joy for all the people."
>
> Luke 2:8–10

Shepherds were ubiquitous in the ancient world. The Old Testament figures, Abel, Abraham, Isaac, Jacob, Moses, and David were all nomadic shepherds; and indeed, the role of the shepherd was laden with unparalleled symbolic significance across the ancient Mediterranean world. In the Old Testament, the wise and watchful shepherd gently steering his flock serves as a metaphor for the ideal ruler. The biblical prophets were also often portrayed as shepherds tending their sheep, and at times even God himself is depicted as a shepherd feeding his flock, Israel.[1] The Old Testament portrays the expected Messiah as a shepherd from the house of David, who "will come to tend the sheep of Israel,"[2] and this allegory paves the way for the shepherd symbolism in the New Testament. A parable from John's Gospel has Jesus saying of himself: "I am the good shepherd" (see Figure 7.1).[3] The medieval church later took up this symbol and adopted the shepherd's crook as the crosier carried by bishops to signify their office.

The figure of the shepherd served as a symbolic representation of the ideal ruler not only in ancient Israel, but also across the entire Near East including Sumer, the Akkadian Empire, Assyria, Babylonia, and Egypt. For example, the Egyptian god Osiris was depicted with a shepherd's crook, and the crook was also an accoutrement of the ruling pharaoh. Homer often referred to the leaders of the Hellenes as "shepherds of the people" – Nestor, Atreus, and above all Agamemnon are given this epithet.[4] Commenting on this, Dio Chrysostom later remarked:

7.1 Statue of the Good Shepherd, third century CE, from the
catacombs of Domitilla, Museo Pio Cristiano, Vatican.

Now it seems to me that Homer was quite right in this as in many other
sayings, for it implies that not every king derives his scepter or this royal
office from Zeus, but only the good king, and that he receives it on no other
title than that he shall plan and study the welfare of his subjects ...
becoming indeed a guide and shepherd of his people, not, as someone has
said, a caterer and banqueter at their expense.[5]

The first-century Roman agronomist Varro remarked on how the great
figures of Greek and Roman mythology had all been shepherds,

mentioning the Trojan prince Paris, the hero Hercules, and the founders of Rome, Romulus and Remus.[6]

Many heroes of Greco-Roman mythology are regularly depicted as abandoned babies suckled by animals and raised by shepherds; indeed, this topos is ubiquitous in ancient literature. Paris, the exiled son of Priam, is raised by shepherds on Mount Ida and spends his youth as a shepherd. Amphion and Zethus, the twin sons of Zeus and Antiope, are found in similar circumstances on Mount Cithaeron by shepherds, who raise them as their children. The royal son Oedipus is given to a shepherd to be exposed, and is raised by the shepherds who find him. Daphnis is abandoned under a laurel tree by his mother (herself a nymph) and subsequently discovered by shepherds, who raise him as their own. Attis, the son of the daughter of the river god Sangarios, is also abandoned as a baby and then raised by shepherds. Telephus, the son of Heracles and Auge, is abandoned on Mount Parthenion, suckled by a doe, and raised by shepherds. Cybele is abandoned as a child and raised by shepherdesses on Mount Cybelon. Semiramis, the daughter of the Syrian goddess Derketo, is similarly abandoned as a child and raised by a shepherd. Daphnis and Chloe, the heroines from Longus' eponymous novel, are also abandoned and then raised by shepherd families. One of Sophocles' lost tragedies involves Tyro, the daughter of Salmoneus, who has given birth to the twins Pelias and Neleus and is forced to abandon them: suckled by a mare and a bitch, they are raised by shepherds. Arcas, the son of Calisto and Zeus, also seems to have been raised by shepherds in Arcadia. The two sons of Melanippe, the twins Boetus and Aeolous, are abandoned by their grandfather shortly after their birth, but then suckled by a cow and raised by shepherds. Romulus and Remus, the sons of the princess Rhea Silvia and Mars, the god of war, are also found and raised by a shepherd (Figure 7.2). Finally, a similar legend surrounds the Persian king Cyrus, who was supposedly abandoned by his parents, suckled by a bitch, and raised by shepherds. It is of particular note that these many foundlings come from much higher social strata than do their rescuers.

Early Roman imperial poetry presents an idealized picture of the shepherd's life. The extent to which this is rooted in contemporary realities rather than in the longings of educated urban elites for a simple rustic life in an idyll far removed from politics and the turmoil of civil war is unclear. It is beyond question that the idealized world of the shepherd in the works of Virgil, Tibullus, Propertius, and Calpurnius Siculus represents a yearning for a return of a golden age (see e.g. Figure 7.3).

7.2 Faustulus finding the she-wolf with the twins Romulus and Remus. Clay relief, second century CE. Antikensammlung, Pergamonmuseum, Staatliche Museen zu Berlin.

To sum up, then, we can state that shepherds were ubiquitous and that their work was undeniably one of the oldest, most widely practiced, and most important occupations in the ancient Mediterranean. When the huge significance of shepherds in our sources is borne in mind, the absence of a sociohistorical study of this occupational group in ancient times seems all the more startling. One possible explanation for this is that the imagery of the Good Shepherd in the New Testament, and its antecedents in the Old Testament, may have dominated research and displaced interest in the real circumstances of shepherding as a way of making a living. In order to be able to understand this imagery as it evolved, however, it is necessary to closely examine the real social and economic situation of ancient shepherds, with which contemporaries were familiar. How, for example, can we understand and correctly interpret the significance of the announcement of the birth of Jesus to shepherds in the Gospel of Luke if we do not know

7.3 A shepherd and his flock. Detail of the Four Seasons mosaic from *ca.* 325 CE found in Daphne (now Antakya, Turkey). Louvre Museum, Paris.

how shepherds and their work were perceived by the author of the Gospel and his contemporary readers?[7]

The Shepherd in Greco-Roman Antiquity

It is surprising that scholars have not yet significantly extended their focus on religious and political imagery centering on shepherds to further encompass a closer look at how shepherds in ancient times actually lived.[8] While there has been a dearth of sociohistorical scrutiny of the status of shepherds in ancient societies, economic aspects of Greco-Roman sheep farming and pastoralism have been better investigated. The Ninth International Congress of Economic History in 1986 was devoted to "Pastoral Economies in Classical Antiquity." The accompanying publication, edited by C. R. Whittaker, did not include any treatment of the subject from a sociohistorical perspective, and in addition ignored the entire Greek East of the Roman Empire, including regions with pastoral traditions known from biblical writings, such as Palestine, Syria, and Egypt.[9] The focus is instead restricted to Greece, Italy, and the western provinces of the Roman Empire, concentrating on transhumance and nomadic pastoralism without considering agro-pastoralism in any depth.

Only James Keenan has concerned himself, in essays from 1985 and 1989, with pastoralism in Roman Egypt, the region for which we possess the most comprehensive sources dealing with shepherding.[10] Keenan focuses primarily on economic and zoological aspects of sheep farming and pays only peripheral attention to shepherds, their position within society, and their work. Other scholars have produced theological and exegetical literature pertaining to the role of shepherds in the Christmas story, which sheds, however, little light on the everyday lives of shepherds in the Roman Empire, and on their economic circumstances.

Various types of source material provide information about the everyday lives of ancient shepherds. Vases, coins, and mosaics bear images of Pan, Daphnis, and Orpheus as shepherds, and we have further visual evidence on late Roman sarcophagi, graffiti in the catacombs, and late antique mosaics (see Figures 7.3–7.5). Further clues are supplied by literary sources: the Hellenistic romance concerning the goatherd Daphnis and the shepherdess Chloe, or the bucolic poetry of Theocritus, Virgil, and Calpurnius Siculus, but also the descriptions of shepherds within the Attic tragedies and Ovid's *Fasti*. The Roman agronomists Varro and Columella also provide detailed descriptions of the economic aspects of small-livestock husbandry.

7.4 Relief of a shepherd with his dog on a Roman sarcophagus dating from the third to fourth century CE. Vatican Museums.

7.5 Relief of a shepherd with his dog, a sheep, and a goat on a Roman sarcophagus dating from the second century CE. Walters Art Museum, Baltimore.

Theocritus gives the following description of the goatherd Lycidas:

> By the Muses' graces we overtook a Kydonian, a man of worth, traveling the same road, called Lycidas, a goatherd, as none could fail to know at first glance, for like nothing but a goatherd did he seem. A tawny skin, stripped from a thick-haired he-goat's shaggy back, he wore upon his shoulders, of fresh rennet reeking still. Across his breast an ancient well-worn tunic was strapped round by a broad belt, and a crooked staff from a wild olive tree he held in his right hand.[11]

Theocritus makes reference more than once to the shepherd's crook, or *pedum*, as a gift made from one shepherd to another.[12] The crook was useful for pulling up fallen sheep by the neck or leg. As noted earlier, the pedum as a religious symbol of benevolent rule turns up in Egypt (where it belonged to the insignia of the pharaoh), in Mithraism, where it was accorded to the *pater*, the highest grade, and in Christianity, where it became part of the insignia of the bishop.[13] The shepherd in Virgil's *Eclogues* plays a tune on a shepherd's flute, the *syrinx*.[14] Shepherds often also carried a sickle, or *falx*, to cut branches as fodder for ill and weak animals or to make camp.[15] Carrying weapons such as spears for defense against wild animals also appears not to have been unusual.[16] Often, shepherds were accompanied by dogs,[17] as Homer puts it in the *Iliad*: "As sheep dogs that watch their flocks when they are yarded and hear a wild beast coming through the mountain forest towards them."[18] Scenes on Attic vases often depict shepherds with a staff and a dog.[19]

The richest sources of information on agro-pastoralism, shepherding as an occupation, and, in particular, the everyday lives of shepherds in the ancient Mediterranean are, however, once again the papyri of Roman Egypt, despite the fact that the geographical conditions – a shortage of space for shepherds and sheep farming in the Nile valley and its surrounding areas – afforded relatively little scope for sheep rearing.[20] The papyri include petitions relating to the theft of livestock or to harvest damage caused by freely grazing sheep, lease agreements pertaining to grazing land or to goats and sheep, private letters touching on livestock husbandry and pastoralism, and small livestock declarations from the Roman period made between the late first century BCE and the middle of the third century CE. It is this latter group of documents which are of most value for our purposes here. Most of them stem from the Oxyrhynchite nome, and the rest are from the Arsinoite nome (the modern Fayum) and from the nome of Hermopolis Magna. Owners had to declare their animals since tax was payable on sheep and goats.[21] Varro reports that owners of herds in late Republican Italy had to ensure their animals had been registered because they could be pastured on common land once the tax due per head had been paid.[22] According to Sherman Wallace, the payment of the sheep tax (*to kathēkon telos*) entitled owners to graze their animals on all the pastures belonging to their district and its nome,[23] while James Keenan comments that the amount of tax payable depended, in Egypt as elsewhere, on the number of animals registered.[24]

Nomadic and Agro-Pastoralism

It is necessary to distinguish between nomadic pastoralists, who are not bound to a particular locality and move regularly, taking their herd to fresh pastures along with their family and household, and agro-pastoralists belonging to settled village communities, who may spend a large part of the year outside with their herds but who move the animals only between local pastures. Although it is not always easy to differentiate between these two forms of pastoralism when we encounter them in ancient sources, the situation is clear for Egypt. Transhumance entails movement between two different climate zones, which provide different seasonal opportunities. In the Nile valley, extensive use of land for grazing was only possible in the less fertile areas immediately adjacent to fertile arable land,[25] so transhumance and forms of nomadic pastoralism including the movement of families and households were not feasible.[26]

The form of pastoralism prevailing in Roman Egypt can be best subsumed under the modern term *agro-pastoralism* (from the Latin *ager*, meaning "field," and *pastor*, meaning "shepherd"), describing a combination of arable and pastoral farming. Animals were pastured on land which was (temporarily) not in use for crops. This required flocks and shepherds to frequently move to new pastures. Grazing was located only a short or moderate distance away from villages. While the majority of the village community was thus settled, shepherds spent their time out with the herds, with tents or huts for shelter.[27]

Pasture land was relatively scarce; fertile land in Egypt was cultivated intensively and the husbandry of goats and sheep competed with arable farming for space. The risk of sheep and goats destroying growing crops or harvests in short order due to carelessness or negligence on the part of their herders was real. Ancient stories and reports are replete with examples of conflicts between settled farmers and shepherds grazing their sheep at the outskirts of the villages.[28]

Shepherds: Hirelings or Owners of Their Herds?

Who were those shepherds mentioned in the papyri? The owners of the herds, or shepherds paid to tend to the flocks of others? The declarations of sheep and goats provide a concrete answer: it is unclear whether owners tended their sheep themselves in Ptolemaic Egypt,[29] but in Roman Egypt it was clearly quite common for owners to engage shepherds to look after their flocks.[30] Owners of flocks that were large enough (between eighty and a hundred animals) engaged a shepherd exclusively for their own animals, while those with fewer animals hired a shepherd together with their neighbors.[31] Small livestock declarations state the location of the grazing land and the name of the hired shepherd.[32]

Many families engaged in arable farming seem also to have owned a few sheep and goats, which supplied wool, milk, and occasionally meat. Owning a small number of animals, which were entrusted to a shepherd – the declarations give numbers ranging from two to forty-two animals – reduced the risk of utter economic ruin following a poor harvest. But as the animals could not be kept near the family homestead or on the land that was cultivated, they were entrusted to a shepherd, who brought the animals of various owners to pastures located at the margins of the fertile land in the

Nile valley and the oases. It is clear, then, that shepherds did not usually own the animals they tended, and that they worked for a range of employers: smallholders, bigger farmers, temples, and, later on, Christian churches and monasteries.[33] While smallholders probably employed shepherds directly, major landowners, who could own several thousand animals, typically leased their flocks to intermediaries, who in turn leased pasture and employed shepherds. A number of agreements survive from which we can infer the nature of the contractual relationships between owners and lessees. In one instance, we have the entire archive of a dynasty of such middlemen containing several papyri referring to the brothers Nilammon and Kalamos and the latter's son Pabous; all were active in this trade in the village of Theadelphia in the Arsinoite nome during the third quarter of the third century.[34] They did not herd sheep themselves, but acted as intermediaries between the owners, who were all large landowners, and the actual shepherds.[35] They had to maintain the head counts of each herd and make twice-yearly lease payments, which fell due after biannual shearing in the fall and spring. In exchange, they were able to keep the proceeds accruing from the sale of wool, milk, cheese, and the meat of the surplus lambs. The actual shepherds formed the final link in this chain of contractual arrangements and gained very little from the entire business. They were probably paid in cash and also received a certain quantity of surplus wool and milk products.[36]

The term normally used in the small livestock declarations to describe those employed to watch over animals belonging to others is *nomeus*. In the exceptional case in which the owner is himself the shepherd, he declares himself *poimēn*.[37] Legal petitions against shepherds regarding the destruction of crops by flocks also use the word *nomeis*.[38] The term *nomeus* as used by Homer, Sophocles, and Theocritus also refers to conventional shepherds who tend the flocks of their masters.[39] The *nomeus* seems to correspond to the *misthōtos*, the hired hand of John's Gospel, who is contrasted with the true shepherd, the *poimēn*, who cares for his sheep.[40] In the papyri, however, the term *poimēn* seems to stand for the middleman rather than the shepherd or the owner of the sheep.[41] Dominic Rathbone determined that tenants were referred to as *poimenes*, but did not look after the animals, their role being restricted to the leasing of pasture land and the employment of shepherds to tend to the flocks.[42] The Greek of Luke's Gospel in turn uses the word *poimenes* to refer to the shepherds who tended their flocks by night close to Bethlehem in Judaea, thereby implying that they were the actual owners of the animals.[43]

It is clear from the papyri that shepherds ranked below smallholders on the social scale. They were recruited from the sons of shepherds, from landless laborers, and from poor farming families who were unable to live from their meager holdings.[44] Even children could work as shepherd auxiliaries for a pittance, although they were not given responsibility for entire herds. One boy living in the Hermopolite nome under Augustus earned half the wages of a grown shepherd for looking after lambs;[45] prior to this, Varro had advised his readers to keep boys and girls close to the homestead and have flocks pastured further away tended by grown men.[46] The teenage sons of farmers were also employed as shepherds.[47] A papyrus from the Oxyrhynchite nome tells of a young boy called Panechotos who watched over the animals of a number of farmers. He is evidently referred to as "minor" (*aphelikos*) in the declaration to stress that he had not reached the age of 14 and was not liable for the poll tax.[48] A further "minor shepherd" (*aphelikos nomeus*) from Oxyrhynchus appears in a papyrus dated 28 CE.[49]

The Composition of Flocks

The flocks of nomadic owner-shepherds could number up to several thousand sheep. Flocks of some hundred animals, such as the flock in the parable of the Good Shepherd, were kept in settled agro-pastoralist societies. The livestock declarations from Egypt demonstrate that an average flock there comprised eighty to a hundred animals. The size of the flock of the Good Shepherd in the parable is congruent with the sizes of the flocks declared in the papyri which were tended by one man.[50] Varro explains why flocks should never be too large: an epidemic could wipe out a large number of animals, he says, so restricting the size of flocks minimized the potential damage and could ward off financial ruin.[51]

Sources indicate that large landowners in both Roman Egypt and Italy could easily own several hundred or several thousand head of livestock.[52] These animals were divided into flocks of between eighty and a hundred, which were each entrusted to individual shepherds. A head shepherd oversaw and coordinated this work. A papyrus from 8 BCE lists an extensive hierarchy of "herdsmen" ranging from a head shepherd at the apex down to ordinary shepherds and a shepherd boy charged with caring for the lambs.[53] In 1 Peter, Jesus himself is cast as the head shepherd (*archipoimēn*) with authority over the group of shepherds:

> I exhort the elders among you to tend the flock of God that is in your charge, exercising the oversight, not under compulsion but willingly, as God would have you do it – not for sordid gain, but eagerly. Do not lord it over those in your charge, but be examples to the flock. And when the chief shepherd appears, you will win the crown of glory that never fades away.[54]

7.6 Fresco of the Good Shepherd from the Catacombs of SS. Marcellino e Pietro, Rome.

Examination of the papyri giving details on herds shows that the great majority of the flocks consisted of sheep and lambs and at least one goat. Why was the number of goats not greater, and why was at least one always included? The declarations document that flocks with between fifty and a hundred animals were usually accompanied by two or three goats. But goats comprised up to a quarter of some flocks (Figure 7.6).

Modern farming guidance suggests reasons for this. The inclusion of more agile, curious, and aggressive goats reduces levels of panic and stress among more timid sheep. Herds consisting entirely of goats are, however, more difficult to control than mixed herds. Finally, goats are less demanding than sheep. While sheep eat only grass, goats also eat the shoots of bushes and thistles.[55] Virgil tells us that goats eat clover and herbage.[56] The existence of such mixed flocks in other regions of the eastern Mediterranean, as well as in Egypt, is attested thus in the Gospel of Matthew: "All the nations will be gathered before him, and he will separate people one from another as a shepherd separates the sheep from the goats."[57]

7.7 Young Egyptian shepherd.

The Tasks of the Shepherd

Unfortunately, we do not possess any written agreements between Roman Egyptian shepherds and flock owners that are like those that have been found for Mesopotamia dating from the Babylonian to the Persian period.[58] We can, however, tell from the declarations of sheep and goats from Roman Egypt that shepherds were usually employed for a year. They drove the sheep to uncultivated land on the edge of villages. The papyri indicate that a shepherd could travel through an entire nome. An employee with no property rights over his charges, he nevertheless operated independently and without any supervision. Out with the animals all day and all night, he probably rarely appeared in the village where he was registered for the poll tax.

According to the literary sources, the tasks of the shepherd comprised leading the sheep to pasture, keeping the flock together, searching for lost sheep, penning them in securely at night, and protecting them from wild animals and thieves. Particular attention had to be paid to weak, pregnant, or injured sheep.[59] The image of the Good Shepherd predates the Christian period and can be found in the works of Roman authors. Writing in the first century CE, Columella recommended that shepherds should be cautious and vigilant, and should treat their animals with kindness; a shepherd ought, he said, to guide his flock with his voice and his staff, and without throwing weapons at the animals – he should remain in close proximity to the flock and should avoid sitting or lying down.[60] According to Virgil, shepherds also needed to ensure that pregnant ewes did not eat any unsuitable fodder, and should keep their animals separate from other flocks so as to prevent diseases.[61] On market days, shepherds took the weaned lambs to the nearest town for sale and also sold the cheese they had produced.[62]

Lambs and kids were born once or twice a year. Shepherds performed the delivery, which Columella describes as being comparable in difficulty to a human birth.[63] According to Isaiah, a shepherd carried lambs not yet able to walk in the folds of his robes,[64] while Calpurnius Siculus advises shepherds to carry ewes who had recently given birth on their shoulders, while the newborn lambs should be carried in the folds of their clothing.[65] Another task for the shepherd was to bring the sheep to shelter at night, sometimes under rock ledges or in a cave which then had rocks rolled across its mouth.[66] A shepherd would sleep next to his flock, not necessarily under the open sky, but close to where the sheep were corralled overnight.[67] When in the open, the flock was housed in a pen built from rocks and covered with thorns to keep out predators and thieves,[68] and the shepherd slept at the entrance.[69] When no danger was present, the animals could sleep outside while the shepherd kept watch.[70]

The sum of all these tasks doubtlessly amounted to a physically demanding occupation. As such, Varro recommended that only men in their prime with strong constitutions should be tasked with looking after sheep; shepherds ought, he opined, to be neither too young nor too old.[71] We know that shepherds in the early sixth-century Egyptian village of Aphrodito were also accorded responsibility for guarding the fields surrounding villages. They reported to the *riparius*, a local police official, and were responsible for these tasks all year round.[72] Operating on the outskirts of the settlements, shepherds might have regularly taken on this responsibility even if it is not documented in our sources.

Socioeconomic Background

The challenging nature of a shepherd's life was not especially compatible with marriage, family, and a steady existence. The very young ages of many of the shepherds recorded in the papyri probably meant that they were too young to marry. As most shepherds possessed neither land nor livestock, and in all likelihood did not even have houses of their own, they were probably not especially sought after as sons-in-law and husbands. Even those shepherds who did manage to start a family would have been separated from their wives and children for much of the year.

Nonetheless, although shepherds spent much of their time in isolated areas, they did not lead lonely lives. The shepherd narratives record how shepherds kept in touch with one another. In Sophocles' *Oedipus Tyrannus*, the shepherd Laios entrusts the abandoned boy Oedipus to another shepherd whose herd grazed alongside his from spring to autumn.[73] In Theocritus' *Idylls* and Virgil's *Eclogues*, shepherds organize competitions during their leisure time. Shepherdesses such as Chloe in the novel by Longus were, however, probably rare. As they had little female company, shepherds were often associated with masturbation. Dio Chrysostom narrates that Hermes taught Pan how to masturbate and that Pan then passed the art on to shepherds.[74] In Longus' novel, on the other hand, the shepherds on Lesbos are all married and lead respectable settled lives tending the flocks of prosperous urbanites. Two married couples adopt the foundlings Daphnis and Chloe; Daphnis is taken in by goatherds and Chloe by a shepherd family. The children grow up together, as the two families live close by. Some shepherds very probably did have children, and the papyri mention sons of shepherds here and there.[75]

It comes as no surprise that shepherds hired to tend animals belonging to others must have lived relatively close to the poverty line. Speaking in Virgil's first *Eclogue*, the goatherd Tityrus complains that he has never seen much reward for his conscientious work, even though his lambs and cheese sell quickly, and that he has never been able to save a *peculium* to buy his freedom.[76] Tityrus makes himself an evening meal from apples, chestnuts, whey, and cheese:[77] he undoubtedly gathered the apples and chestnuts during his progress through the meadows, while the whey and cheese would have come from his flock. He sleeps on a bed of leaves next to his animals. The goatherd Meliboeus, from the same book, lives, Virgil tells us, in a poor hut with a roof of grass.[78] While Virgil's Tityrus is a slave, the shepherds attested by the papyri were all freeborn men. Paid in kind, they were permitted to keep a proportion of the milk and wool produced. This practice was touched on by the Apostle Paul, who used it as an analogy in support of his ministry: "Or who tends a flock and does not get any of its milk?"[79]

One papyrus, a farmer's account book from the Hermopolite nome dating from the reign of Augustus, lists five shepherds who tended five flocks totaling 566 sheep and 25 goats.[80]

> Paid for from the sum named above for the wages of five shepherds: twenty-four drachmas per flock per month makes one hundred and twenty drachmas.

Paid to Pausiris, the foreman, a further twenty-four drachmas. Paid to the boy who looked after the lambs, twelve drachmas. Total monthly expenditure one hundred and fifty-six drachmas. Total sum of the expenditure for twelve months: one thousand, eight hundred and seventy-two drachmas.

Each shepherd thus tended an average of a hundred sheep and five goats, and was employed for a period of twelve months. They all earned 24 drachmas a month, the same as the wage paid to the foreman. The young boy (*paidarion*) who helped the shepherds with the lambs was only paid half this sum, namely 12 drachmas.[81] With the average monthly wage of an ordinary first-century worker standing at around 30 drachmas per month, a shepherds' earning power was clearly below average. Another papyrus (from 57 CE) from Philadelphia in the Arsinoite nome specifies a shepherd's monthly wage as a mere 16 drachmas. This particular shepherd tended a flock of 89 sheep and 22 lambs.[82]

The relative underpayment of shepherds was a state of affairs that changed little over the centuries that followed. Diocletian's *Edict on Maximum Prices* (301 CE) orders that shepherds should be paid no more than 20 denarii plus board, less than the 25 denarii plus board earned even by agricultural laborers or water carriers. A carpenter, stone mason, or baker could expect to be paid 50 denarii per day.

Shepherds clearly needed experience and expertise to perform their work, certainly more so than fieldhands or water carriers did. Moreover, the strenuous nature of the occupation demanded round-the-clock availability with no free days. While they were able to augment their wages through the sale of surplus wool and milk products and thus had an incentive to do a good job, they were not permitted to keep lambs for themselves from among the new births; all animals were counted carefully and subject to the biannual registration requirement.[83]

Shepherds were, in all likelihood, even held financially liable for any animals lost on their watch. From the lease agreements surviving on papyrus, it is plain that the livestock entrusted to the shepherd were declared to be "immortal" (*athanatoi*), in other words, leased on the basis of immortality.[84] Joachim Hengstl comments that this implies that a shepherd was to return animals in the same number and of the same type as those originally entrusted to him. Within such a legal framework, thefts and losses to wild animals could prove costly, and an epidemic even more so. It would appear that some form of financial forfeiture was far from uncommon.[85] The athanatos clauses available to us come from the third century BCE to the fourth century CE.[86] The question is whether the burden imposed by the athanatos clause was borne by middlemen or passed on to shepherds. Did a shepherd have to hand back the precise number of animals he had been entrusted with, replacing livestock which had died at his own expense if necessary? The settlement of accounts from Philadelphia mentioned above certainly states the precise number of animals (male and female adult sheep and lambs) which were entrusted to the shepherd Pnepheros in column 1 and notes the number he lost in each month and year.[87]

The existence of a shepherd's guild (*koinon*) has been documented in the village of Aphrodito in the Antaiopolite nome (Thebaid) for the sixth century CE. Keenan considers that this village could have specialized in sheep breeding, and the large concentration of shepherds documented as having been active in the area at the same time supports his hypothesis.[88] In 514 CE thirteen shepherds were registered in this guild,[89] in a village in which wool was probably produced more for trade than to meet local demand. We can see how significant the raw products supplied by shepherds were to ancient societies when we consider the number of specialist trades dedicated to their processing. While the shepherds themselves processed the milk produced by their herds and sold the produce at local markets, wool was worked on by spinners, dyers, weavers, and, ultimately, tailors.

Conflicts between Arable Farmers and Shepherds

Conflicts between the two main pillars of subsistence agriculture, arable farmers and shepherds, have arisen since time immemorial, and are also attested in the papyri from Roman Egypt. A petition from the second half of the fourth century from Hermopolis, which was directed against two shepherds (*poimenes*) from the village of Thelbontis, accuses them of repeatedly driving their livestock into the planted fields of a neighboring village. When they led their animals to water in this neighboring village, the local shepherd who protested was apparently beaten up and had his clothes stolen. This seems to have been no ordinary assault, but an incident in an ongoing dispute over access to fodder and water.[90] The petition was found in the archive of the *beneficiarius* Flavius Isidorus from Hermopolis, who had already lodged a complaint five months earlier against the owner of these same animals, which had repeatedly destroyed his harvest.[91]

Many similar cases involving flocks grazing in arable fields – be it because shepherds were careless or because they deliberately took advantage of farmers – appear in the papyri.[92] In one case, a landowner's administrator lodged a complaint against a shepherd whose animals had ruined the fields of his master.[93] In another, sheep destroyed two hundred olive saplings growing on the property of the imperial family. One of the two shepherds held responsible for this also broke into the toolshed on the property and made off with farm implements and silver drachmas.[94] A series of similar reports from Euhemeria in the Arsinoite nome notified the authorities of crop destruction by flocks in the period 28–42 CE – complaints against negligent shepherds constituted the second most common source of conflicts (after theft) lodged with the authorities in this agrarian village in the Fayum.[95] All in all, it seems plain that shepherds tending their flocks close to settlements repeatedly came into conflict with villagers – a phenomenon typical for agro-pastoralism in many premodern societies in which different forms of economic activity take place in close proximity to each other.

Shepherds as Highwaymen

It was often suspected that shepherds supplemented their income with banditry. As they had a large radius of activity, carried weapons, had excellent local knowledge of even the most remote areas, and lived on the periphery of society in more ways than one, they were prime suspects.[96] The nomadic lifestyle of shepherds also meant minimal contact with the authorities and tax evasion. Shepherds returned to their home villages only intermittently, and spent most of their time driving their herds through the nome – a task that took them away for days, weeks, or even months at a stretch. The shepherds listed in the small livestock declarations were registered in the Roman household census, but others may have been able to evade the procedure with relative ease. The census data available to us does not expressly mention any individuals working as shepherds, but it seems likely that the possible candidates would have been older men who were officially registered in the household of their brother or unmarried young men registered in the households of their fathers but absent from them for long periods.

The *Codex Theodosianus* contains a number of laws aimed specifically at shepherds, which seem to place them under blanket suspicion of brigandage. They were, for example, forbidden to use horses.[97] As it was "generally known" that shepherds engaged in dishonest schemes, they were also barred from accepting foster children.[98] References to this discrimination against shepherds in imperial law do not, however, appear in the papyri.[99] The common complaints relating to sheep damage may have been triggered by the incompetence of shepherds or, in times when fodder was scarce, by intentional acts on their part, but the various accusations do not in any way add up to a picture of shepherds as brigands.

The case of Bentetis of Oxyrhynchus is frequently advanced in the literature as an example of a violent shepherd who confirms their poor image as

criminals and bandits.[100] The plaintiff Thouonis, from Areos Kome, a hamlet in the Arsinoite nome, claimed that Bentetis had refused to pay him the agreed wages (probably wool and milk products in addition to money) and had attacked him and his pregnant wife – with fists and not merely with words – during the argument which ensued over this. The plaintiff's wife had suffered a stillbirth in consequence and was, according to the petition, now fighting for her life. Bentetis was, however, not an ordinary shepherd, but a *probatokthnotrophos*, a sheep breeder or livestock dealer who did not tend sheep but merely leased them and then hired shepherds to look after them. Thouonis, the plaintiff, may well have been a shepherd, since he says himself that he worked for the sheep breeder Bentetis.[101]

Conclusions

In many ancient nomadic societies across the Near East the shepherd stood as a symbol for the ideal ruler. This imagery developed at a time when shepherds were the owners of flocks that could contain thousands of animals. With the transition from nomadic lifestyles to settled agro-pastoralism, the role of shepherds changed dramatically: they were now hired hands recruited from the lowest social strata who tended to sheep entrusted to them by others. By New Testament times, agro-pastoralism had come to dominate in both Palestine and other parts of the ancient Mediterranean world.

At the bottom of the ancient social hierarchy, shepherding was a livelihood at the outer reaches of society. Living for long stretches in remote or hilly pastures far from the centers of social interaction, shepherds had no fixed abode, were often entirely without a family, and interacted only with animals or the socially excluded. Furthermore, they were often suspected of being thieves or robbers. A number of shepherds in Roman Italy appear to have been slaves, while in Greco-Roman Egypt they were usually freemen. Paid in cash and a certain quantity of surplus wool and milk products, shepherds rarely owned their own animals, and if they did, only in small numbers. Roman pastoral poetry reveals the urban view of the coarse and penniless shepherd; a life spent sleeping rough in forests, far from culture and civilization, and surviving on hard, dirty work.

This new reality is already reflected in the New Testament. In the parable of the Good Shepherd, the shepherd tends the kind of flock of some one hundred animals that was often entrusted to a hired hand (see Figure 7.7). He does not have control over thousands of animals, as in

7.8 Shepherds milking goats. Mosaic, sixth century CE. Great Palace Mosaic Museum, Istanbul.

the times of the Patriarchs. That the news of Christ's birth is first proclaimed to shepherds can, in this context, be read as a piece of social criticism which is congruent with the depiction of Jesus later choosing to associate with tax collectors, prostitutes, and lepers. It was not the emperor, his governor, King Herod, or the scribes who were the first to hear the news, but simple folk at the margins of society.

CHAPTER VIII

Afterword

Most New Testament scholars agree that the early Christian writings can only be understood within their historical context. However, the vast majority of studies that have concerned themselves so far with these issues have focused exclusively on political and religious aspects. They have explored how the accounts of Jesus' life fit into the context of Second Temple Judaism, the political intricacies of Herod's client kingdom, the influences of Hellenism, Jewish sectarianism, and finally Roman occupation and riots and uprisings against Roman rule.

Comparatively little attention has been paid to the influence of Jesus' socialization in the form of his social and family background and networks, his everyday life in childhood and youth amidst local tradesmen, merchants, farmers, and shepherds, the education and training in the carpenter's workshop he received, and the places where he lived and worked. This book establishes firm foundations for a social history of the New Testament and its early readership in the history of everyday life.

Cooperation on problems in this field has long been hampered by disciplinary boundaries. New Testament scholars and church historians have tended to shy away from the territory of ancient history. While they have the linguistic and hermeneutic skills required for intense close reading of the New Testament and other early Christian texts, they are not trained in historical theories and methods required to situate their knowledge of these narratives within the broader historical context of the administration of the Roman provinces. The details gleaned from early Christian texts on the social and economic history of Judaea and Palestine require historical comparison with the current research on other eastern Roman provinces. Widespread reluctance to draw on papyrological evidence has presented a further impediment to progress: many ancient historians are loath to do so because of its perceived inaccessibility, and New Testament scholars may find the prospect of working with Egyptian papyri even more

daunting, especially in the light of the prevalence of texts not yet translated into any modern language.

Ancient historians are similarly prone to eschewing both the New Testament and the apocryphal gospels as source groups complementing the wide variety of other sources we have for the early Roman imperial period. Historical research on early Christian narratives has been hobbled by fears of the undertaking becoming bogged down in fruitless arguments with devout Christians and theologians. These factors explain why only a handful of scholars have dedicated themselves to this research, and why so many important topics have yet to receive the thorough analysis of their social, cultural, and economic history that they merit.

In focusing on the protagonists and key episodes of the New Testament literature, this book has explored the world of its protagonists and early Christian readership in a way that usefully supplements traditional exegetical research while remaining a work of ancient history and not of biblical exegesis or New Testament studies. It has focused on the everyday lives and daily concerns and difficulties of members of the lower and middle classes, people like a carpenter with his family or a shepherd herding animals out in the fields. It has concerned itself with ordinary women who dared to speak up in a man's world, with common men or women undertaking journeys without the financial means and social networks that facilitated the smooth passage of the elite, and with villagers subject to the efficient grip of Roman rule who were forced to register their households in the Roman provincial census. Finally, it has looked at young Christian men who enjoyed a similar upbringing to St. Antony in comfortably well-off Christian families in the rural hinterland of the province of Egypt in the first half of the third century, but then went on to live ordinary rather than highly exceptional lives. These men who followed their fathers and grandfathers as estate managers or into positions of political leadership on city councils are surely as worthy of study as Antony, the founding father of monasticism, precisely because their careers represent the prevailing norm and not the exception.

Everyday history is at times dismissed as arbitrary in its approach and trivial in its results by critics who perceive an element of randomness in the choices made by historians to study or not study particular aspects of everyday life. My choice of topics for this book, made on the basis of key episodes from the New Testament, may suffice to counter such objections: the study of everyday life is of intrinsic relevance for understanding the everyday concerns of the common people who are the protagonists in these narratives. The authors of the early Christian texts took care to

present the miracles worked by Jesus in the context of plausible, believable scenarios. Only once these scenarios are situated in their historical context does it become possible to understand them and to reconstruct how a contemporary reader in the Roman provinces would have understood them. The analysis presented here provides a window on to aspects of the socioeconomic and domestic contexts of the Jesus tradition, using papyri recovered from the Egyptian desert sands over the past 130 years. The evidence we have for Galilee is meager and fragmentary, but papyri from contemporary Roman Egypt can provide us with, at the very least, useful initial insights into the complex web of participants and arrangements making up local society. They help us to understand everyday living conditions, social differences and economic hardships experienced by ordinary people, as well as the influence of the Roman state on their everyday lives.

I have explored the social and cultural environment of the early first centuries in several case studies in this book. Many more aspects of the Gospels could be analyzed in a similar way, however. The Galilean fishing economy and its importance for the socialization of Jesus and his disciples is one obvious example. Economic and social issues arising from the lived reality of fishermen and their families have been widely neglected up to now in the scholarly literature, in spite of the strong association between Jesus and his followers with fish and fishing in first-century Galilee in the New Testament tradition and the various references made by Jesus in the Gospels to fishermen and their daily lives.

Finally, the chapters of this book contain original research on papyrus documents from Roman Egypt that both enhance our knowledge of multiple aspects of everyday life in a Roman province and generate insights relevant to issues well beyond the scope of New Testament scholarship. As such, I trust that the volume will also be of interest to Roman social historians more generally.

Notes

I Egypt and the Social World of the New Testament

1. Stambaugh and Balch 1992; Stegemann and Stegemann 1995; Harrison 2003; Theißen 2004; Erlemann et al. 2004–2007; Kloppenborg 2006; Bienert et al. 2008; Öhler 2011; Last 2016.
2. Scheidel and Friesen 2009. For a recent discussion see Harper 2011: 55–56.
3. For the coinage "quotidian turn" as well as an account of the various trajectories and approaches to everyday history in the humanities and social sciences, see Tweed 2015.
4. Despite this situation, the papyri do not provide an overview of the entire province of Egypt; climatic variations mean we only have information from the Fayum area in Middle Egypt, Oxyrhynchus on the Tomis canal, Hermopolis and Antinoopolis, the region of Thebes, and the Dakhla and Kellis oases in the Western Desert.
5. The volumes relating to the New Testament cover the Pauline epistles: Phil. (Arzt-Grabner 2003), 1 Cor. (Arzt-Grabner 2006), 2 Thess. (Kreinecker 2010), and 2 Cor. (Arzt-Grabner 2014).
6. Transl. Shipley 1924.
7. Tac. *Hist.* 1.11 (transl. A.J. Church and W.J. Brodribb 1876).
8. For the Roman magistrate of Egypt, the *praefectus Aegypti*, see Jördens 2009, 11–58.
9. Tac. *Ann.* 2.59 (transl. A.J. Church and W.J. Brodribb 1876).
10. Wilcken 1912, xv. See also Vogt 1929. Modrzejesky 2001 positions himself in this tradition when he entitles his chapter on Egypt in the volume edited by Lepelley on the regions of the Roman Empire "The Special Position of Egypt." Cf. Modrzejesky 2001, 459: "The circumstances of the conquest conferred on Egypt a special position within the Empire in terms of the constitution and the prevailing socio-economic and religious conditions, which permeates all aspects of this chapter."
11. See again Modrzejesky 2001, 511, who argues for the distinctive status of Egypt within the empire as a result, as well, of its economic idiosyncrasies.

12. Wilcken 1912, xv; see also Vogt 1929, introduction.
13. For example Lewis 1984; Geraci 1989, 55–88; Bagnall 1995, 11–13; Cribiore 2001, 6; Bowman 2005, 313–314; Hanson 2005, 85; Keenan, 2009, 17–92. Cf. Rathbone 2013, who considers changes in Egypt from Ptolemaic to Roman times in the context of wider developments in the Roman Empire.
14. Goodman 1997, 275.
15. Diod. Sic. 1.31.8.
16. Euseb. *Hist. Eccl.* 2.16. (Transl. McGiffert 1890).
17. Bausi and Camplani 2013, *HEpA* §§1–5.
18. Lang 2008, 12–14.
19. Acts 18:24–28 NIV. Cf. Choat 2019.
20. Acts 2:9–10 NIV.
21. Cf. Acts 2:41.
22. Von Harnack 1924, 706.
23. Grenfell and Hunt 2007.
24. Now classed as apocryphal, it is clear that the arbiters of the New Testament canon had rejected them for various reasons. They were all lost for more than a millennium until their rediscovery in the papyrus excavations of the late nineteenth and early twentieth centuries.
25. Roberts 1935; Roberts 1979; Hurtado 2003; Nongbri 2005; Barker 2011; Orsini and Clarysse 2012; Porter 2013; Nongbri 2018.
26. See Chapter II P. Bas. II.43 and SB 16. 12497.
27. Huebner 2005; Bagnall et al. 2016.
28. Naldini 1998; Wipszycka 1974.
29. Barnes 1989; Modrzejewski 1997; Pucci Ben Zeev 2005; Horbury 2014; Jakab 2001b.
30. Tilly 2008, 56–57.
31. Smallwood 1981, 516–517; Haas 1997, 108–109.
32. Roberts 1979; Broeck 1996; Pearson 1986; Pearson 2004; Pearson 2007.
33. Klauck 2003, 55.
34. Hippol. *Ref. omnium haer.* 7.2.
35. Clem. Al. *Strom.* 7.17. Cf. Pearson 2005; Löhr 2013; Choat 2019.
36. Orig. *in Luc. Hom.* 1.2: "Basilides too dared to write a *Gospel according to Basilides.*"
37. Epiph. *Pan.* §31.
38. Tert. *Adv. Val.* 4. Cf. Markschies 1992, 294–311.
39. Lang 2008, 28–31.
40. See below, chap. IV.
41. Euseb. *Hist. Eccl.* 6.11.3. Cf. Wipszycka 2006, 87–88.
42. Euseb. *Hist. Eccl.* 6.1.1.

43. Euseb. *Hist. Eccl.* 6.15 and 6.31. Eutychius *Annals* 9.5. Cf. Wipszycka 2015, 59; Choat 2019.

44. Dionysius in Euseb. *Hist. Eccl.* 7.21. Origen attributed the local uprisings to the increasing number of Christians, and to the fact that the Roman authorities did not persecute them as they had in previous times (Orig. *Contra Celsum* 3.15).

45. Bell 1944, 205; Luijendijk 2008, 168–174; Choat et al. 2014, 194. See also Schubert 2016.

46. Claytor and Bagnall 2015.

47. Rathbone 1991, 7. See Chapter II on *P.Bas.* II.43.

48. Euseb. *Hist. Eccl.* 6.40.4.

49. Euseb. *Hist. Eccl.* 6.41.

50. Euseb. *Hist. Eccl.* 6.42.1 (Transl. McGiffert 1890).

51. Three papyri from the Valerian persecution have survived. P.Oxy. 43. 3119; P.Oxy. 42.3035 and possibly P.Mil. Vogl. 6, 287 (cf. Huebner 2019c) See also Luijendijk 2008, 174–188; Blumell 2013.

52. Euseb. *Hist. Eccl.* 7.11.1–11.

53. Euseb. *Hist. Eccl.* 7.11.13.

54. Euseb. *Hist. Eccl.* 7.11.15–17. Cf. Choat 2012, 482.

55. *P. Oxy.* 42.3035; *P. Oxy.* 43.3119. Cf. Luijendijk 2008, 180–188. See Chapter II for a discussion of a Christian community in the Fayum in the 250s CE.

56. Euseb. *Hist. Eccl.* 7.21.1–10.

57. For the dating of the two relevant letters by bishop Dionysius on the outbreak of the plague in Alexandria (Euseb. *Hist. Eccl.* 7.21.1–10 and 7.22.1–11), see von Harnack 1893; Feltoe 1904; Schwartz 1909; Oost 1961, 9; Lane Fox 1986, 555 n. 17; Tissot 1997, 51–65; Jakab 2001a, 31–32; Legutko 2003, 33; Baumkamp 2014, 79–85 against Bienert 1978; Strobel 1993, 171–184, and most recently, Harper 2017, 119–160, who dates the outbreak of the plague in Alexandria to 249 CE.

58. Dionysius in Euseb. *Hist. Eccl.* 7.21: "And though they see the race of man on earth thus dwindling ever and being exhausted, they do not tremble, as its total extinction proceeds and draws near." Transl. McGiffert 1890. Cf. Cyprian, *De mort.* 14–16.

59. Cf. Parkin 1992, 63–64. The *Historia Augusta* speaks of 5,000 people dying each day in Rome (*HA, Vit. Gall.* 5.5). The suffering during the multiple waves of plague that hit the Alexandrian population sometime in the late 250s and early 260s CE are graphically described by the patriarch Dionysius of Alexandria in Thucydidean terms (Euseb. *Hist. Eccl.* 7.21–22. Cf. Thuc. 2.48–54). Strobel (1993, 185–187) has argued that this letter by Dionysius does not describe an actual plague event.

60. Duncan-Jones 1996, 120–121. The papyrological evidence attests to significant population decreases due to the Antonine plague; mortality and the subsequent flight of survivors having substantially impacted tax revenues. For further discussions of the papyrological evidence, see Littman and Littman 1973, 243–255; Bagnall 2000, 288–292; Van Minnen 2001; Bruun 2007.

61. Bagnall 1982, 105–124; Wipszycka 1986; Bagnall 1987; Wipszycka 1988; Bagnall 1995, 279, n. 113; Bagnall 2009, 20. See also Hopkins 1998.

62. Depauw and Clarysse 2013; cf. for a critical discussion Frankfurter 2014.

63. Bausi and Camplani 2013: 240–242.

64. Dionysius in Euseb. *Hist. Eccl.* 7.22 "They deserted those who began to be sick, and fled from their dearest friends. And they cast them out into the streets when they were half dead, and left the dead like refuse, unburied." Transl. McGiffert 1890. Cf. Cyprian *De mort.* See also Rébillard 2009, 93–95.

65. *P.Oxy.* 36.2785. See Luijendijk 2008, 94–102.

66. Hope 2012, 3727.

67. Cf. Schmelz 2002, 319.

68. Bausi and Camplani 2013, *HEpA* §§15–16. *PG* 111.982, at 332; Cf. Choat et al. 2014, 191.

69. Bausi and Camplani 2013, *HEpA* §16.

70. Bausi and Camplani 2013, *HEpA* §§17–24.

71. Bausi and Camplani 2013, *HEpA* §18.4.5.

72. Bausi and Camplani 2013, *HEpA* §21.12.14.

II The Social Milieu of Early Christians in Egypt

1. An early dating was proposed by, among others, Bell 1944 and Roberts 1979. Bagnall 2009 argues for a later dating to the late second century at the earliest. See now also Nongbri 2018.

2. See Huebner 2019b, Huebner forthcoming b + c.

3. 250–275 CE: *PSI* 9.1041; *PSI* 3.208; *P.Oxy.* 36.2785; *P.Alex.* 29. See Bagnall 2009, 8. The possibility of a Christian author for *P.Oxy.* 42.3057, which is dated to the first or second century, was convincingly rejected by Blumell in 2010; see also Luijendijk 2008, 29.

4. *P.Bas.* II.43.

5. Lewis 1982.

6. Huebner 2019b, Huebner forthcoming b + c. See also Verreth and Vandorpe 2013.

7. Rathbone 1991, 71.

8. *BGU* 4.1030. See also *P.Prag inv. Gr.* 3.8 + 574 verso from Theadelphia, edited by Vanthieghem 2014/2015. *P.Mich.* 11.620 = *SB* 8.9898 from 239/40 CE. For information on Valerius Titanianus, see *P.Gen.* 1.1.1 and Schubert 2007,

161–162, with a list of occurrences in papyri and inscriptions. Cf. also *P.Ryl.* 2.245 (undated). See Huebner forthcoming b + c.

9. *P.Lond.* 3.948 R from 236 CE; see also *BGU* 4.1030 – Letter from Arius to the soldier Sarapammon – undated. Rathbone 1991, 65 and 69.

10. For Roman education, cf. Cribiore 1996; Cribiore 2001.

11. *P.Bas.* II.43: l.19–21: ἐρρῶσθαί σε εὔχομαι ὁλοκληρ[οῦν]τα ἐν κ(υρί)ῳ)

12. Cf. Hurtado 1998. Choat (2006, 43–125) also studies genuine Christian markers in documentary papyri. See also Bagnall 2009, 24.

13. Choat 2006, 119–125; Bagnall 2009, 24. Also see Choat and Nobbs 2001–2005, 39.

14. Cf. Nevius 2001, 1046. *Nomina sacra* for *Iesous, pater,* and *huios* were added to the canon only later.

15. *P.Alex.* 29 from 350 to 375 CE; *PSI* 3.208 from 250 to 325 CE; *PSI* 9.1041 from 250 to 325 CE; *P.Oxy.* 36.2785 from 250 to 330 CE; *PSI* 15.1560 from 250 to 399 CE; *SB* 16.12304 from 275 to 325 CE; *P.Oxy.* 8.1162 from 300 to 399 CE; *P.Oxy.* 56.3857 from 300 to 399 CE. See Luijendijk 2008, 81–151; Blumell 2012, 50 n. 112.

16. *P.Oxy.* 50.3523 (John 18:36–19:7); *P.Ryl.* 3.457 (John 18:31–33; 37–38). The latter was bought on the antiquities market, so its provenance from Oxyrhynchus is not secure.

17. According to the Gospel of John, this uncommon expression refers to Jesus himself (John 6:55–56). Here Jesus says: "Those who eat my flesh and drink my blood abide in me, and I in them."

18. A search for the name "Paulus" on Trismegistos reveals that during the first two centuries of Roman rule it was extremely rare. It became slightly more popular in the third century, grew to be widespread in the fourth century, and finally reached its highest popularity in the fifth century CE.

19. Dionysius in Euseb. *Hist. Eccl.* 7.24. See Bagnall 1982, 108; Luijendijk 2008, 41.

20. Bagnall 1982, 109; Luijendijk 2008, 40–42.

21. The letter from Alexander also includes greetings from Narcissus, the former bishop of Jerusalem who died shortly after relinquishing the see to Alexander.

22. Euseb. *Hist. Eccl.* 6.14.8–9.

23. Bowman 1971, 18–19.

24. Which was the most likely figure according to Tacoma 2006, 138.

25. Athan. *Vit. Ant.* §2.

26. Cf. Bowman 1971, 98–107.

27. Cf. van Minnen 1994, 76, commenting on *SB* 16.12497.

28. See Chapter VI.

29. See Chapter VI, and also Lewis 1983, 63–64; Parkin and Pomeroy 2007, 140–142.

30. See Luijendijk 2008, 58: "in several instances the people using *nomina sacra* in their private letters also wrote and owned literary manuscripts."

31. *SB* 16.12497 from Arsinoe, a list of nominations to liturgies that probably dates to the later years of the first half of the third century. For a detailed discussion of this text, see Sijpesteijn 1980, 341; van Minnen 1994, 74–77; Huebner 2019c and Huebner forthcoming c.

32. Cf. Lactantius with regard to Jesus' epithet "Christ," which the "ignorant" change into "Chrestus" (*Div. Inst.* 4.7.5).

33. Luijendijk 2008, 38 and 141: "As a marker of identity, the epithet indicates that one stands out as "Christian."

34. In *PSI* 14.1412.10, from the third quarter of the third century CE, the likely pagan author of the document refers to Sotas, the bishop of the Oxyrhynchite nome, as the "Christian" (δι<ὰ> Σώτου τοῦ χρησια[. . .] (Luijendijk 2008, 138, 180–181).

35. Euseb. *Hist. Eccl.* 7.21.2. Cf. Choat 2012, 484; Choat et al. 2014, 194.

36. Wipszycka 1996, 85–86.

37. Euseb. *Hist. Eccl.* 7.21.2.

38. Euseb. *Hist. Eccl.* 7.24.6–9.

39. Euseb. *Hist. Eccl.* 7.24.1.

40. Euseb. *Hist. Eccl.* 7.24.9: ὅ τε τῆς διδαχῆς ταύτης ἀρχηγὸς καὶ εἰσηγητής.

41. From the Arsinoite nome: *P.Strasb. Gr.* 8.793 from 100 to 199 CE (Arsinoite); *P. Mich.* 4.224 from November 16, 173 CE (Karanis); *P.Mich.* 4.225, col. 159.2852 from March 26, 175 CE (Karanis); *P.Mich.* 4.225, 1769 from March 26, 175 CE (Karanis), *P.Flor.* 1.21 from November 29, 239 CE (Theadelphia). From the Oxyrhynchite nome: *PSI* 12.1259 from 120 to 225 CE (Oxyrhynchus).

42. *P.Flor.* 1.21 from November 29, 239 CE.

43. *PSI* 12.1259.

44. Bastianini 1969, 149–182; Rowlandson 1998, 111–112.

45. Cf. Huebner 2019c and Huebner forthcoming b + c for further research into this matter.

46. Several book-length studies focusing on Christians in documentary texts from the city of Oxyrhynchus in Middle Egypt have been published in recent years. Luijendijk 2008 concentrates on the pre-Constantinian material from the city consisting of papyri dating from the late third to the beginning of the fourth centuries CE. She also studies the Oxyrhynchite evidence pertaining to the Decian persecution at Oxyrhynchus, above all the *libelli* – certificates of pagan worship required under Decius – from the city as well as documents relating to confiscations under Valerian and the great persecution under Diocletian. Blumell 2012 examines Christians from the Oxyrhynchite nome during the period 300–700 CE. See also Schmelz 2002 and Choat 2012. For the *libelli* more generally, see Schubert 2016.

47. See Chapter I, pp. 3–4, 9–10.
48. Luijendijk 2008. See also Choat 2006, 119–25.
49. Blumell repeatedly and wrongly claims that the Ethiopian manuscript reports that Sotas was ordained by Theon. Blumell 2012, 114; Blumell 2014, 84, n. 2; Blumell and Wayment 2015, 479, n. 133. Cf. Luijendijk 2017, 107, n. 18.
50. *PSI* 3.208; *PSI* 9.1041; *P. Oxy.* 36.2785; *P.Alex.* 29.
51. *P. Oxy.* 8.1162; *P. Oxy.* 56.3857; *P. Congres.* 15.20; *P. Oxy.* 12.1493; *P. Oxy.*12.1592; *P. Oxy.* 31.2601; *P. Oxy.* 63.4365. Luijendijk 2008, 62–64. See also Luijendijk 2017.

III The Herodian Kingdom and the Augustan Provincial Census System

1. Liv. *epit.* 134: "Caesar having called a meeting of the states at Narbo, a census was made of the three Gauls, which were conquered by his father" (transl. McDevitte 1850).
2. Livy reports that the census in Gaul had sparked rebellion (*tumultus*). Liv. *epit.* 137: "The insurrections, excited by the taxes levied in Gaul, were suppressed."
3. Str. 17.153. In 36 CE a tribe in Cappadocia also rebelled against a Roman census (Tac. *Ann.* 6.41), as did, in 61 CE, the Iceni in Britain. (Tac. *Ann.* 14.31; cf. Cass. Dio 62.2.3–4; Rathbone 1993, 88.)
4. Jos. *Ant.* 18.1–8.
5. The Book of Acts, which may well also have been written by Luke, also makes reference to Judas of Galilee, the rebel leader active during the census of Quirinius (Acts 5:37): "After him Judas the Galilean rose up at the time of the census and got people to follow him; he also perished, and all who followed him were scattered."
6. Luke 1:5: "In the days of King Herod of Judea, there was a priest named Zechariah, who belonged to the priestly order of Abijah. His wife was a descendant of Aaron, and her name was Elizabeth."
7. Matt. 2:1–2: "In the time of King Herod, after Jesus was born in Bethlehem of Judea, wise men from the East came to Jerusalem, asking, 'Where is the child who has been born king of the Jews? For we observed his star at its rising, and have come to pay him homage.'"
8. Sartre 2005, 95–96, nn. 39 and 40.
9. Renan 1863, 36.
10. Luke's account is dismissed as unhistorical by, for example, Davies and Sanders 1999 and Bickermann in his *Studies in Jewish and Christian History*. The New Testament scholars Theißen and Merz (2001, 149–150) also assume that Luke "mistakenly harmonized pieces of chronological information that do not fit together." This summarizes the dominant scholarly view at this time.

11. See, for an argument defending Luke's credibility, Ramsay 1898. Several recent German-language publications on the topic of Rome and the Jews refrain entirely from adopting a position of their own on the question thrown up by the different perceptions recorded by Josephus and in the New Testament; they include Schuol 2007; Bernett 2007; Wilker 2007, and the volume of essays edited by Böttrich and Herzer 2007.

12. Luke 1:1–4.

13. On the Roman census see: Tenny 1924; Jones 1953; Wiseman 1969; Unruh 2001.

14. *R. Gest. div. Aug.* 8.2–4. The imperial census held in 28 BCE counted 4,063,000 male and female Roman citizens in total. The enormous difference between this figure and the results of earlier censuses – in 70 BCE, 910,000 citizens had been counted – presumably resulted from Augustus having included women and children in the numbers for the first time. By the time of the next census of the Roman people, in 8 BCE, the number had already risen to 4,233,000. The imperial census in 14 CE, the year of Augustus' death, arrived at a figure of 4,937,000 Roman citizens. This increase had less to do with natural population growth than with the gradual extension of Roman citizenship to ever larger swathes of the population. Tac. *Ann.* 11.25. Cf. Tenny 1930, 313–324; Brunt 1971. The census conducted under Emperor Claudius in 47 CE later counted almost 6 million (5,984,072) Roman citizens, a million more than in the time of Augustus. The last *lustrum* for Roman citizens took place under Vespasian in 73 CE, when he acted as censor together with his son Titus.

15. Wallace 1938b; Hombert and Preaux 1952; Montevecchi 1970; Bagnall and Frier 2006; Claytor and Bagnall 2015.

16. For more on the census in the Ptolemaic period, see Clarysse and Thompson 2006.

17. It is only through the unique discovery of the archive of the Jew Babatha in the "Cave of Letters" near Ein-Gedi to the west of the Dead Sea, which also included Babatha's tax return from December 2, 127 CE, that scholars have learnt more about the functioning of the Roman provincial census in the province of Arabia (Lewis, Yadin, and Greenfield 1989; Rosen 1995, 5–7).

18. Cf. Braunert 1957, 202.

19. *SB* 1.5661 (trans. APIS); cf. Bagnall and Frier 2006: 33-Ar-2.

20. Rathbone 1993, 87.

21. Luke 2:3–5.

22. *P.Lond.* 3.904.

23. Joh. Chrys. *Hom. in diem nat.* (Migne *PG* 49, col. 351).

24. Luke 2:1.

25. *R. Gest. div. Aug.* 8 (transl. Shipley 1924): "As consul for the fifth time, by order of the people and the senate I increased the number of the patricians. Three times I revised the roll of the senate. In my sixth consulship, with Marcus Agrippa as my colleague, I made a census of the people. I performed the *lustrum* after an interval of forty-one years. In this lustration 4,063,000 Roman citizens were entered on the census roll. A second time, in the consulship of Gaius Censorinus and Gaius Asinius, I again performed the *lustrum* alone, with the consular imperium. In this *lustrum* 4,233,000 Roman citizens were entered on the census roll. A third time, with the consular imperium, and with my son Tiberius Caesar as my colleague, I performed the *lustrum* in the consulship of Sextus Pompeius and Sextus Apuleius. In this *lustrum* 4,937,000 Roman citizens were entered on the census roll."

26. *CIL* 14.3613 = *ILS* 918 = *Inscr. Ital.* 4.1, no. 130.

27. Mommsen 1883, 161–178.

28. Groag 1924, 458–459; Syme 1934, 133; Alföldy 1997, 199–200; Eck 2007, 1105.

29. Luke 3:1–2: "In the fifteenth year of the reign of Emperor Tiberius, when Pontius Pilate was governor of Judaea, and Herod was ruler of Galilee, and his brother Philip ruler of the region of Ituraea and Trachonitis, and Lysanias ruler of Abilene, during the high priesthood of Annas and Caiaphas, the word of God came to John son of Zechariah in the wilderness."

30. This opinion has been advanced in recent years by scholars of ancient history including, principally, Baltrusch 2012, Günther 2005; 2009, Weber 2003, Vogel 2002, Schalit 2001 and contributors to the volume of essays edited by Jacobson and Kokkinos 2009.

31. Tacitus, *Ann.* 6.41. Transl. Church and Brodribb 1876.

32. While evidence is lacking, it seems quite probable that Augustus also had censuses conducted in other client kingdoms such as Thrace, Commagene, and Mauretania.

33. Baltrusch 2012.

34. Only in 8 or 7 BCE did Herod succeed in regaining the favor of Augustus through sending his trusted court historian Nicolaus of Damascus to Rome as an envoy.

35. Jos. *Ant.* 17.2.4. See Baltrusch 2012.

36. Justin *Apol.* 1.34 (transl. Schaff 1885).

37. P.Lond. 2.324 l. 1–24 and l. 25–29 (Bagnall and Frier 2006, 131-Pr-1 and 145-Pr-1); cf. *P.Lond.* 2.324 from 161 CE.

38. Eck 2007, 79–103.

39. Tert. *Adv. Marc.* 4.19 (transl. Evans 1972). Cf. Evans 1973, 24–39.

40. Jos. *Ant.* 17.1.

41. Jos. *Ant.* 18.2–4; Jos. *BI* 2.117–118. See also Cotton 1999, 75–91; Hengel 2011, 143–149.

42. Liv. *epit.* 137; Millar 1993, 46–47.
43. Luke 2:1: Ἐγένετο δὲ ἐν ταῖς ἡμέραις ἐκείναις ἐξῆλθεν δόγμα παρὰ Καίσαρος Αὐγούστου ἀπογράφεσθαι πᾶσαν τὴν οἰκουμένην. 2. αὕτη ἀπογραφὴ πρώτη ἐγένετο ἡγεμονεύοντος τῆς Συρίας Κυρηνίου.

IV Discrimination and the Struggle for Women's Equality in Early Christianity

1. *P. Oxy.* 50.3525.
2. Roberts 1938; Roberts 1970; Roberts 1979; Parrott 1979; Parsons 1983; Lührmann 1988; Schmid 1990; Tuckett 2007.
3. *P. Ryl.* 3.463.
4. For the codex's gradual replacement of the traditional book form of the ancient world, the papyrus scroll, from the first to the sixth century CE, see Roberts and Skeats 1983; Bagnall 2009.
5. Coptic is the latest form of the Egyptian language, developed in the first or second century CE, written with Greek letters and several signs borrowed from Demotic. The most common dialect of Coptic was Sahidic, belonging to Upper Egypt.
6. *Papyrus Berolinensis* 8502, also known as the Akhmim Codex.
7. The codex contains parts of the gospel according to Mary, the *Apocryphon of John*, the *Sophia of Jesus Christ*, and the *Acts of Peter*. Cf. Lang 2008, 33.
8. The two most recent and authoritative books on the *Gospel of Mary* offering their own translation of the entire text are King 2003b and Tucket 2007.
9. See King 2003a, 3–12.
10. De Boer 2004; De Boer 2006; King 2003a and 2003b; Meyer 2004; Tuckett 2007.
11. De Boer 2004 and 2006; King 2003b, 74.
12. Cf. King 2003a, 3–12.
13. Cf. King 2003a, 6–7.
14. This includes the writings from the Nag Hammadi Library, which date to the middle of the fourth century. The writings were first found by chance in 1945 by farmers near the small Egyptian village of Nag Hammadi, in Upper Egypt.
15. For women in Greco-Roman Egypt, see: Pomeroy 1981; Pomeroy 1984; Rowlandson 1998; Bagnall and Cribiore 2006; Huebner 2009a; Huebner 2009b; Huebner 2013.
16. Cf. Huebner 2009.
17. Bagnall and Cribiore 2006.
18. Rowlandson 1998, 55. Cf. Cenival 1977, 29–30; Bowman 1996, 165–202; Messerer 2019.
19. Rowlandson 1998 as well as Bagnall and Cribiore 2006 follow Harris (1989, 24 and 279) in the assumption that the great majority of Roman Egyptian

women could not read and write, and that their proportion of the total literate population lay far below that of men. Before Harris, Calderini 1950 and Cole 1981 had already argued for the widespread illiteracy of women. Cf. Cribiore 2002; Bar-Ilan 2003, 117–180; Bagnall and Cribiore 2006, 48–55; Yiftach 2016. Cf. also Chapter V below and Huebner 2018.

20. See as evidence the various letters sent by women to family members, business partners and officials, in Bagnall and Cribiore 2006.

21. Rowlandson 1998, 280.

22. On the status of Jewish women in ancient Judaism, see: Wegner 1988; Wegner 1991.

23. King 2003a.

24. Eisen 1996.

25. Cf. Elm 1994, 248.

26. For the role of women in early Christianity, see Cohick 2009.

27. 1 Tim. 3:11; Plin. *Ep.* 10.96.8.

28. C Nic., *can.* 19.

29. *Ap. Const.* 3.11.3; 8.19–20.

30. See Huebner 2005, 45–49.

31. *Nov. Iust.* 3.1. See Gelzer 1893, 120; Schmelz 2002, 36.

32. As already noted, there was a long tradition of educating women in various forms of writing in Egypt, a practice which was apparently not interrupted by the Christianization of Egyptian society (Haines-Eitzen 2000). Luijendijk (2008, 74–78) identifies a female Christian letter writer of the late third century from Oxyrhynchus as a professional book author by her handwriting, and Eusebius also reports that Origen had enlisted the help of seven female calligraphers in order to copy his writings at the start of the third century. Cf. Euseb. *Hist. Eccl.* 6.23.2.

33. Wipszycka 1996, 232–233.

34. Griggs 1991 does not address the role of women in the Christianization of Egypt; they are only addressed in relation to the founding of a women's convent by Pachomius, and the absence of female members of the secular clergy is not discussed (154). Harmless 2004 examines the role of women in Egyptian monasticism in a five-page appendix, but does not discuss the absence of women in the secular clergy.

35. Schmelz 2002.

36. Huebner 2005.

37. 1 Tim. 5:5–10; 1 Cor. 7:8; Ambr. *De viduis*; Aug. *Bon. vid.*; Joh. Chrys. *Ep. Ad vid. iun.*; Joh. Chrys. *Hom. 13 in 1 Tim.*.

38. *Nov. Iust.* 3.1.

39. Clem. Al. *Paed.* 1.4; cf. Ferguson 1974, 72; Osborne 2005, 214–215.

40. Orig. *Comm. in Rom* 16:1–2 (Rufinus).

41. Wipszycka 2009, 567; cf. Wipszycka 2002.
42. *PSI* 6.698 from 391/392 CE.
43. *P.Lips.* 43 from before 371 CE; *P.Lips.* 60 from 371 CE.
44. *P.Oxy.* 44.3203 from 400 CE.
45. Cf., for example, the *Canons of Pseudo-Athanasius*, a work written in Egypt between 350 and 450 CE, or the *Gnomai of the Council of Nicaea*, an anonymously written work from the end of the fourth century.
46. Cf. John Chrysostom's and Ambrosius' *De Virginitate*.
47. Pall. *Laus.* 41.
48. See also Chapter I.
49. Wipszycka 2015, 69.
50. *P.Oxy.* 3.405 from the late second/early third century CE.

V The Family and Household of a Craftsman

1. Cf. for example Cic. *Off.* 1.42.
2. By far the most comprehensive account of the carpenter's craft comes from Ulrich 2007. Here, based on literary sources, visual representations, and archeological finds, Ulrich traces the practice of skilled crafts, including a study of the usage and application of a carpenter's tools and the products created; he does not examine the social position of carpenters or their everyday lives, however.
3. *SB* 14.11625 from the first century CE; *P.Mil.Vogl.* 2.66 R from Tebtunis (Arsinoites) from the second century CE.
4. Bagnall 1993, 18. Cf. López 2013, 85–86 and nn. 67–69. Their invention supposedly dates back to the Greek engineers of the fourth and third centuries BCE. Cf. Ritti et al. 2007, 138–163; Hochspringen 1984; Hochspringen 2000.
5. Huebner 2016.
6. *T.Mom.Louvre* 40; 943; 978; 1178. *SB* 1.3862 = *C. Étiq. Mom.* 305.
7. Ulrich 2007, 17–58.
8. Ulrich 2007, 13–16.
9. Carpenters appear with gooseherds, basket makers, cheese makers, cattle herders, shepherds, threshers, coppersmiths, barbers, potters, flute players, embalmers, dyers, water-guards, bag weavers, engineers, repairmen, donkey herdsmen, brickmakers, and butchers in *P.Corn.* 22 from the early first century CE; *P. Strasb.* 9.829 of Theadelphia (Arsinoite) from 138–161 CE; *O.Leid.* 292 from the second/third century CE; *O.Theb.* 146 from the second century CE; *O. Claud.* 4.715 (Mons Claudianus) from 98–117 CE; *SB* 1.5220 from the Arsinoite nome from the first to fourth centuries CE; *SB* 10.10563 from Tebtunis from the second century CE; and *SB* 18.13145 after 110 CE from Euhemeria (Arsinoite).

10. *SPP* 22.173 (Soknopaiou Nesos) from 40 CE.
11. Neef 1990, 305.
12. Jos. *BI* 1.407.
13. Roller 1998.
14. See Chapter III, note 15.
15. Bagnall and Frier 2006, 66.
16. Bagnall and Frier 2006, 67, table 3.2.
17. Cf. Eckerman 2011.
18. For example, *O.Claud.* 4.715 (Mons Claudianus) from 98 to 117 CE as well as *O.Claud.* 4.686, 4.697, 4.698, and 4.722.
19. Mark 1:9: "In those days Jesus came from Nazareth of Galilee and was baptized by John in the Jordan"; Luke 2:39: "When they had finished everything required by the law of the Lord, they returned to Galilee, to their own town of Nazareth"; Matt. 2:33: 'There he made his home in a town called Nazareth, so that what had been spoken through the prophets might be fulfilled, He will be called a Nazorean"; John 1:45: "Jesus, son of Joseph from Nazareth."
20. According to Procopius of Gaza, craftsmen who produced and sold things for everyday needs were counted among groups legally known as *negotiatores* (Procop. *Pan.* 13). Cf. *CTh* 13.1.10 from 374 CE. Tax amounts were calculated according to the size of a craftsman's capital. This included work tools, cattle, slaves, the tradesmen themselves, and their family members (Jones 1964, I.432).
21. Zos. 2.38.
22. Rich long-distance merchants, who could and should pay this tax, escaped by sea. Only the poor craftsman stayed behind with his work tools, with which he could hardly survive. Cobblers were considered to be particularly poor men, but even on the shoemaker's knife, representing their only capital, the unrelenting tax collectors raised their taxes (Lib. *Or.* 46.22).
23. Lib. *Or.* 46.22–23. On another occasion we learn that Libanius represented the craftsmen in relation to taxes, protecting the weaker people from the wealthier guild members, who had assumed responsibilities for taxation and protecting the employees of the great entrepreneurs against unjust tax claims from their employers (Lib. *Or.* 36.4; Cf. Liebeschuetz 1972, 54).
24. Zos. 2.38. In the sixth century Zonaras also reported how badly the trade-related income taxes burdened people of earlier periods. This is why Anastasius abolished these taxes upon his accession to power in 491 CE (Zon. 14.3).
25. *Nov. Maior.* 7.3 from 458; cf. Jones 1964, II.858–859; Zimmermann 2002. Only the highly specialized trades, which required a special training and aptitude, did not have to pay this tax. Tradesmen were given the opportunity to improve their skills and educate their sons in their crafts, for

there was a considerable shortage of men who were competent in these fields (*CTh* 13.4.1–2 from 334 to 337 CE; cf. Jones 1964, II.1014).

26. Lib. *Or.* 36.4; 46.21; cf. also *Or.* 33.33. Some of the tasks were to make rivers traversable again, to build a local fire department, to keep drainpipes clean and to re-erect columns, to provide the facilities and workers required by the accommodation at the stations of the *cursus publicus*, and, if necessary, to be ready to have soldiers and officials as lodgers (Jones 1964, II.859 with further references at n. 83).

27. Cf. Joh. Chrys. *Hom. in 1 Cor.* 20:16–18; Lib. *Or.* 46.11–13; 24 for state officials who took advantage of their rank and, for example, did not pay for their drinks in taverns (Liebeschuetz 1972, 53, 58).

28. Matt. 13:55–56; Mark 6:3. References to Jesus' family (including his mother and brothers) are generally found in Matt. 12:46–50 and Mark 3:31. Cf. also John 7:5; 1 Cor. 9:5, 15:7; and Acts 1:14.

29. Cf. Chapter III above and Huebner 2013.

30. Matt. 13:55.

31. John 19:26–27: "When Jesus saw his mother and the disciple whom he loved standing beside her, he said to his mother, 'Woman, here is your son.' Then he said to the disciple, 'Here is your mother.' And from that hour the disciple took her into his own home."

32. Parkin 1992; Frier 2000; Scheidel 2001; Bagnall and Frier 2006.

33. See Bagnall and Frier 2006.

34. Herlihy and Klapisch Zuber 1985.

35. Huebner 2010.

36. Saller 1994; Parkin 2003; Pudsey 2012; Pudsey 2013.

37. For an overview of the demographic profile of the ancient world, see Saller 1994; Parkin 2003; Bagnall and Frier 2006; Pudsey 2012; Pudsey 2013.

38. Bagnall and Frier 2006, 77, table 4.1 – Model West, Level 2, females.

39. Saller 1994, 52, table 3.1.e – Male, "ordinary," Level 3 West: proportion having living kin.

40. Saller 1994, 51, table 3.1.d – Male, "ordinary," Level 3 West: mean number of living kin.

41. Cf. Tropper 2006.

42. It was still very unusual to have four living brothers by the age of 30, yet we still find some examples of this in the Roman Egyptian censuses. In 187 CE, for example, Herod and his wife and sister Eirene, who were both in their fifties, lived in Arsinoe, the area's metropolis. They lived in a household with their five sons, who ranged in age from 7 to 29 years, as well as two adult daughters, their brother's children, and several grandchildren. They also had tenants (P.Strasb. 5.313 from 189 CE; cf. also SB 10.10759 from 35 CE (Fig. 3.3)). Eirene was a full sister with the same father and mother as Herod. There are no other examples of

families with this many daughters in the preserved census records, although it is noted that daughters commonly left the household when they married between the ages of 14 and 18, while married sons remained in their parents' house (Bagnall and Frier 2006, 121–122; Huebner 2013, 48–50).

43. Saller 1994, 49, table 3.1.b – Female, "ordinary," Level 3 West: proportions having living kin.

44. Saller 1994, 52, table 3.1.e – Male, "ordinary," Level 3 West: proportion having living kin.

45. Luke 4:16–17.

46. Cf. for example Kelly 2004, 164–165. Cf. also Hanson 1991 and Hopkins 1991.

47. Bowman 1991, 121–123. He perhaps emphasizes Egypt's exceptional position too strongly.

48. For example, Sentia Asklatarion, *P.Sot.* 19–21.

49. Youtie 1966, 252.

50. Cribiore 2001, 159.

51. Rowlandson 1998, 301.

52. Youtie 1966.

53. Youtie 1966, 127–143.

54. Wipszycka 1996, 108: "Les individus appartenant à une même couche, à une même groupe social, peuvent savoir écrire ou non, phénomène que l'on ne saurait expliquer autrement que par les inclinations ou facultés personnelles de tel ou tel."

55. Saller 2008, 84: "The chief point is that the Romans did not attempt mass publicly funded education, restricting basic education to children of families with some surplus income to pay teachers."

56. For the school system in Greco-Roman Egypt, see Mitteis and Wilcken 1912, 136–138; Morgan 1998, 48–49; Cribiore 2001; Parca 2013, 474–476. Some years ago, an excavation project run by Columbia and New York Universities at Amheida in the Dakhla Oasis discovered what was perhaps the first schoolroom located next to a private house for the local elite. The schoolroom with benches along the walls dates from 329/30 CE. On the room's plastered walls are verses presumably written by the teacher himself in red, which are preserved to this day (Cribiore et al. 2008).

57. Saller 2008.

58. Comparisons with other premodern and early modern societies confirm these hypotheses: "the majority, or a near majority of skilled craftsmen are literate, while women and unskilled laborers and peasants are mainly not, this being the situation which prevailed in most of the educationally more advanced regions of Europe and North America from the sixteenth to the eighteenth century" (Harris 1989, 8).

59. These figures are confirmed by the other 316 *hypographai* Yiftach studied. They came from the Roman *grapheion*, which was the public archive for legal documents. Nearly a quarter of these written documents, or 81 out of a total of 326, were written by the contracting parties themselves, while the others were done by a representative skilled at writing. While 34 percent of men signed in their own hands, only 6.7 percent of women did so (Yiftach 2016).

60. In addition, see Fewster 2002.

61. Cohen 1993; Satlow 2012.

62. Hezser 2001; Eshel and Edwards 2004.

63. Mark 6:3.

64. Matt. 13:55.

65. Pl. *Rep.* 5.467A; Saller 2008, 81.

66. *P.Mich.* 5.346b. Cf. Eckerman 2011.

67. *MAMA* III.463.

68. *MAMA* III.760.

69. *MAMA* III.336.

70. *MAMA* III.582.

71. *MAMA* III.643.

72. *MAMA* III.226.

73. *SEG* 37 (1987) 1292.

74. *MAMA* III.506.

75. Gr. Naz. *Ep.* 9.

76. Gr. Naz. *Ep.* 98.

77. Bas. *Ep.* 198.1.

78. Schmelz 2002, 232–241.

79. *Vita Ioh. Eleem.* (in Dawes and Baynes 1948) 44A.

80. *CTh* 16.2.8 from 343 CE. Constantius probably refers to the general privilege of the clergy issued by his father in 313 (*CTh* 16.2.2).

81. *CTh* 16.2.8 from 343 CE; *CIust* 1.3.2.1 from 357 CE. See also Noethlichs 1972, 140.

82. *CTh* 16.2.10 from 346 CE.

83. Huebner 2013, 107–114; 169–170.

84. Huebner (forthcoming a) on the right of residence (*habitatio*) in Roman Egypt.

85. See Huebner 2013, 141–161 on the difficult relationship between mothers- and daughters-in-law.

86. Huebner 2013, 122–140; 169–174.

87. Cf., for example, how Jesus gave a widow immeasurable joy when he raised her son (Luke 7:11–17).

88. Huebner 2013, 118–121.

89. For example *P.Giss.* 43 = *SB* 10.10630: A 70-year-old man named Harpokration, who came from the village of Tanyaithis in the

Apollonopolite nome, married a wife who was thirty-one years his junior; he was already over 50 years old and she was not much older than 20. For more examples see Huebner 2013, 107–140.

90. Huebner 2013, 187–196.

VI Travel by the Lower Classes in Roman Times

1. For an investigation of such trips, see in particular the studies by Stoffel 1994 and Kolb 1997, Kolb 2000, and Kolb 2001.
2. Millar 1981; Blumell 2011.
3. Hor. *Sat.* 1.5.
4. For more on this, see especially Kotsifou 2000; Elsner and Rutherford 2010; Rutherford 2012.
5. Sijpesteijn 1987.
6. *O.Flor.* 14 from the early second century CE.
7. *P.Oxy.* 36.2791 from the second century CE.
8. *P.Fouad* 1.75 from 64 CE.
9. See Elsner and Rutherford 2010 for more on this.
10. *P.Oxy.* 1.112 (transl. Grenfell and Hunt 1898) from the third or early fourth century CE. In a later text we read of Mikke's preparations to travel by boat to spend Lent and Easter with her mother (*SB* 12.10840; cf. Bagnall and Cribiore 2006, 82, 385).
11. For more detail on trips to attend court hearings in Alexandria, see *P.Mich.* 9 533 from 137 CE; *P.Tebt.* 2.407 from 199 CE; *P.Oxy.* 77.5117 from 264 CE.
12. Cf. for example *P.Mich.* 8.490 from the late second century CE.
13. *P.Lond.* 3.904 from 104 CE.
14. See for example *P.Tebt.* 2.384 from 10 CE; *P.Wisc.* 1.4 from 53 CE; *SB* 18.13305 from 271 CE. Cf. Westermann 1914; Bradley 1991; Venticinque 2010; Freu 2011.
15. For example *P.Oxy.* 18.2190 = *SB* 22.15708 from *ca.* 100 CE. Cf. Lewis 1983, 63–64; Parkin and Pomeroy 2007, 140–142.
16. Cf. Epp 1991.
17. *SB* 3.6263 from the second half of the second century CE.
18. *P.Mich.* 8.484 (transl. APIS) from the second century CE.
19. *P.Sarap.* 86 from 90 to 133 CE.
20. Cf. for example *P.Mich.* 3.217 from 297 CE.
21. *P.Oxy.* 18.2191 from the second century CE; cf. also *BGU* 1.27 and *BGU* 2.423.
22. *P.Mich.* 8.490 (transl. APIS) from the late second century CE.
23. Hdt. 2.97.1 (transl. Godley 1920).
24. *P.Oxy.* 33.2680.10–12 (transl. Bagnall and Cribiore 2006).
25. Cf. Bagnall 1985a; Bowman 2013, 219–254. See also Adams 2007.

26. Cf. the letters written by women in Bagnall and Cribiore 2006, 81–83.
27. *SB* 14.11580.
28. Transl. Bagnall and Cribiore 2006, 284.
29. *BGU* 1.261 from the second century CE. Cf. Bagnall and Cribiore 2006, 189.
30. *P. Oxf.* 19 after 208 CE (transl. Bagnall and Cribiore 2006, 272). Verbatim in this letter: "son." Bagnall and Cribiore, however, consider that "son" is not to be taken literally (2006, 272).
31. On migration within Greco-Roman Egypt, see Braunert 1964.
32. *P. Oxy.* 33.2680 from the second/third century CE (transl. Bagnall and Cribiore 2006, 300).
33. Wilkinson 2006; Brodersen 2016.
34. *OIM* 25622 (transl. APIS).
35. Bagnall 1985b, 1–6.
36. *P. Oxy.* 1.112 from the third or fourth century CE.
37. *BGU* 16.2604 from 7 BCE; *P. Oxy.* 1.112 from the third or fourth century CE; *P. Dub.* 16 from the second or third century CE; *P.Lille* 1.25 from the third century CE.
38. *P. Oxy.* 14.1773, cf. Bagnall and Cribiore 2006, 82 and 371.
39. *P. Oxy.* 7.1068 from the third century CE.
40. Cf. Bagnall 1993, 37–38.
41. *P.Bas.* II.19 from 141 CE.
42. Bagnall 1985b. For donkey drivers, see for example *P.Coll.Youtie* 1.17; *P.Oxy.* 77.5121; *P.Oxy.* 12.1425.
43. *SB* 12.10840 from the fourth century CE. Cf. Bagnall and Cribiore 2006, 385.
44. *O.Flor.* 17 from the second century CE (60 drachmas for passage by boat from the Fayum to Alexandria or the Thebaid was twice what an ordinary laborer earned in a month). *P.Amh.* 2.131 from the second century CE (a man traveling from the Fayum to Alexandria paid 54 drachmas for a boat trip including taxes, i.e. tolls).
45. Bagnall 1993, 36.
46. Bagnall 1985b.
47. Kolb 2001.
48. *BGU* 7.1680 from the third century CE (transl. Bagnall and Cribiore 2006, 365).
49. *PSI* 5.514; *PSI* 5.502; *P.Mich.* 1.48. Cf. Epp 1991, 53–55. Another woman called Takalis reported in a letter to her brother that she had reached Alexandria in six days. It is not clear where she had departed from – perhaps also from the Fayum or from Oxyrhynchus, 50 miles further upstream (*BGU* 3.843 from the first or second century CE).
50. *P.Cair.Zen.* 1.59029 from 257 CE.
51. *P.Cair.Zen.* 1.59251 from 252 CE.

52. *Epigr.* 7.61.
53. *P.Oxy.* 17.2109 from 261 CE: opening of a public inn in Oxyrhynchus. *P.Col.* 4.83 from 254/3 BCE: a certain Antipatros from Philadelphia reports he has opened a public inn in Hermopolis. *P.Genova* 3.126 from the third century BCE: public inn in Crocodilopolis. *P.Iand.Zen.* 19 from 254 BCE: construction of a public inn in Philadelphia (Arsinoites). *P.Tebt.* 1.43 from 117 BCE: public inn in Kerkeosiris (Arsinoites); cf. *P.Tebt.* 1.230 from the period 125–100 BCE.
54. *P.Tebt.* 1.43 from 117 BCE: four men from the village of Kerkeosiris met a guest from Krokodilopolis/Arsinoe in a hostelry in the village for dinner. This hostelry in Kerkeosiris is also mentioned as a place where disputes had taken place: *P.Tebt.* 1.230 from the late second century BCE.
55. Also Egeria, whose pilgrim journey to Jerusalem, Egypt, and Mesopotamia has already been mentioned, reports in detail on the beauty of the landscape she traveled through and mentions many details about the places she visited. But even she mentions only that the monks were hospitable and gave blessed food to the members of her group; she does not tell us what these meals consisted of or where the members of her group slept at night.
56. *P.Oxy.* 33.2680; *P.Mich.Zenon* 103, col. 1.2–8; *P.Haun.* 2.19; *P.Oxy.* 1.118.
57. For more on banditry in Egypt, cf. Nachtergael 1988; McGing 1998; Blumell 2008.
58. *P.Mich.* 3.214 from 297 CE.
59. *P.Lille* 1.6 from the third century BCE.
60. *SB* 8.9792 from 162 BCE. Transl. HGV.
61. *P.Lond.* 7.2009 from 246 BCE.
62. *P.Oxy.* 10.1291 (transl. Bagnall and Cribiore 2006, 334).
63. *P.Fayum* 108 from 171 CE.
64. *P.Fuad.inv.* 1.26 from 59 CE.
65. *BGU* 13.2350 probably from the second century CE (transl. Bagnall and Cribiore 2006, 366).
66. *P.Enteux.* 79 from 218 BCE (transl. Winter 1933, 115–116). On this incident see also Adams 2001, 156.
67. *P.Wisc.* 2.74; cf. Bagnall and Cribiore 2006, 387.
68. *P.Ryl.* 4.624 from the early fourth century CE; cf. Matthews 2006, 27 (transl. HGV).
69. *SB* 5.8027 (transl. Bagnall and Cribiore 2006, 82).
70. The elites of the province did, however, take part in culture and study trips. For more on these, see Foertmeyer 1989.
71. *P.Oxy.* 1.119 from the second or third century CE (transl. Parsons 2007, 129).
72. The Old Testament contains multiple references to Egypt as a place where people could take refuge from persecution by their rulers (Öhler 2008, 61–62).

For the significance of the Flight into Egypt in salvation history, see Assmann 2013, 131–142.

73. Ps.-Matt. 19:2 (transl. Cleveland Coxe 1886).
74. Ps.-Matt. 20 (transl. Cleveland Coxe 1886).
75. Ps.-Matt. 18 (transl. Cleveland Coxe 1886).
76. Ps.-Matt. 20:1 (transl. Cleveland Coxe 1886).
77. Ps.-Matt. 22 (transl. Cleveland Coxe 1886).
78. Thuc. 3.68.3; Rosenfeld 1998; Claytor 2012.
79. Rosenfeld 1998, 134.
80. For a detailed analysis of the so-called Archive of Theophanes, see Matthews 2006.
81. Kaiser 2010, 64–65.
82. Luke 10:30–35.
83. In Latin they were referred to as: *caupona, thermopolium, diversorium, taberna,* or *stabulum.*
84. Cf. Ar. *Ran.* 549–578.
85. For the history of *pandocheion*, see Constable 2003.
86. Str. 17.1.16 (transl. Roller 2014).
87. Casson 1974, 56–57; 65–94; 115–121; 340–341; Schaps 1979, 61–62.
88. Apul. *Met.* 1.6–19.
89. Pomeroy 2010, 192.
90. Bremmer 2001, 81–82.
91. *Vita Theod. Syk.* (in Dawes and Baynes 1948) 3.
92. *Acts of John* 60–61.
93. Acts 21:7–9.
94. Acts 9:43; 10:5–6.
95. Acts 10:22.
96. Acts 18:24–27.
97. *P.Mich.* 1.33 from January 4, 254 CE (transl. APIS).
98. Ps.-Clem. *Recogn.* 9.38 (transl. Smith 1885).
99. Cf. Blumell 2011.

VII An Occupation on the Margins of Society

1. For example Ps. 23: "The Lord is my shepherd, I shall not want. He makes me lie down in green pastures; he leads me beside still waters; he restores my soul. He leads me in right paths for his name's sake. Even though I walk through the darkest valley, I fear no evil; for you are with me; your rod and your staff – they comfort me." Ps. 78:52: "Then he led out his people like sheep, and guided them in the wilderness like a flock." See also Ezek. 34:24; Ezek. 37:22, 24; Jer. 3:15; Jer. 23:4.

2. Ezek. 34:23: "I will set up over them one shepherd, my servant David, and he shall feed them: he shall feed them and be their shepherd." Ezek. 37:24: "My servant David shall be king over them; and they shall all have one shepherd. They shall follow my ordinances and be careful to observe my statutes."

3. John 10: 11–14.

4. ποιμένες λαῶν for example Hom. *Il.* 2.85, 105, 254, 772 etc.

5. Dio Chrys. 1.12–13 (transl. Cohoon 1932).

6. Varro *Rust.* 2.1.6 (transl. Hooper 1934): "Of the ancients the most illustrious were all shepherds, as appears in both Greek and Latin literature, and in the ancient poets, who call some men 'rich in flocks,' others 'rich in sheep,' others 'rich in herds.'"

7. Luke 2:17–18: "When they saw this, they made known what had been told them about this child; and all who heard it were amazed at what the shepherds told them."

8. Sociohistorical studies of shepherding in ancient times are lacking. The *Encyclopedia of Ancient History, Oxford Classical Dictionary* and *Neue Pauly* all lack entries for "shepherd" (or its German equivalent, "Hirte"), despite covering most other occupational groups. The *EAH* article "Stock rearing, Roman Empire" by King does not include the eastern provinces and does not work with any papyrus sources. This also applies, unfortunately, to the *EAH* entry "Cheese" by Paulas.

9. Whittaker 1988. See also Howe 2008.

10. See also Van Lith 1974 and Samuel 1979.

11. Theoc. *Id.* 7.13–19 (transl. Trevelyan 1947).

12. Theocritus receives a shepherd's crook from his friend Lycidas (*Id.* 7.128); Mopsus makes a gift of a shepherd's crook to Theocritus (*Id.* 5. 88–90).

13. See for the shepherd's staff Ps. 23:4 (staff); 1 Sam. 17:40 (staff and sling); Varro *Rust.* 2.10.1, 3. The crook also plays a central role in a letter from Emperor Marcus Aurelius to his friend Fronto in 143 CE (Fronto *Ad M. Caes.* 2.12), where the emperor recounts traveling with a friend along a country road on horseback and coming upon two shepherds and their four dogs. Upon spying the riders, one shepherd had said to the other, "Careful of these riders – they are usually out to steal." Incensed, Marcus Aurelius had ridden into the center of the herd, which scattered in panic. He reports that one shepherd had thrown his *furca*, a two-pronged spear usually translated as a shepherd's crook, but hit only the horse behind Marcus Aurelius. The point of the story for Aurelius was that the shepherd had feared losing a few sheep but had ended up losing his crook. This punchline only works if we accept that the crook was more important to the shepherd than the sheep. And this importance persisted; in the seventeenth and eighteenth centuries the district shepherds

in the Allgäu region of southern Germany were presented with their crooks as a symbol of their responsibilities in an official ceremony (Maul 2013, 32).

14. Virg. *Ecl.* 1.1–2.

15. Ov. *Fasti* 4.753–755.

16. Liv. 9.36.6; cf. Frayn 1984, 66–78. On the symbolism of the shepherd's crook, cf. Buchholz 2012, 272–280.

17. "There is left," said Atticus, "of the discussion of quadrupeds only the topic of dogs; but it is of great interest to those of us who keep fleece-bearing flocks, the dog being the guardian of the flock, which needs such a champion to defend it. Under this head come especially sheep but also goats, as these are the common prey of the wolf, and we use dogs to protect them." Varro *Rust.* 2.9.1 (transl. Hooper 1934).

18. Hom. *Il.* 10.183–184 (transl. Butler 1898).

19. Shepherds in Egypt were also accompanied by dogs. In his *Historia Lausiaca* from the late fourth century, Palladius narrates that the barking of a shepherd's dog prevented the thief Moses from making off with his booty. Moses exacts revenge by killing almost the entire herd and selling the remaining animals. Pall. *Laus.* 19. See also *P.Laur.* 4.189.2–4 from 200–399 CE.

20. Bagnall 1993, 142–143.

21. *P.Princ.* 2.24 (Oxyrhynchus) from 21 CE. See Kloppenborg 2010, 58; Balconi 1984, 35–60, esp. 39; Arzt-Grabner 2010, 24.

22. Varro *Rust.* 2.1.16.

23. *P.IFAO* 1.40; *P.Princ.* 24.20–21; *PSI* 1.56.130; *P.Amh.* 1.73 = *P.Sarap.* 4; *P.Sarap.* 5. See Wallace 1938a.

24. See for example *P.Princ.* 2.24, and also Keenan 1989, 182.

25. As such, we are dealing with what Mireille Corbier describes as "un secteur pastorale d'une agriculture sedentaire," which she views as one of three forms of pastoralism practiced in ancient societies (Corbier 1988, 216).

26. See Bagnall 1994, 142–143.

27. Keenan 1989, 179: "the shepherd's mobility is a function of his employers' sedentarism." The archeologist Anna Boozer has recently produced a study of these temporary shelters for Roman Egypt (in Huebner and Laes 2019).

28. For example, the Old Testament conflict between Cain and Abel can be read in this context: (Gen. 4:2): "Now Abel was a keeper of sheep, and Cain a tiller of the ground. In the course of time Cain brought to the Lord an offering of the fruit of the ground, and Abel for his part brought of the firstlings of his flock, their fat portions." Complaints about negligent shepherds also appear quite frequently in the papyri of the Roman period.

29. *P.Frankf.* 5; *P.Hibeh.* 33; *P.Petrie* 3.72b; *SB* 6314–6318.

30. Avogadro 1935, 193.

31. *P.Berl.Möller* 7. A small livestock declaration (probably from the Oxyrhynchite nome) from 8/7 BCE registers some seventy-five sheep to three men (twenty-five per man) who were probably brothers. The first of the three men also registered a goat (*P.IFAO* 1.40). Further examples of joint declarations of sheep flocks and goat herds are found in *P.Oxy.* 2.245 and *SB* 4.7344.

32. Hagedorn conducted a study of the formulations characteristic for every nome, but the paucity of source material means that we can only reach reliable conclusions for three nomes: the Oxyrhynchite, Arsinoite, and Hermopolite. The standard formulation for the Oxyrhynchite nome (for which we have the most data) was: so-and-so owns so many sheep and so many goats with their lambs and kids, which need to be grazed around the village so-and-so and throughout the nome; this is to be performed by the shepherd so-and-so, who is registered in the village so-and-so (Hagedorn 1976, 159). The formula applied in the Arsinoite nome: "so-and-so owns so many sheep and goats with their lambs and kids, which I will also graze on other pastures, wherever I wish to go (within the nome) and which will mix with other sheep; their shepherd is so-and-so" (Hagedorn 1976, 160). Hagedorn reproduces the formulation prevalent in the Hermopolite nome as: the grazing area is the whole area (in the nome or toparchy), currently as pasture, for which I pay so much tax due in the toparchy. Under the shepherd so-and-so" (Hagedorn 1976, 164).

33. In one case from 8/9 CE, Ptollis, the owner of the animals, also tended his neighbor's animals (*P.Berl.Möller* 7 from 8/9 CE). Petermouthis from Theadelphia owned a number of animals, which he looked after himself together with his neighbor in the Arsinoite nome (*P.Corn.* 15 from 128/9 CE). Lykos from Euhemeria in the Arsinoite nome was also the owner of the animals he tended (*P.Alex.Giss.* 4 from 140 CE).

34. For the village Theadelphia see Chapter II, pp. 21–23.

35. Schwartz 1964; Rathbone 1991, 202–206, 209–211.

36. The shepherds mentioned in the papyri were often drawn from the same village as the owner of the animals (*P.Oxy.* 55.3778, *P.Oxy.* 55.3779), or at least from the same toparchs, a few miles from their pasture land (*P.Oxy.* 2.350), but some also came from other villages in the nome (*P.Princ.* 2.24; *P.Ross. Georg.* 2.13) or from different nomes to their employer and separated by a journey on foot of several days (*P.Oxy.* 2.352).

37. The προβατοκτηνοτρόφος is the trader or breeder: he owns the animals, the care of which he entrusts to a shepherd (*P.Mich.* 5.228).

38. *P.Heid.* 7.394 (Moithymis in the Memphite nome) from 214 BCE.

39. Hom. *Od.* 4.413: Proteus as a herder of the seals of Poseidon; Soph. *Oed. Tyr.* 1118: shepherd of Laios; Theocr. *Id.* 9.29.

40. John 10:12.
41. *P.Cair.Masp.* 1.67112; *P.Cair.Zen.* 3.59340 from 246 BCE; *P.Lond.* 3.851; *P. Strasb.* 1.24 from 118 CE; *SB* 5.8087 from 279 CE.
42. Rathbone 1991, 206. The *poimēn* also leased land on which to graze his own animals (e.g. *P.Cair.Masp.* 1.67112), whereas a hired hand would not do this. This differentiation appears not to have been possible in Latin: while *pastor* remains the general designation for the shepherds of small animals, *opilio/upilio* was the name applied to the herders of sheep (Virg. *Ecl.* 10.19).
43. Luke 2:8: Καὶ ποιμένες ἦσαν ἐν τῇ χώρᾳ τῇ αὐτῇ ἀγραυλοῦντες καὶ φυλάσσοντες φυλακὰς τῆς νυκτὸς ἐπὶ τὴν ποίμνην αὐτῶν; *et pastores erant in regione eadem vigilantes et custodientes vigilias noctis supra gregem suum.*
44. A papyrus from late second-century Theadelphia tells of the shepherd (*poimēn*) Kiapis, referred to as *apator*, who can only be identified by the name of his mother Thakautos (*BGU* 9.1900 from 196 to 198 CE).
45. *P.Lond.* 3.1171 from 8 BCE.
46. Varro *Rust.* 2.10; see Keenan 1989, 187 n. 51.
47. In *P.Oxy.* 1.245 the shepherd is the son of one of the three owners. In *P.Oxy.* 2.356 it is also the son of the owner who tends the fifty sheep and seven goats belonging to his father. The biblical David was the youngest of eight sons and tended his father's animals (1 Sam. 16:11); the seven daughters of the Priest of Midian watered their father's sheep (2 Ex. 2:16–18).
48. *P.Oxy.* 38.2850 from 29 CE.
49. *P.Oxy.* 2.351: διὰ νομέως Νικοστράτου τοῦ . . . εὐρίος, ἀφηλίκου. The two sons of sheep owners who each watched over sheep belonging to their father and to some belonging to another owner may well have still been teenagers (*P.Oxy.* 1.245; *P.Oxy.* 2.356). Symeon the Stylite, born *ca.* 390 CE in Sis (now Kozan in Turkey), grew up tending the sheep of his father. Theodoret reports on Symeon's childhood: "There is a village lying on the border between our region and Cilicia; they call it Sisa. Originating from this village, he was taught by his parents first to shepherd animals, so that in this respect too he might be comparable to those great men the patriarch Jacob, the chaste Joseph, the lawgiver Moses, the king and prophet David, the prophet Micah and the inspired men of their kind. Once when there was much snow and the sheep were compelled to stay indoors, he took advantage of the respite to go with his parents to the house of God" (Theod. *Hist. rel.* 26.2 [transl. Price 1985]).
50. See Kloppenborg 2010, 50, especially n. 11.
51. Varro *Rust.* 2.3.9.
52. Varro *Rust.* 2.10.
53. *P.Lond.* 3.1171.
54. 1 Pet. 5:2–4.

55. Comparing sheep and goats, Varro writes: "The care of this animal in the matter of feeding is about the same as that of the sheep, though each has certain peculiarities; thus, the goat prefers wooded glades to meadows, as it eats eagerly the field bushes and crops the undergrowth on cultivated land. Indeed, their name *capra* is derived from *carpere*, to crop" (*Rust.* 2.3.6–7 [transl. Hooper and Ash 1934]).

56. Virg. *Ecl.* 1.78.

57. Matt. 25:32. A papyrus in the Dioscorus archive from the late sixth century records the goatherd Jacob (δ(ιὰ) Ἰακυβίο(υ) [α]ἰγοβόσκο(υ)) who hands a herd of thirty-one goats over to the shepherd Apollos (Ἀπολλῶτι ποιμ(ένι)) (*P.Cair.Masp.* 2.67141.6 V). The herd was composed of eighteen large goats belonging to Jacob, seven small goats belonging to Jacob's father, and six kids. The different occupational titles ascribed to the keepers of the two herds is remarkable. Jacob appears to have specialized in goat breeding, while Apollos to have tended sheep and goats. Keenan (1989, 180 n. 20) does not comment on the divergent terms applied to the shepherds and views all thirty-one goats handed over as a single herd.

58. Postgate 1975; Van De Mieroop 1993; Van Driel 1993; Matthews and Benjamin 1995.

59. Ezek. 34:11–16: "For thus says the Lord God: I myself will search for my sheep, and will seek them out. As shepherds seek out their flocks when they are among their scattered sheep, so I will seek out my sheep. I will rescue them from all the places to which they have been scattered on a day of clouds and thick darkness. I will bring them out from the peoples and gather them from the countries, and will bring them into their own land; and I will feed them on the mountains of Israel, by the watercourses, and in all the inhabited parts of the land. I will feed them with good pasture, and the mountain heights of Israel shall be their pasture; there they shall lie down in good grazing land, and they shall feed on rich pasture on the mountains of Israel. I myself will be the shepherd of my sheep, and I will make them lie down, says the Lord God. I will seek the lost, and I will bring back the strayed, and I will bind up the injured, and I will strengthen the weak, but the fat and the strong I will destroy. I will feed them with justice."

60. Columella 7.3.26.

61. Virg. *Ecl.* 1.50.

62. Virg. *Ecl.* 1.20–21.

63. Columella 7.3.16. Sheep normally lamb in the fall. In her article on the declarations of small livestock, Balconi (1988, 47–50) assumed that Egyptian sheep lambed twice a year, in March/April and then again in October/November (cf. Avogadro 1935).

64. Isa. 40:11: "He shall feed his flock like a shepherd: he shall gather the lambs with his arm, and carry them in his bosom, and shall gently lead those that are with young." See also Virg. *Ecl.* 1.14–15.

65. Calp. *Ecl.* 5.39–42.

66. 1 Sam. 24:3; Zeph. 2:6; Luke 2:8.

67. See Varro *Rust.* 2.10.6; Calp. *Ecl.* 2.60.

68. Ezek. 34:14; John 10:1–3.

69. John 10:7.

70. Gen. 31:39; Luke 2:8.

71. Varro *Rust.* 2.10.3.

72. *P.Cair.Masp.* 1.67001; 1.67090; 3.67328. Keenan (1989) assumes that shepherds had long performed this role in previous centuries and that the arrangement was merely formalized in the early sixth century.

73. Soph. *Oed. Tyr.* 1110–1185.

74. Dio 6.20. This association of shepherds and masturbation was by no means confined to the ancients: an eighteenth-century directive issued by the regional authorities in Heiligenberg (Oberallgäu) remarked that shepherds and other boys would have to be given a strict talking-to in this regard (Maul 2013, 26).

75. For example *SB* 18.13320, a sixth-century papyrus from Aphrodito in the Antaiopolite nome, which refers to the progeny of the shepherd Andreas. It is striking that, in registers of names, frequently the only man to have his occupation expressly noted next to his name is the herdsman. See *P.Princ.* 1.10 from Philadelphia (Arsinoite) from 34 BCE: col. II, l. 21: Onnophris son of Horos, cowherd; col. IV, l. 15: Heracles, the son of Horion, shepherd; col. IV, l. 25: Apynchis, son of Mysthas, Swineherd; *P.Ross.Georg.* 4.21 from Aphrodito (Antaiopolite) from the early eighth century CE: Victor, the son of Marcus, shepherd.

76. Virg. *Ecl.* 1.32–35.

77. Virg. *Ecl.* 1.80–81.

78. Virg. *Ecl.* 1.68.

79. 1 Cor. 9:7.

80. *P.Lond.* 3.1171 from 8 BCE.

81. For a monthly wage in the third century BCE, see *PSI* 4.368 (Philadelphia) from 250/49 BCE, from the Zenon archive.

82. *SB* 20.14525.

83. *SB* 22.15339 (Arsinoite) from 271 CE.

84. Hengstl 1979.

85. *P.Oxy.* 1.74; *P.Oxy.* 12.1458; *P.Amh.* 1.73; *BGU* 1.133.

86. *PSI* 4.377 from 250/49 BCE; *P.Cair.Zen.* 3.59328 from 248 BCE; *P.Cair.Zen.* 3.59422 from the third century BCE; *P.Amst.* 1.41, col. 1 = SB 12.11248 from 10

BCE; *SB* 5.8086 from 268 CE; *P.Strasb.* 1.30 from 276 CE; *P.Thead.* 8 from 306 CE; *P.Princ.* 3.151 from 341 CE.

87. *SB* 20.14525.

88. Keenan 1989, 186–187.

89. *P.Cair.Masp.* 1.67001.

90. *P.Col.* 7.171 from June 6, 324 CE; see Bryen 2013, 270, no. 16.

91. *P.Cair.Isid.* 78 from January 30, 324 CE; see also *P.Cair.Isid.* 79.

92. For example *P.Cair.Masp.* 1.67087; see Keenan 1985, 245–259.

93. *P.Cair.Isid.* 78.

94. *P.Ryl.* 2.138.

95. Sheep destroyed twenty artabas of young *aracus* (*P.Ryl.* 2.143); elsewhere, twelve artabas of barley were destroyed (*P.Ryl.* 2.147), five artabas of vegetable seedlings (*P.Ryl.* 2.149), and an entire olive grove (*P.Ryl.* 2.152).

96. Herz 1988, 221–241; Grünewald 1999, 57; Kloppenborg 2010, 61–62.

97. *CTh* 9.30.2; *CTh* 9.30.5.

98. *CTh* 9.31.1 from 409 CE.

99. See also Kloppenborg 2010, 61–62.

100. *P.Mich.* 5.228 (47 CE).

101. If the plaintiff Thouonis was a shepherd, he lived with his wife in the Arsinoite nome, while he worked for the sheep breeder Bentetis in the Oxyrhynchite nome.

Bibliography

Adams, C. 2001, "'There and back again': getting around in Roman Egypt," in C. Adams and R. Laurence, eds., *Travel and Geography in the Roman Empire*. London and New York.

Adams, C. 2007, *Land Transport in Roman Egypt: A Study of Economics and Administration in a Roman Province*. Oxford.

Alföldy, G. 1997, "Un celebre frammento epigrafico Tiburtino anonymo (P. Sulpicius Quirinius)," in I. di Stefano Manzella, ed., *Le iscrizioni dei cristiani in Vaticano: Materiali e contributi scientifici per una mostra epigrafica*. Vatican City: 199–208.

Arzt-Grabner, P. 2003, *Philemon*, Papyrologische Kommentare zum Neuen Testament 1, ed. P. Arzt-Grabner, J. S. Kloppenborg, and M. Pesce. Göttingen.

Arzt-Grabner, P. 2006, *1. Korinther*, Papyrologische Kommentare zum Neuen Testament 2, ed. P. Arzt-Grabner, J. S. Kloppenborg, and M. Pesce. Göttingen.

Arzt-Grabner, P. 2010, "Papyrologische und Neutestamentliche Wissenschaft: Einige Beispiele aus neueren Papyruseditionen," in P. Arzt-Grabner and C. M. Kreinecker, eds., *Light from the East. Papyrologische Kommentare zum Neuen Testament*. Wiesbaden: 11–26.

Arzt-Grabner, P. and C. M. Kreinecker, eds. 2010, *Light from the East. Papyrologische Kommentare zum Neuen Testament*. Wiesbaden.

Arzt-Grabner, P. with R. E. Kritzer, 2014, *2. Korinther*, Papyrologische Kommentare zum Neuen Testament 4, ed. P. Arzt-Grabner, J. S. Kloppenborg, and M. Pesce. Göttingen.

Assmann, J. 2013, "Aus Ägypten habe ich meinen Sohn gerufen," in Th. Söding, ed., *Zu Bethlehem geboren?* Freiburg: 131–142.

Avogadro, S. 1935, "Le ἀπογραφαί di proprietà dell'Egitto greco-romano," *Aegyptus* 15: 131–206.

Bagnall, R. S. 1982, "Religious conversion and onomastic change in Early Byzantine Egypt," *Bulletin of the American Association of Papyrologists* 19: 105–124.

Bagnall, R. S. 1985a, "Agricultural productivity and taxation in Later Roman Egypt," *Transactions of the American Philological Association* 115: 289–308.

Bagnall, R. S. 1985b, "The camel, the wagon and the donkey in Later Roman Egypt," *Bulletin of the American Association of Papyrologists* 22: 1–6.

Bagnall, R. S. 1987, "Conversion and onomastics: a reply," *Zeitschrift für Papyrologie und Epigraphik* 69: 243–250.

Bagnall, R. S. 1991, "The beginnings of the Roman census in Egypt," *Greek, Roman and Byzantine Studies* 32: 255–265.

Bagnall, R. S. 1992, "The periodicity and collection of the chrysargyrion," *Tyche* 7: 15–17.

Bagnall, R. S. 1993, *Egypt in Late Antiquity*. Princeton, NJ.

Bagnall, R. S. 1995, *Reading Papyri, Writing Ancient History*. London and New York.

Bagnall, R. S. 2000, "P.Oxy. 4527 and the Antonine plague in Egypt: death or flight?," *Journal of Roman Archaeology* 13: 288–292.

Bagnall, R. S. 2009, *Early Christian Books in Egypt*. Princeton, NJ, and Oxford.

Bagnall, R. S. and R. Cribiore 2006, *Women's Letters from Ancient Egypt. 300 BC–AD 800*. Ann Arbor, Mich.

Bagnall, R. S. and B. W. Frier 2006, *The Demography of Roman Egypt*, 2nd edn. Cambridge.

Bagnall, R. S., R. Casagrande-Kim, A. Ersoy, C. Tanriver, and B. Yolaçan, eds. 2016, *Graffiti from the Basilica in the Agora of Smyrna*. New York.

Bähr, C. 1898, *Herodot – Neun Bücher zur Geschichte*. Berlin.

Balconi, C. 1984, "'Apographai probaton kai aigon' dell'età di Tiberio e Caligola (*P.Oxy.* 354; 356; 352; 355)," *Aegyptus* 64: 35–60.

Balconi, C. 1988, "Bis gravidae pecudes. Dichiarazioni di ovini demotiche con annotazione greca," *Aegyptus* 68: 47–50.

Baltrusch, E. 2012, *Herodes. König im Heiligen Land. Eine Biographie*. Munich.

Bar-Ilan, M. 1992, "Illiteracy in the Land of Israel in the first centuries C.E.," in S. Fishbane et al., *Essays in the Social Scientific Study of Judaism and Jewish Society*, vol. 11. Hoboken, NJ: 46–61.

Barker, D. 2011, "The dating of New Testament papyri," *New Testament Studies* 57: 571–582.

Barnes, T. D. 1989, "Trajan and the Jews," *Journal of Jewish Studies* 40: 145–162.

Bastiani, G. 1969, "La carriera di Sarapion alias Apollonianus," *Aegyptus* 49: 149–182.

Bauer, W. 1934, *Rechtgläubigkeit und Ketzerei im ältesten Christentum*. Tübingen.

Bauer, W. 1971, *Orthodoxy and Heresy in Earliest Christianity*, trans. and ed. R. Kraft and G. Krodel. Philadelphia, Penn.

Baumkamp, E. 2014, *Kommunikation in der Kirche des 3. Jahrhunderts. Bischöfe und Gemeinden zwischen Konflikt und Konsens im Imperium Romanum*. Tübingen.

Bausi, A. and A. Camplani 2013, "New Ethiopic documents for the history of Christian Egypt," *Zeitschrift für Antikes Christentum* 17: 215–247.

Bell, H. I. 1944, "Evidences of Christianity in Egypt during the Roman period," *Harvard Theological Review* 37: 185–208.

Bernett, M. 2007, *Der Kaiserkult in Judäa unter den Herodiern und Römern. Untersuchungen zur politischen und religiösen Geschichte Judäas von 30 v. bis 66 n.Chr*. Tübingen.

Bickermann, E. 1976, 1980, 1986, *Studies in Jewish Christian History*. 3 vols. Leiden.

Bienert, W. A. 1978, *Dionysius von Alexandria*. Berlin.

Bienert, D. C., J. Jeska and T. Witulski, eds. 2008, *Paulus und die antike Welt. Beiträge zur zeit- und religionsgeschichtlichen Erforschung des paulinischen Christentums. Festgabe für Dietrich-Alex Koch zum 65. Geburtstag.* Göttingen.

Blumell, L. H. 2008, "Beware of bandits! Banditry and land travel in the Roman Empire," *Journeys* 8: 1–20.

Blumell, L. H. 2010a, "A note on Dionysius of Alexandria's letter to Novatian in light of third-century papyri," *Zeitschrift für Antike und Christentum* 17: 356–361.

Blumell, L. H. 2010b, "Is *P.Oxy.* XLII 3057 the earliest Christian letter?," in T. J. Kraus and T. Nicklas, eds., *Early Christian Manuscripts. Examples of Applied Method and Research.* Leiden: 97–113.

Blumell, L. H. 2011, "Christians on the move in late antique Oxyrhynchus," in P. A. Harland, ed., *Travel and Religion in Antiquity.* Waterloo, Ont.: 235–254.

Blumell, L. H. 2012, *Lettered Christians: Christians, Letters, and Late Antique Oxyrhynchus.* Leiden and Boston, Mass.

Blumell, L. H. 2013, "The Date of P.Oxy. XLIII 3119 the Deputy Prefect Lucius Mussius Aemilianus, and the Persecution of Christians by Valerian and Gallienus," *Zeitschrift für Papyrologie und Epigraphik* 186: 111–113.

Blumell, L. H. 2014, "P. Birmingham inv. 317: an addendum to the fourth-century bishops of Oxyrhynchus?," *Journal of Juristic Papyrology* 44: 83–92.

Blumell, L. H. and T. A. Wayment, eds. 2015, *Christian Oxyrhynchus: Texts, Documents, and Sources.* Waco, Tex.

Böttrich, C. and J. Herzer, eds. 2007, *Josephus und das Neue Testament. Wechselseitige Wahrnehmungen. II. Internationales Symposium zum Corpus Judaeo-Hellenisticum. 25.–28. Mai 2006, Greifswald.* Tübingen.

Bowman, A. K. 1971, *The Town Councils of Roman Egypt.* Toronto.

Bowman, A. K. 1991, "Literacy in the Roman Empire: mass and mode," in J. H. Humphrey, ed., *Literacy in the Roman World.* Journal of Roman Archaeology, supplementary series 3. Ann Arbor, Mich.: 119–131.

Bowman, A. K. 1996, *Egypt after the Pharaohs.* London.

Bowman, A. K. 2005, "Egypt from Septimius Severus to the death of Constantine," in *The Cambridge Ancient History XII²: The Crisis of Empire, A.D. 193–337.* Cambridge: 313–326.

Bowman, A. K. 2013, "Agricultural production in Egypt," in A. K. Bowman and A. Wilson, eds., *The Roman Agricultural Economy: Organization, Investment, and Production.* Oxford: 219–254.

Bradley, K. R. 1991, *Discovering the Roman Family: Studies in Roman Social History.* Oxford and New York.

Braunert, H. 1957, "Der römische Provinzialzensus," *Historia: Zeitschrift für Alte Geschichte* 6: 192–214.

Braunert, H. 1964, *Die Binnenwanderung – Studien zur Sozialgeschichte Ägyptens in der Ptolemäer- und Kaiserzeit.* Bonn.

Bremmer, J. 2001, "The Acts of Thomas. Place, date and women," in J. Bremmer, ed., *The Apocryphal Acts of Thomas.* Leuven: 74–90.

Brodersen, K. 2016, *Aetheria/Egeria: Reise in das Heilige Land.* Lat./German. Berlin and Boston, Mass.

Broek, R. van den 1996, *Studies in Gnosticism and Alexandrian Christianity*. Leiden, New York and Cologne.

Brown, P. 1988, *Power and Persuasion in Late Antiquity. Towards a Christian Empire*. Madison, Wis.

Brunt, P. A. 1971, *Italian Manpower 225 BC–AD 14*. Oxford.

Bruun, C. 2007, "The Antonine plague and the 'Third-Century Crisis,'" in O. Hekster, G. de Kleijn, and D. Slootjes, eds., *Crises and the Roman Empire: Proceedings of the Seventh Workshop of the International Network Impact of Empire* (Nijmegen, June 20–24, 2006). Leiden and Boston, Mass.: 201–17.

Bryen, A. 2013, *Violence in Roman Egypt: A Study in Legal Interpretation. Empire and After*. Philadelphia, Penn.

Buchholz, H.-G. 2012, *Erkennungs-, Rang- und Würdezeichen*. Göttingen.

Calderini, R. 1950, "Gli agrammatoi nell'Egitto greco-romano," *Aegyptus* 30: 14–41.

Callon, C. and J. S. Kloppenborg 2010, "The parable of the shepherd and the transformation of pastoral discourse," *Early Christianity* 1: 218–260.

Casson, L. 1974, *Travel in the Ancient World*. London.

Cenival, F. de 1977, *Les associations religieuses en Égypte d'après les documents démotiques*. Paris.

Choat, M. 2006, *Belief and Cult in Fourth Century Papyri*. Turnhout, Belgium.

Choat, M. 2012, "Christianity," in C. Riggs, ed., *The Oxford Handbook of Roman Egypt*. Oxford: 474–492.

Choat, M. 2019, "Egypt's Role in the rise of Christianity, Monasticism and Regional Schisms," in K. Vandorpe, ed., *Blackwell Companion to Greek, Roman, and Byzantine Egypt*. Chichester, England: (in press).

Choat, M. and A. Nobbs 2001–2005, "Monotheistic formulae of belief in Greek letters on papyrus from the second to the fourth century," *Journal of Greco-Roman Christianity and Judaism* 2: 36–51.

Choat, M., J. Dijkstra, C. Haas, and W. Tabbernee 2014, "The world of the Nile," in W. Tabbernee, ed., *Early Christianity in Contexts. An Exploration across Cultures and Continents*. Grand Rapids, Mich.: 181–209.

Clarysse, W. and D. Thompson 2006, *Counting the People in Hellenistic Egypt*, vol. I, *Population Registers (P. Count)*. vol. II, *Historical Studies*. Cambridge.

Claytor, W. G. 2012, "Inn," in R. S. Bagnall, C. Champion, A. Erskine, and S. R. Huebner, eds., *Encyclopedia of Ancient History* vol. VI. Oxford: 3465–3466.

Claytor, W. G. and R. S. Bagnall 2015, "The beginnings of the Roman provincial census: a new declaration from 3 BCE," *Greek, Roman and Byzantine Studies* 55: 637–653.

Cleveland Coxe, A. 1886, *Ante-Nicene Fathers*, vol. VIII, *The Twelve Patriarchs, Excerpts and Epistles, The Clementina, Apocrypha, Decretals, Memoirs of Edessa and Syriac Documents, Remains of the First Ages*, ed. A. Roberts and James Donaldson. New York.

Cohen, S. J. D. 1993, *The Jewish Family in Antiquity*. Providence, RI.

Cohick, L. 2009, *Women in the World of the Earliest Christians. Illuminating Ancient Ways of Life*. Grand Rapids, Mich.

Cole, S. G. 1981, "Could Greek women read and write?," in H. P. Foley, ed., *Reflections of Women in Antiquity*. Philadelphia: 219–245.

Constable, O. R. 2003, *Housing the Stranger in the Mediterranean World. Lodging, Trade, and Travel in Late Antiquity and the Middle Ages*. Cambridge.

Corbier, M. 1988, "Intervention," in C. R. Whittaker, ed., *Pastoral Economies in Classical Antiquity*. Cambridge: 216–218.

Cotton, H. M. 1999, "Some aspects of the Roman administration of Judaea/Palaestina," in W. Eck, ed., *Lokale Autonomie und römische Ordnungsmacht in den kaiserlichen Provinzen vom 1. bis 3. Jahrhundert*. Munich: 75–91.

Cribiore, R. 1996, *Writing, Teachers, and Students in Graeco-Roman Egypt*. Atlanta, Ga.

Cribiore, R. 2001, *Gymnastics of the Mind: Greek Education in Hellenistic and Roman Egypt*. Princeton, NJ.

Cribiore, R. 2002, "The women in the Apollonios Archive and their use of literacy," in H. Melaerts and L. Mooren, eds., *Le rôle et le statut de la femme en Égypte hellénistique, romaine et byzantine*. Leuven: 149–166.

Cribiore, R., P. Davoli, and D. M. Ratzan 2008, "A teacher's dipinto from Trimithis (Dakhleh Oasis)," *Journal of Roman Archaeology* 21: 171–191.

Cyrus, Theodoret von 1926, *Mönchsgeschichte. Aus dem Griechischen übersetzt von K. Gutberlet*. Munich.

Davies, W. D. and E. P. Sanders 1999, "Jesus: from the Jewish point of view," in W. Horbury, W. D. Davies, and J. Sturdy, eds., *The Cambridge History of Judaism*, vol. 111, *The Early Roman Period*. Cambridge: 618–677.

Dawes, E. and N. H. Baynes 1948, *Three Byzantine Saints: Contemporary Biographies of St. Daniel the Stylite, St. Theodore of Sykeon and St. John the Almsgiver*. London.

De Boer, E. A. 2004, *The Gospel of Mary: Beyond a Gnostic and a Biblical Mary Magdalene*. London.

Depauw, M. and W. Clarysse 2013, "How Christian was fourth-century Egypt? Onomastic perspectives on conversion," *Vigiliae Christianae* 67: 407–435.

Dickey, E. 2004, "Literal and extended use of kinship terms in documentary papyri," *Mnemosyne* 57: 131–176.

Duncan-Jones, R. P. 1996, "The impact of the Antonine plague," *Journal of Roman Archaeology* 9: 108–136.

Eck, W. 2007, *Rom und Judaea*. Tübingen.

Eck, W. 2016, "s.v. Sulpicius II 13 (P. S. Quirinius)," *Der Neue Pauly*, http://refe renceworks.brillonline.com/entries/der-neue-pauly/sulpicius-e1125490 (accessed January 19, 2016).

Eckerman, C. 2011, "Apprenticeship contract for carpentry," *Bulletin of the American Society of Papyrologists* 48: 47–49.

Eisen, U. 1996, *Kirchliche Amtsträgerinnen im frühen Christentum*. Göttingen.

Elm, S. 1994, *"Virgins of God." The Making of Asceticism in Late Antiquity*. Oxford.

Elsner, J. and I. Rutherford, eds. 2010, *Pilgrimage in Graeco-Roman and Early Christian Antiquity: Seeing the Gods*. Oxford.

Engemann, J. 1991, "Hirt," in *Reallexikon für Antike und Christentum* 15. Stuttgart: c. 577–607.

Epp, E. J. 1991, "New Testament papyrus manuscripts and letter carrying in Greco-Roman times," in B. A. Pearson, G. W. E. Nickelsburg, and N. R. Petersen, eds., *The Future of Early Christianity* (essays in honor of H. Koester). Minneapolis, Minn.: 35–56.

Erlemann, K., K. L. Noethlichs, K. Scherberich, and J. Zangenberg, eds. 2004–2007, *Neues Testament und Antike Kultur*, 5 vols. Neukirchen-Vluyn.

Eshel, E. and D. R. Edwards 2004, "Language and writing in early Roman Galilee: social location of a potter's abecedary from Khirbet Qana," in D. R. Edwards, ed., *Religion and Society in Roman Palestine. Old Questions, New Approaches.* London and New York: 49–55.

Evans, C. F. 1973, "Tertullian's references to Sentius Saturninus and the Lukan census," *Journal of Theological Studies* 24: 24–39.

Feltoe, C. L. 1904, *ΔΙΟΝΥΣΙΟΥ ΛΕΙΨΑΝΑ. The Letters and other Remains of Dionysius of Alexandria.* Cambridge.

Ferguson, J. 1974, *Clement of Alexandria.* New York.

Fewster, P. 2002, "Bilingualism in Roman Egypt," in J. N. Adams, M. Janse, and S. Swain, eds., *Bilingualism in Ancient Society: Language Contact and the Written Text.* Oxford: 220–245.

Foertmeyer, V. A. 1989, "Tourism in Greco-Roman Egypt," dissertation, Princeton University.

Frankfurter, D. 2014, "Onomastic statistics and the Christianization of Egypt: a response to Depauw and Clarysse," *Vigiliae Christianae* 68: 284–289.

Frayn, J. M. 1984, *Sheep Rearing and the Wool Trade in Italy during the Roman Period.* Liverpool.

French, D. H. 1994, "Acts and the Roman Roads of Asia Minor," in D. W. Gill and C. Gempf, eds., *The Book of Acts in its Graeco-Roman Setting*, vol. 11. Grand Rapids, Mich.:49–58.

Freu, C. 2011, "Apprendre et exercer un métier dans l'Égypte romaine (Ier–VIe siècles après J.-C.)," in N. Tran and N. Monteix, eds., *Les savoirs professionnels des hommes de métier romains.* Naples: 27–40.

Frier, B. W. 2000, "Demography," in A. K. Bowman, P. Garnsey, and D. Rathbone, eds., *The Cambridge Ancient History*, vol. XI, *The High Empire, AD 70–192*, 2nd edn. Cambridge: 787–816.

Gelzer, H. 1893, *Leontios' von Neapolis Leben des Heiligen Johannes des Barmherzigen Erzbischofs von Alexandrien.* Freiburg and Leipzig.

Geraci, G. 1989, "L'Egitto romano della storiografia moderna," in G. Geraci and L. Criscuolo, eds., *Egitto e storia antica dall'ellenismo all'età Araba: Bilancio di un confronto.* Bologna: 55–88.

Ghedini, G. 1923, *Lettere Christiane dai papyri greci del III e IV secolo.* Milan.

Giebel, M., ed. 1980, *Res gestae. Tatenbericht (Monumentum Ancyranum). Lateinisch, griechisch und deutsch.* Stuttgart.

Goodman, M. 1997, *The Roman World 44 BC–AD 180.* London.

Grenfell, B. P. and A. S. Hunt 1899, "Graeco-Roman branch: excavations for papyri in the fayum; the position of Lake Moeris," *Egypt Exploration Fund. Archaeological Report*: 8–15.

Grenfell, B. P. and A. S. Hunt 2007, "Excavations at Oxyrhynchus (1896–1907)," in: A. K. Bowman, R. A. Coles, N. Gonis, D. Obbink, and P. Parsons eds. *Oxyrhynchus: A City and its Texts*. London, 345–368.

Griggs, C. W. 1991, *Early Egyptian Christianity: From its Origins to 451 CE*. Leiden, New York, and Cologne.

Groag, E. 1924, "Prosopographische Beiträge, VII. M. Plautius Silvanus," *Jahreshefte des österreichischen archäologischen Instituts in Wien* 21–22: 445–478.

Grünewald, T. 1999, *Bandits in the Roman Empire: Myth and Reality*. London and New York.

Günther, L.-M. 2005, *Herodes der Große*. Darmstadt.

Günther, L.-M. 2009, *Herodes und Jerusalem*. Stuttgart.

Haas, C. 1997, *Alexandria in Late Antiquity: Topography and Social Conflict*. Baltimore, Md. and London.

Hagedorn, D. 1976, "Zum Formular der Kleinviehdeklarationen," *Zeitschrift für Papyrologie und Epigraphik* 21: 159–165, 165–167.

Haines-Eitzen, K. 2000, *Guardians of Letters: Literacy, Power, and the Transmission of Early Christian Literature*. New York and Oxford.

Hansen, M. H. 1986, *Demography and Democracy. The Number of Athenian Citizens in the Fourth Century BC*. Herning, Denmark.

Hanson, A. E. 1989, "Declarations of sheep and goats from the Oxyrhynchite nome," *Aegyptus* 69: 61–69.

Hanson, A. E. 1991, "Ancient illiteracy," in J. H. Humphrey, ed., *Literacy in the Roman World*. Ann Arbor, Mich.: 159–198.

Hanson, A. E. 2005, "The widow Babatha and the poor orphan boy," in R. Katzoff and D. Schaps, eds., *Law in the Documents of the Judaean Desert*. Leiden: 85–104.

Harmless, W. 2004, *Desert Christians – An Introduction to the Literature of Early Monasticsm*. Oxford and New York.

Harper, K. 2011, *Slavery in the Late Roman World, AD 275–425*. Cambridge.

Harper, K. 2017, *The Fate of Rome. Climate, Disease, and the End of an Empire*. Princeton, NJ.

Harris, W. V. 1989, *Ancient Literacy*. Cambridge, Mass.

Harrison, J. 2003, *Paul's Language of Grace in its Graeco-Roman Context*. Tübingen.

Hengel, M. 2011, *Die Zeloten. Untersuchungen zur jüdischen Freiheitsbewegung in der Zeit von Herodes I. bis 70 n.Chr*. Tübingen.

Hengstl, J. 1979, "Die *athanatos*-Klausel," in J. Bingen and G. Nachtergael, eds., *Actes du XV Congrès international de papyrologie*, vol. IV, *Papyrologie documentaire*. Brussels: 231–239.

Herlihy, D. and C. Klapisch-Zuber 1985, *Tuscans and their Families: A Study of the Florentine Catasto of 1427*. New Haven, Conn.

Herz, P. 1988, "*Latrocinium* und Viehdiebstahl. Soziale Spannungen und Strafrecht in römischer Zeit," in I. Weiler, ed., *Soziale Randgruppen und Außenseiter*. Graz: 221–241.

Hezser, C. 2001, *Jewish Literacy in Roman Palestine*. Tübingen.

Hobson, D. 1979, "Sheep grazing on the estate of Germanicus," *Zeitschrift für Papyrologie und Epigraphik* 33: 227–228.

Hobson, D. 1984, "Agricultural land at Soknopaiou Nesos," *Bulletin of the American Association of Papyrologists* 21: 89–109.

Hochspringen, J. P. O. 1984, *Greek and Roman Mechanical Water-lifting Devices: The History of a Technology*. Toronto.

Hochspringen, J. P. O. 2000, "Water-lifting," in Ö. Wikander, ed., *Handbook of Ancient Water Technology, Technology and Change in History*. Leiden: 217–302.

Hombert, M. and C. Préaux 1952, *Recherches sur le recensement dans l'Égypte romaine (Pap.Lugd.Bat. V)*. Leiden.

Hope, C. A. 2012, "s.v. Kellis," in R. S. Bagnall, C. B. Champion, A. Erskine and S. R. Huebner, eds., *Encyclopedia of Ancient History*. Oxford: 3726–3728.

Hopkins, K. 1991, "Conquest by book," in J. H. Humphrey, ed., *Literacy in the Roman World*. Ann Arbor, Mich: 133–158.

Hopkins, K. 1998, "Christian number and its implications," *Journal of Early Christian Studies* 6: 185–226.

Horbury, W. 2014, *Jewish War under Trajan and Hadrian*. Cambridge.

Horsley, G. H. R. 1987, "Name change as an indication of religious conversion," *Atomen* 34: 1–17.

Howe, T. 2008, *Pastoral Politics. Animals, Agriculture and Society in Ancient Greece*. Claremont, Calif.

Huebner, S. R. 2005, *Der Klerus in der Gesellschaft des spätantiken Kleinasiens*. Stuttgart.

Huebner, S. R. 2009a, "Callirhoe's dilemma: remarriage and stepfathers in the Graeco-Roman East," in S. R. Huebner and D. M. Ratzan, eds., *Growing up Fatherless in Antiquity*. Cambridge: 61–82.

Huebner, S. R. 2009b, "Female circumcision as *rite de passage* in Egypt – continuity through the millennia?," *Journal of Egyptian History* 2: 149–171.

Huebner, S. R. 2010, "Household and family in the Roman East and West," in B. Rawson, ed., *A Companion to Families in the Greek and Roman Worlds*. Oxford: 73–91.

Huebner, S. R. 2013, *The Family in Roman Egypt: A Comparative Approach to Intergenerational Solidarity and Conflict*. Cambridge.

Huebner, S. R. 2016, "Egypt as part of the Mediterranean? Domestic space and household structures in Roman Egypt," in S. R. Huebner and G. Nathan, eds., *Mediterranean Families in Antiquity: Households, Extended Families, and Domestic Space*. Oxford: 154–173.

Huebner, S. R. 2018, "Frauen und Schriftlichkeit im römischen Ägypten," in A. Kolb, ed., *Literacy in Ancient Everyday Life – Schriftlichkeit im antiken Alltag*. Berlin: 163–178.

Huebner, S. R. 2019a, "The Basel papyrus collection and its history," in S. R. Huebner, W. G. Claytor, I. Marthot, and M. Müller, eds., *Texts from the Basel Papyrus Collection in Greek, Latin, Coptic, Hieratic, and Persian (P.Bas. II)*. Berlin (in press).

Huebner, S. R. 2019b, "*P.Bas.* II.43 R," in S. R. Huebner, W. G. Claytor, I. Marthot, and M. Müller, eds., *Texts from the Basel Papyrus Collection in Greek, Latin, Coptic, Hieratic, and Persian (P.Bas.II)*. Berlin (in press).

Huebner, S. R. 2019c, "Soter, Sotas, and Dioscorus before the Roman Governor," *Journal of Late Antiquity* 12: 2–24.

Huebner, S. R. forthcoming a "Habitatio: Transfer of Houses and Rights of Residence in Roman Egypt," in C. E. Barrett and J. C. Carrington, eds., *Households of Ptolemaic and Roman Egypt in Context*. Cambridge.

Huebner, S. R. forthcoming b, "The first Christian family of Egypt," in H. Flower and A. Luijendijk, eds., *Subjects of Empire: Political and Cultural Exchange in Imperial Rome*. Cambridge.

Huebner, S. R. forthcoming c, "Χρηστιανὸς ἔστ(ιν): self-identification and formal categorization of the first Christians in Egypt," in M. Brand and E. Scheerlinck, eds., *Late Antique Religion in Practice: Papyri and the Dynamics of Religious Identification*. Cambridge.

Huebner, S. R. and C. Laes, eds. 2019, *The Single Life in the Roman and Later Roman Worlds*. Cambridge.

Hurtado, L. W. 1998, "The origin of the *Nomina Sacra*: a proposal," *Journal of Biblical Literature* 117: 655–673.

Hurtado, L. W. 2003, "P52 (P. Rylands Gr 457) and the *nomina sacra*: method and probability," *Tyndale Bulletin* 54: 1–14.

Jacobson, D. M. and N. Kokkinos, eds. 2009, *Herod and Augustus. Papers Presented at the IJS Conference, 21st–23rd June 2005*. Leiden.

Jakab, A. 2001a, "Denys d'Alexandrie," *Recherches Augustiniennes* 32: 3–37.

Jakab, A. 2001b, *Ecclesia Alexandrina. Evolution sociale et institutionelle du christianisme alexandrine (IIe et IIIe siècles)*. Bonn.

Jones Hall, L. 2004, *Roman Berytus: Beirut in Late Antiquity*. London.

Jones, A. H. M. 1953, "Census records of the Later Roman Empire," *Journal of Roman Studies* 43: 49–64.

Jones, A. H. M. 1964, *The Later Roman Empire, 284–602: A Social Economic and Administrative Survey*. Oxford.

Jördens, A. 2009, *Statthalterliche Verwaltung in der römischen Kaiserzeit. Studien zum praefectus Aegypti*. Stuttgart.

Kaiser, A.-M. 2010, "'Ich bitte Dich, Herr. Habe ihn vor Augen wie mich selbst ...' Empfehlungsbriefe auf Papyrus," in C. Kreuzsaler, B. Palme, and A. Zdiarsky, eds., *Stimmen aus dem Wüstensand. Briefkultur im griechisch-römischen Ägypten*. Vienna: 61–68.

Keenan, J. G. 1985, "Village shepherds and social tension in Byzantine Egypt," *Yale Classical Studies* 28: 245–259.

Keenan, J. G. 1989, "Pastoralism in Roman Egypt," *Bulletin of the American Association of Papyrologists* 26: 175–200.

Keenan, J. G. 2009, "Egypt's special place," in E. P. Cueva, S. N. Byrne, and F. Benda, eds., *Jesuit Education and the Classics*. Newcastle upon Tyne: 17–92.

Kelly, C. 2004, *Ruling the Later Roman Empire*. Cambridge, Mass.

King, K. L. 2003a, *The Gospel of Mary of Magdala: Jesus and the First Woman Apostle*. Santa Rosa, Calif.

King, K. L. 2003b, "Why all the controversy? Mary in the Gospel of Mary," in F. S. Jones, ed., *Which Mary? The Marys of Early Christian Tradition*. Leiden and New York: 53–74.

King, K. L. 2014, "Jesus said to them, 'My wife . . .' A new Coptic gospel papyrus," *Harvard Theological Review* 107: 131–159.

Klauck, H.-J. 2003, *Apocryphal Gospels: An Introduction*. London and New York.

Kloppenborg, J. S. 2006, *The Tenants in the Vineyard: Ideology, Economics, and Agrarian Conflict in Jewish Palestine*. Tübingen.

Kloppenborg, J. S. 2010, "Pastoralism, papyri, and the parable of the shepherd," in P. Arzt-Grabner and C. M. Kreinecker, eds., *Light from the East. Papyrologische Kommentare zum Neuen Testament*. Wiesbaden: 47–70.

Kolb, A. 1997, "Der *cursus publicus* in Ägypten," in B. Kramer, W. Luppe, and H. Maehler, eds., *Akten des 21. Internationalen Papyrologenkongresses*. Leipzig: 533–540.

Kolb, A. 2000, *Transport und Nachrichtentransfer im Römischen Reich*. Berlin.

Kolb, A. 2001, "Transport and communication in the Roman state: the *cursus publicus*," in C. Adams and R. Laurence, eds., *Travel and Geography in the Roman Empire*. London and New York: 95–105.

Kotsifou, C. 2000, "Papyrological evidence of traveling in Byzantine Egypt," in A. McDonald and C. Riggs, eds., *Current Research in Egyptology*. Oxford: 57–64.

Kreinecker, C. M. 2010, "2. Thessaloniker," in P. Arzt-Grabner, J. S. Kloppenborg, and M. Pesce, eds., *Papyrologische Kommentare zum Neuen Testament 3*. Göttingen.

Lane Fox, R. 1986, *Pagans and Christians in the Mediterranean World from the second century AD to the Conversion of Constantine*. London.

Lang, M. 2008, "Das frühe ägyptische Christentum: Quellenlage, Forschungslage und perspektiven," in M. Öhler, W. Pratscher, and M. Lang, eds., *Das ägyptische Christentum im 2. Jahrhundert*. Vienna: 9–43.

Last, R. 2016, *The Pauline Church and the Corinthian Ekklesia: Greco-Roman Associations in Comparative Context*. Cambridge.

Legutko, P. A. 2003, "The letters of Dionysius: Alexandrian and Christian identity in the mid-third century AD," *Ancient World* 34: 27–41.

Lepelley, C. 1998, "Le patronat épiscopal aux IVe et Ve siècles: continuités et ruptures avec le patronat classique," in E. Rebillard and C. Sotinel, eds., *L'évêque dans la cité. Image et autorité*. Paris: 17–33.

Lewis, N. 1982, *The Compulsory Public Services of Roman Egypt*. Florence.

Lewis, N. 1983, *Life in Egypt under Roman Rule*. Oxford.

Lewis, N. 1984, "The Romanity of Roman Egypt: a growing consensus," in *Atti del XVIIº Congresso Internazionale di Papirologia*. Naples: 1077–1084.

Lewis, N. 1989, *The Documents from the Bar Kokhba Period in the Cave of Letters. Greek Papyri (with Aramaic and Nabatean Signatures and Subscriptions)*, ed. Y. Yadin and J. C. Greenfield. Jerusalem.

Liebeschuetz, J. H. W. G. 1972, *Antioch, City and Imperial Administration in the Later Roman Empire*. Oxford.

Littman, R. J. and M. L. Littman 1973, "Galen and the Antonine Plague," *American Journal of Philology* 94: 243–255.

Löhr, W. 2013, "Christliche 'Gnostiker' in Alexandria in zweiten Jahrhundert," in T. Georges, F. Albrecht, and R. Feldmeier, eds., *Alexandria*. Tübingen: 413–433.

López, A. G. 2013, *Shenoute of Atripe and the Uses of Poverty: Rural Patronage, Religious Conflict and Monasticism in Late Antique Egypt*. Berkeley, Calif., Los Angeles, and London.

Lührmann, D. 1988, "Die griechischen Fragmente des Mariaevangeliums *POxy* 3525 und *PRyl* 463," *Novum Testamentum* 30: 321–338.

Luijendijk, A. 2008, *Greetings in the Lord: Early Christians and the Oxyrhynchus Papyri*. Cambridge, Mass.

Luijendijk, A. 2017, "On and beyond duty: Christian clergy at Oxyrhynchus (*c.* 250–400)," in J. Rüpke, R. Gordon, and G. Petridou, eds., *Beyond Priesthood. Religious Entrepreneurs and Innovators in the Roman Empire*. Berlin: 103–128.

Markschies, C. 1992, *Valentinus Gnosticus?: Untersuchungen zur valentinianischen Gnosis mit einem Kommentar zu den Fragmenten Valentins*. Tübingen.

Markschies, C. 2001, *Die Gnosis*. Munich.

Martin, A. 1970, "L'église et la khora égyptienne au IVe siècle," *Revue des Études Augustéennes* 25: 3–26.

Martin, A. 1981, "Aux origines de l'église copte: l'implantation et le développement de christianisme en Egypte (Ie–IVe siècles)," *Revue des Études Anciennes* 83: 35–56.

Martin, A. 1996, *Athanase d'Alexandrie et l'église d'Égypte au IVe siècle (328–373)*. Rome.

Matthews, J. 2006, *The Journey of Theophanes: Travel, Business, and Daily Life in the Roman East*. New Haven, Conn.

Matthews, V. H. and D. C. Benjamin 1993, *Social World of Ancient Israel 1250–587 BCE*. Peabody, Mass.

Maul, H. 2013, *Hirtenleben zwischen Idylle und Wirklichkeit: die Geschichte der Gemeindehirten im Allgäu*. Bad Schussenried.

McGing, B. 1998, "Bandits, real and imagined, in Greco-Roman Egypt," *Bulletin of the American Association of Papyrologists* 35: 159–183.

Messerer, C. 2019, *Corpus des papyrus grecs sur les relations administratives entre le clergé égyptien et les autorités romaines Vol.II*. Leiden and Boston.

Meyer, M. 2004, *The Gospel of Mary*. San Francisco.

Millar, F. 1981, "The world of the Golden Ass," *Journal of Roman Studies* 71: 63–75.

Millar, F. 1993, *The Roman Near East: 31 BC–AD 337*. Cambridge, Mass.

Minehart, M. 2012, "*P. Oxy.* XLII 3057: letter of Ammonius. The [mis]identification of an Oxyrhynchus papyrus [as the earliest Christian letter]," in P. Schubert, ed.,

Actes du 26e Congrès international de papyrologie. Genève, 16–21 août 2010, Geneva: 543–548.

Modrzejewski, J. M. 1997, *The Jews of Egypt: From Rameses II to Emperor Hadrian*, trans. R. Cornman. Princeton, NJ.

Modrzejewski, J. M. 2001, "Ägypten," in C. Lepelley, ed., *Rom und das Reich in der Hohen Kaiserzeit 44 v.Chr.–260 n.Chr.*, vol. ii, *Die Regionen des Reiches*. Munich and Leipzig.

Mommsen, Th. 1883, *Res Gestae Divi Augusti. Ex monumentis Ancyrano et Apolloniensi*. Berlin.

Montevecchi, O. 1976, "Il censimento romano d'Egitto," *Aevum* 50: 72–84.

Morgan, T. 1998, *Literate Education in the Hellenistic and Roman Worlds*. Cambridge.

Nachtergael, G. 1988, "Un aspect de l'environnement en Égypte gréco-romaine: les dangers de la circulation," *Ludus Magistralis* 21: 19–54.

Naldini, M. 1998, *Il cristianesimo in Egitto: lettere private dei papyri dei secoli II–IV*, 2nd edn. Florence.

Neef, R. 1990, "Introduction, development and environmental implications of olive culture: the evidence from Jordan," in S. Bottema, G. Entjes-Nieborg, and W. van Zeist, eds., *Man's Role in the Shaping of the Eastern Mediterranean Landscape*. Rotterdam: 295–307.

Nevius, R. C. 2001, "On using the nomina sacra as a criteria for dating early Christian papyri," *XXII congresso internazionale di papirologia*, vol. ii. Florence: 1045–1050.

Noethlichs, K. L. 1972, "Zur Einflussnahme des Staates auf die Entwicklung eines christlichen Klerikerstandes. Schicht- und berufsspezifische Bestimmungen für den Klerus im 4. und 5. Jahrhundert in den spätantiken Rechtsquellen," *Jahrbuch für Antike und Christentum* 16: 28–59.

Nongbri, B. 2005, "The use and abuse of P52: papyrological pitfalls in the dating of the fourth gospel," *Harvard Theological Review* 98: 23–48.

Nongbri, B. 2011, "Grenfell and Hunt on the dates of early Christian codices: setting the record straight," *Bulletin of the American Society of Papyrologists* 48: 149–162.

Nongbri, B. 2014, "The limits of palaeographic dating of literary papyri: some observations on the date and provenance of *P. Bodmer II (P66)*," *Museum Helveticum* 71: 1–35.

Nongbri, B. 2018, *God's Library. The Archaeology of the Earliest Christian Manuscripts*. New Haven and London.

Öhler, M. 2008, "Jesus in Ägypten," in W. Pritscher, M. Öhler, and M. Lang, eds., *Das ägyptische Christentum im 2. Jahrhundert*. Berlin: 59–79.

Öhler, M. 2011, *Aposteldekret und antikes Vereinswesen. Gemeinschaft und ihre Ordnung*. Tübingen.

Öhler, M., W. Pratscher, and M. Lang, eds. 2008, *Das ägyptische Christentum im 2. Jahrhundert*. Vienna.

Oost, S. I. 1961, "The Alexandrian seditions under Philip and Gallienus," *Classical Philology* 56: 1–20.

Orsini, P. and W. Clarysse 2012, "Early New Testament manuscripts and their dates: a critique of theological palaeography," *Ephemerides Theologicae Lovanienses* 84: 443–474.

Orth, 1921, "Schaf," in *Realencyclopädie der classischen Altertumswissenschaft*. N.p.: vol. 1: 373–379.

Osborn, E. 2005, *Clement of Alexandria*. Cambridge.

Parca, M. 2013, "Children in Ptolemaic Egypt: what the papyri say," in J. Evans Grubbs and T. Parkin, eds., *The Oxford Handbook of Childhood and Education in the Classical World*. Oxford: 465–483.

Parkin, T. G. 1992, *Demography and Roman Society*. Baltimore, Md. and London.

Parkin, T. G. 2003, *Old Age in the Roman World. A Cultural and Social History*. Baltimore, Md. and London.

Parkin, T. G. and A. Pomeroy 2007, *Roman Social History. A Sourcebook*. London and New York.

Parrott, D. M., ed. 1979, *Gospel of Mary*. Leiden.

Parsons, P. J. 1983, "3525: Gospel of Mary," in *The Oxyrhynchus Papyri 50*. London: 12–14.

Parsons, P. J. 2007, *City of the Sharp-nosed Fish*. London.

Paulas, J. 2012, "Cheese," in R. S. Bagnall, C. Champion, A. Erskine, and S. R. Huebner, eds., *The Encyclopedia of Ancient History*, vol. III. Oxford: 1445–1446.

Pearson, B. A. 1986, "Earliest Christianity in Egypt: some observations," in B. A. Pearson and J. E. Goehring, eds., *The Roots of Egyptian Christianity*. Philadelphia: 132–134.

Pearson, B. A. 2004, *Gnosticism and Christianity in Roman and Coptic Egypt*. New York.

Pearson, B. A. 2005, "Basilides the Gnostic," in A. Marjanan and P. Luomanen, eds., *A Companion to Second-century Christian "Heretics."* Leiden and Boston, Mass.: 1–31.

Pearson, B. A. 2007, "Earliest Christianity in Egypt: further observations," in J. E. Goehring and J. A. Timbie, eds., *The World of Early Egyptian Christianity: Language, Literature and Social Context*. Washington, DC: 97–112.

Pearson, B. A. and J. E. Goehring, eds. 1986, *The Roots of Egyptian Christianity*. Philadelphia, Penn.

Pfeiffer, S. 2012, "The imperial cult in Egypt," in C. Riggs, ed., *The Oxford Handbook of Roman Egypt*. Oxford: 83–100.

Pikoulas, Y. 2007, "Traveling by land in ancient Greece," in C. Adams and J. Roy, eds., *Travel, Geography and Culture in Ancient Greece, Egypt and the Near East*. Oxford: 78–87.

Pomeroy, S. 1981, "Women in Roman Egypt: a preliminary study based on papyri," in H. Foley, ed., *Reflections of Women in Antiquity*. London: 303–322.

Pomeroy, S. 1984, *Women in Hellenistic Egypt from Alexander to Cleopatra*. New York.

Pomeroy, S. B. 2010 (1975), *Goddesses, Whores, Wives and Slaves: Women in Classical Antiquity*. London.

Porter, S. E. 2013, "Recent efforts to reconstruct early Christianity on the basis of its papyrological evidence," in S. Porter and A. Pitts, eds., *Christian Origins and Graeco-Roman Culture*. Leiden: 71–84.

Postgate, J. N. 1975, "Some Old Babylonian shepherds and their flocks," *Journal of Semitic Studies* 20: 1–21.

Pucci Ben Zeev, M. 2005, *Diaspora Judaism in Turmoil, 116/117 CE. Ancient Sources and Modern Insights*. Leuven.

Pudsey, A. 2012, "Death and the family: widows and divorcees in Roman Egypt," in L. Larsson Lovén and M. Harlow, eds., *Families in the Imperial and Late Antique Roman Worlds*. London and New York: 157–180.

Pudsey, A. 2013, "Children in Roman Egypt," in J. Evans Grubbs and T. G. Parkin, eds., *Handbook of Children and Education in the Classical World*. Oxford: 484–509.

Ramsay, W. M. 1898, *Was Christ Born at Bethlehem? A Study on the Credibility of St. Luke*. London.

Rapp, C. 2011, "Early monasticism in Egypt: between hermits and cenobites," in G. Melville and A. Müller, eds., *Female Vita Religiosa between Late Antiquity and the High Middle Ages. Structures, Developments and Spatial Contexts*. Münster: 21–42.

Rapske, B. M. 1994, "Acts, travel and shipwreck," in D. W. Gill and C. Gempf, eds., *The Book of Acts in its Graeco-Roman Setting*. Grand Rapids, Mich.: vol. II: 1–47.

Rathbone, D. W. 1991, *Economic Rationalism and Rural Society in Third-century AD Egypt: The Heroninos Archive and the Appianus Estate*. Cambridge.

Rathbone, D. W. 1993, "Egypt, Augustus and Roman taxation," *Cahiers du Centre G. Klotz* 4: 86–99.

Rathbone, D. W. 2013, "The Romanity of Roman Egypt: a faltering consensus?," *Journal of Juristic Papyrology* 43: 73–91.

Rébillard, E. 2009, *The Care of the Dead in Late Antiquity*. Ithaca, NY.

Renan, E. 1863, *The Life of Jesus*. London.

Ritti, T., K. Grewe, and P. Kessener 2007, "A relief of a water-powered stone saw mill on a sarcophagus at Hierapolis and its implications," *Journal of Roman Archaeology* 20: 138–163.

Roberts, C. H. 1935, *An Unpublished Fragment of the Fourth Gospel in the John Rylands Library*. Manchester.

Roberts, C. H. 1938, "Gospel of Mary," in *Catalogue of the Greek and Latin Papyri in the John Rylands Library*, vol. III. Manchester: 18–23.

Roberts, C. H. 1970, "Books in the Graeco-Roman world and in the New Testament," in P. R. Ackroyd, ed., *The Cambridge History of the Bible*, vol. I, *From the Beginnings to Jerome*. Cambridge: 48–66.

Roberts, C. H. 1979, *Manuscript, Society and Belief in Early Christian Egypt*. Oxford.

Roberts, C. H. and T. C. Skeat 1983, *The Birth of the Codex*. Oxford.

Roller, D. W. 1998, *The Building Programme of Herod the Great*. Berkeley, Calif.

Rosen, K. 1995, "Jesu Geburtsdatum. Der Census des Quirinius und eine jüdische Steuererklärung aus dem Jahr 127 n.Chr.," *Jahrbuch für Antike und Christentum* 38: 5–15.

Rosenfeld, B.-Z. 1998, "Inn-keeping in Jewish society in Roman Palestine," *Journal of the Economic and Social History of the Orient* 41: 133–158.

Rowlandson, J. 1998, *Women and Society in Greek and Roman Egypt: A Sourcebook.* Cambridge.

Rubensohn, O. 1905, "Aus griechisch-römischen Häusern des Fayum," *Jahrbuch des Deutschen Archäologischen Instituts* 20: 1–25.

Rutherford, I. C. 2012, "Travel and pilgrimage," in C. Riggs, ed., *The Oxford Handbook of Roman Egypt.* Oxford: 701–716.

Saller, R. P. 1994, *Patriarchy, Property and Death in the Roman Family.* Cambridge.

Saller, R. P. 2008, "Human capital and economic growth," in W. Scheidel, ed., *The Cambridge Companion to the Roman Economy.* Cambridge: 71–86.

Samuel, D. H. 1979, "Sheep grazing on the estate of Germanicus at Socnopaiou Nesos: a note on *P.Lond.* 312 (II, p. 80)," *Zeitschrift für Papyrologie und Epigraphik* 33: 227–228.

Sartre, M. 2005, *The Middle East under Rome*, trans. Catherine Porter and Elizabeth Rawlings. Cambridge, Mass.

Satlow, M. L. 2012, "Family, Jewish," in R. S. Bagnall, C. Champion, A. Erskine, and S. R. Huebner, eds., *Encyclopedia of Ancient History*, vol. v. Oxford: 2629–2630.

Schalit, A. 2001, *Herodes. Der Mann und sein Werk*, 2nd edn. Berlin.

Schaps, D. M. 1979, *Economic Rights of Women in Ancient Greece.* Ann Arbor, Mich.

Scheidel, W. 2001, *Death on the Nile: Disease and the Demography of Roman Egypt.* Leiden.

Scheidel, W, and S. J. Friesen 2009, "The size of the Economy and the Distribution of Income in the Roman Empire," *Journal of Roman Studies* 99: 61–91.

Schenke, H.-M., ed. 1972, *Die gnostischen Schriften des koptischen Papyrus Berolinensis 8502.* Berlin.

Schmelz, G. 2002, *Kirchliche Amtsträger im spätantiken Ägypten nach den Aussagen der griechischen und koptischen Papyri und Ostraka.* Munich and Leipzig.

Schmid, R. 1990, *Maria Magdalena in gnostischen Schriften.* Munich.

Schubert, P. 2007, *Philadelphie. Un village égyptien en mutation entre le IIe et le IIIe. siècle ap. J.-C.* Basel.

Schubert, P. 2016, "On the form and content of the certificates of pagan sacrifice," *Journal of Roman Studies* 106: 172–198.

Schuol, M. 2007, *Augustus und die Juden. Rechtsstellung und Interessenpolitik der kleinasiatischen Diaspora.* Berlin.

Schwartz, E. 1909, *Die Kirchengeschichte. Eusebius' Werke*, vol. II. Leipzig.

Schwartz, J. 1964, "Une famille de chepteliers au IIIe S.p.C.," *Recherches de Papyrologie* 3, 49–96. (*P. Chept.* 1–20.)

Sharp, M. 1999, "The village of Theadelphia in the Fayyum: land and population in the second century," in A. K. Bowman and E. Rogan, eds., *Agriculture in Egypt from Pharaonic to Modern Times*. Oxford: 159–192.

Shipley, F. W. 1924, *Velleius Paterculus and Res Gestae Divi Augusti*. Cambridge, Mass.

Sijpesteijn, P. J. 1980, "List of nominations to liturgies," R. Pintaudi, ed., *Miscellanea Papyrologica*. Florence: 341–347.

Sijpesteijn, P. J. 1987, *Custom Duties in Graeco-Roman Egypt*. Zutphen, Netherlands.

Smallwood, E. M. 1981, *The Jews under Roman Rule. From Pompey to Diocletian: A Study in Political Relations*. Leiden and Boston, Mass.

Stambaugh, J. W. and D. L. Balch 1992, *Das soziale Umfeld des Neuen Testaments*. Göttingen.

Stegemann, E. W. and W. Stegemann 1995, *Urchristliche Sozialgeschichte. Die Anfänge im Judentum und die Christusgemeinden in der mediterranen Welt*. Stuttgart.

Stoffel, P. 1994, *Über die Staatspost, die Ochsengespanne und die requirierten Ochsengespanne. Eine Darstellung des römischen Postwesens auf Grund der Gesetze des Codex Theodosianus und des Codex Iustinianus*. Bern.

Strobel, K. 1993, *Das Imperium Romanum im "3. Jahrhundert": Modell einer historischen Krise? Zur Frage mentaler Strukturen breiterer Bevölkerungsschichten in der Zeit von Marc Aurel bis zum Ausgang des 3. Jh.n.Chr*. Stuttgart.

Syme, R. 1934, "Galatia and Pamphylia under Augustus: the governorships of Piso, Quirinius and Silvanus," *Klio* 27: 122–148.

Tacoma L. E. 2006, *Fragile Hierarchies. The Urban Elites of Third-century Roman Egypt*. Leiden.

Tenney, F. 1924, "Roman census statistics," *Classical Philology* 19: 329–341.

Tenney, F. 1930, "Roman census statistics from 508 to 225 BC," *American Journal of Philology* 51: 313–324.

Theißen, G. 2004, *Die Jesusbewegung. Sozialgeschichte einer Revolution der Werte*. Gütersloh, Germany.

Theißen, G. and A. Merz 2001, *Der historische Jesus: ein Lehrbuch*. Göttingen.

Tibiletti, G. 1979, *Le lettere private nei papiri greci del III e IV secolo d.C.: Tra paganesimo e cristianesimo*. Milan.

Till, W. 1955, *Die gnostischen Schriften des koptischen Papyrus Berolinensis 8502*. Berlin.

Tilly, M. 2008, "Das ägyptische Judentum von der römischen Annexion bis zum Partherkrieg Trajans," in W. Pratscher, M. Öhler, and M. Lang, eds., *Das ägyptische Christentum im 2. Jahrhundert*. Vienna: 45–58.

Tissot, Y. 1997, "Le rapt de Denys d'Alexandrie et la chronologie de ses lettres festales," *Revue d'Histoire et de Philosophie Religieuses* 77: 51–65.

Tropper, A. 2006, "Children and childhood in light of the demographics of Jewish family life in Late Antiquity," *Journal for the Study of Judaism* 37: 299–343.

Tuckett, C. 2007, *The Gospel of Mary*. Oxford.

Tweed, T. A. 2015, "After the quotidian turn: interpretive categories and scholarly trajectories in the study of religion since the 1960s," *Journal of Religion* 95: 361–385.

Ulrich, R. U. 2007, *Roman Woodworking*. New Haven, Conn.

Unruh, F. 2001, *"Dass alle Welt geschätzt würde" – Volkszählung im Römischen Reich*. Stuttgart.

Van De Mieroop, M. 1993, "Sheep and goat herding according to the Old Babylonian texts from Ur," *Bulletin on Sumerian Agriculture* 7: 161–182.

Van den Berg-Onstwedder, G. 1990, "Diocletian in the Coptic tradition," *Bulletin de la Société d'Archaeologie Copte* 29: 88–122.

Van den Brock, R. 1996, "The Christian 'School' of Alexandria in the second and third centuries," in J. W. Drijvers and A. A. MacDonald, eds., *Studies in Gnosticism and Alexandrian Christianity*. Leiden.

Van Driel, G. 1993, "Neo-Babylonian sheep and goats," *Bulletin on Sumerian Agriculture* 7: 219–258.

Van Lith, S. M. E. 1974, "Lease of sheep and goats / nursing contract with accompanying receipt," *Zeitschrift für Papyrologie und Epigraphik* 14: 145–162.

Van Minnen, P. 1994, "The roots of Egyptian Christianity," *Archiv für Papyrusforschung* 40: 71–85.

Van Minnen, P. 2001, "*P.Oxy.* LXVI 4527 and the Antonine plague in the Fayyum," *Zeitschrift für Papyrologie und Epigraphik* 135: 175–177.

Vanthieghem, N. 2014/2015, "Contributions à la reconstitution, à l'édition et à l'étude des archives papyrologiques dites d'Hèrôninos," dissertation, Université Libre de Bruxelles.

Venticinque, P. F. 2010, "Family affairs: guild regulations and family relationships in Roman Egypt," *Greek, Roman and Byzantine Studies* 50: 273–294.

Verreth, H. and K. Vandorpe 2013, "Heroninos, estate manager," Trismegistos http://www.trismegistos.org/arch/archives/pdf/103.pdf (accessed July 13, 2017).

Vogel, M. 2002, *Herodes. König der Juden, Freund der Römer*. Leipzig.

Vogt, J. 1929, *Römische Reichspolitik in Ägypten*. Leipzig.

Von Harnack, A. 1893, *Geschichte der altchristlichen Litteratur bis Eusebius*. Leipzig.

Von Harnack, A. 1924, *Die Mission und Ausbreitung des Christentums in den ersten drei Jahrhunderten*, 4th edn. Leipzig.

Wallace, S. L. 1938a, "Census and Poll-Tax in Ptolemaic and Roman Egypt," *American Journal of Philology* 59: 418–422.

Wallace, S. L. 1938b, *Taxation in Egypt from Augustus to Diocletian*. Princeton, NJ.

Weber, F. 2003, *Herodes – König von Roms Gnaden? Herodes als Modell eines römischen Klientelkönigs in spätrepublikanischer und augusteischer Zeit*. Berlin.

Wegner, J. R. 1988, *Chattel or Person? The Status of Women in the Mishna*. Ann Arbor, Mich.

Wegner, J. R. 1991, "The image and status of women in classical Judaism," in J. Baskin, ed., *Jewish Women in Historical Perspective*. Detroit: 68–93.

Westermann, W. L. 1914, "Apprentice contracts and the apprentice system in Roman Egypt," *Classical Philology* 9: 295–315.

White, J. L. 1972, *The Form and Function of the Body of the Greek Letter: A Study of the Letter-Body in Non-literary Papyri and in Paul the Apostle*. Missoula, Mont.

Whittaker, C. R., ed. 1988, *Pastoral Economics in Classical Antiquity*. Cambridge.

Wilcken, U. 1912, *Grundzüge und Chrestomatie der Papyruskunde I: Historischer Teil, Zweite Hälfte: Chrestomatie*. Leipzig and Berlin.

Wilfong, T. G. 2002, *Women of Jeme: Lives in a Coptic Town in Late Antique Egypt*. Ann Arbor, Mich.

Wilker, J. 2007, *Für Rom und Jerusalem. Die herodianische Dynastie im 1. Jahrhundert n.Chr.* Frankfurt am Main.

Wilkinson, J. 2006, *Egeria's Travels*. Oxford.

Winter, J. G. 1933, *Life and Letters in the Papyri*. Ann Arbor, Mich.

Wipszycka, E. 1974, "Remarques sur les lettres privées chrétiennes des IIe–IV siècles: à propos d'un livre de M. Naldini," *Journal of Juristic Papyrology* 18: 203–221.

Wipszycka, E. 1986, "La valeur de l'onomastique pour l'histoire de la christianisation de l'Egypte: à propos d'une étude de R. S. Bagnall," *Zeitschrift für Papyrologie und Epigraphik* 62: 173–181.

Wipszycka, E. 1988, "La christianisation de l'Égypte aux IVe–VIe siècles: aspects sociaux et ethniques," *Aegyptus* 68: 117–165. Reprinted in E. Wipszycka 1996: 63–106.

Wipszycka, E. 1996, *Études sur le christianisme dans l'Égypte de l'antiquité tardive*. Rome.

Wipszycka, E. 2002, "L'ascétisme féminin dans l'Égypte de l'Antiquité tardive: topoi littéraires et formes d'ascèse," in H. Melaerts and L. Mooren, eds., *Le rôle et le statut de la femme en Égypte hellénistique, romaine et byzantine*. Leuven: 355–396.

Wipszycka, E. 2006, "The origins of the monarchic episcopate in Egypt," *Adamantius* 12: 71–90.

Wipszycka, E. 2007, "The institutional church," in R. S. Bagnall, ed., *Egypt in the Byzantine World, 300–700*. Cambridge: 331–349.

Wipszycka, E. 2009, *Moines et communautés monastiques en Égypte (IVe–VIIIe siècles)*. Warsaw.

Wipszycka, E. 2015, *The Alexandrian Church. People and Institutions*. Warsaw.

Wiseman, T. P. 1969, "The census in the first century BC," *Journal of Roman Studies* 59: 59–75.

Witherington, B. 1988, *Women in the Earliest Churches*. Cambridge.

Wolter, M. 2009, "Die Hirten in der Weihnachtsgeschichte (Lk 2.8–20)," in M. Wolter, ed., *Theologie und Ethos im frühen Christentum. Studien zu Jesus, Paulus und Lukas*. Tübingen: 355–372.

Yiftach, U. 2016, "Quantifying literacy in the early Roman Arsinoitês: the case of the *grapheion* document," in D. M. Schaps, U. Yiftach, and D. Dueck, eds., *When West Met East. The Encounter of Greece and Rome with the Jews, Egyptians, and Others. Studies Presented to Ranon Katzoff in Honor of his 75th Birthday*. Triest: 269–284.

Youtie, H. C. 1966, "Pétaus, fils de Pétaus, ou le scribe qui ne savait pas écrire," *Chronique d'Egypte* 41: 127–143.

Zimmermann, C. 2002, *Handwerkervereine im griechischen Osten des Imperium Romanum*. Mainz.

Index Locorum

Ambrose, *De viduis*, 148n
Apophthegmata Patrum, 61
Apostolic Constitutions
  3.11.3, 59
  8.19–20, 59
Apuleius, *Met.*, 88
  1.6–19, 111
Athanasius, *Vit. Ant.* §2, 142n
Ps.-Athanasius, *De virginitate*, 61
Augustine, *Bon. vid.*, 148n

Basil, *Ep.* 198.1, 153n
BGU
  1.133, 163n
  1.261, 155n
  3.843, 155n
  4.1030, 141n, 142n
  7.1680, 155n
  9.1900, 161n
  13.2350, 156n
  16.2604, 155n

C. Étiq. Mom. 305, 149n
Calpurnius Siculus, *Ecl.*
  2.60, 163n
  5.39–42, 163n
Cassius Dio 62.2.3–4, 144n
CIL 14.3613, 146n
Clement of Alexandria
  Paed. 1.4, 148n
  Strom. 7.17, 139n
Ps.-Clementine, *Recogn.* 9.38, 113n
Codex Iustinianus 1.3.2.1, 153n
Codex Theodosianus
  9.30.2, 164n
  9.30.5, 164n
  9.31.1, 164n
  13.1.10, 150n
  13.4.1–2, 151n
  16.2.2 153n

16.2.8, 153n
16.2.10, 153n
Columella
  7.3.16, 162n
  7.3.26, 128
Council of Chalcedon, *can.* 15, 59
Council of Nicaea, *can.* 19, 59

Didascalia Apostolorum, 58
Dio Chrysostom
  1.12–13, 115–116
  6.20, 129
Diodorus Siculus 1.31.8, 139n

Epiphanius, *Panarion* §31, 139n
Eusebius, *Hist. Eccl.*
  2.16, 8
  6.1.1, 139n
  6.11.3, 139n
  6.14.8–9, 142n
  6.15, 140n
  6.23.2, 148n
  6.31, 140n
  6.40.4, 140n
  6.41, 140n
  6.42.1, 140n
  7.2, 141n
  7.11.1–11, 140n
  7.11.13, 140n
  7.11.15–17, 140n
  7.21, 140n
  7.21.1–10, 140n
  7.21.2, 143n
  7.21–22, 140n
  7.22.1–11, 140n
  7.24, 142n
  7.24.1, 143n
  7.24.6–9, 143n
  7.24.9, 143n
Eutychius, *Annals* 9.5, 140n

General Index

For EU product safety concerns, contact us at Calle de José Abascal, 56–1°,
28003 Madrid, Spain or eugpsr@cambridge.org.